How to Have Better Relationships

Steven Kessler

Also by Steven Kessler:

The 5 Personality Patterns
*Your Guide to Understanding Yourself and Others
and Developing Emotional Maturity*

How to Have Better Relationships

The Skills You Need, the Actions to Take
based on The 5 Personality Patterns

STEVEN KESSLER

BODHI TREE PRESS

Copyright © 2024 by Steven Kessler. All rights reserved. Except for brief quotes used in a review, no portion of this book may be reproduced, stored in a retrieval system, or transmitted in any form or by any means — electronic, mechanical, photocopying, recording, or otherwise — without the written permission of the copyright holder.

Published by Bodhi Tree Press
Richmond, California
www.BodhiTreePress.com

ISBN: 978-1-961678-04-0

Library of Congress Control Number: 2024917483

Publisher's Cataloging-In-Publication Data
Names: Kessler, Steven (Psychotherapist), author.
Description: Richmond, California: Bodhi Tree Press, [2024] |
    Includes bibliographical references and index.
Identifiers: ISBN: 978-1-961678-04-0 (print) | LCCN: 2024917483
Subjects: LCSH: Personality--Social aspects. | Interpersonal relations--
    Psychological aspects. | Social skills. | Typology (Psychology) |
    Self-management (Psychology) | LCGFT: Self-help publications. |
    BISAC: SELF-HELP / Personal Growth / General. |
    SELF-HELP / Communication & Social Skills. |
    PSYCHOLOGY / Interpersonal Relations.
Classification: LCC: BF698.9.S63 K47 2024 | DDC: 155.2--dc23

For information on speaking, workshops, and trainings, please visit www.The5PersonalityPatterns.com or contact the author at info@The5PersonalityPatterns.com.

Your experience of life
is determined mostly by
your habits of attention
and the patterned flow
of your life energy.

– *Steven Kessler*

Contents

Introduction 1

- 1 - Our Two Big Mistakes............................. 5
What's Your Habitual View? 6
Safety.. 8

- 2 - The Skills You Need to Manage Yourself............. 9
Develop Your Inner Witness 9
Learn to Attend to Your Raw Sensory Experience........... 10
Disidentify from Your Inner Critic 13
The Basic Energy Skills.................................. 18
    The Centering Breath – the doorway to core............ 18
    Core – how to know your self 20
    Grounding – your source of support.................... 25
    Edge – your protection & shield 32
    Me / Not Me – how to differentiate yourself 34
Learn to Manage Your Own Inner State.................... 36
What is Needed to be a Healthy Adult 39
Questions 41

- 3 - The Skills You Need when Interacting with Others ... 43
The 6 Levels of Relationship............................. 43
Relationship is Voluntary................................ 46
The 4 Levels of Communication 47
The Basic Communication Skills........................... 50
    The Steps of Communication 50
    Be Honest 51
    Use 'I Statements' Instead of 'You Statements'........ 52
    Listen for the Embedded Statements 55
    The Skill of Negotiating.............................. 56
    Communication 101 58

Notice Their Ways of Thinking and Perceiving. 59
Respect Their Autonomy 66
Adjust Your Approach to Suit Them 68
Holding Space for Someone 69

- 4 - About the Personality Patterns 74
Pattern vs Presence. 74
You Are Not Your Personality Patterns 76
The 5 Safety Strategies 77
How Do Kids Choose? 78
A Brief Overview of the Personality Patterns. 80
Primary and Secondary Patterns 86
People in Different Patterns Live in Different Worlds 87
How to Discern Your Own and Others' Patterns. 90
Questions 94

- 5 - How to Understand and Interact with Each Pattern . . 98

- 6 - Relating to the Leaving Pattern 103
The Origins of The Leaving Pattern 105
The Gifts of The Leaving Pattern. 108
Communicating with Someone Caught in the Pattern 112
How to Relate to Them Successfully 115
Questions 126

- 7 - Relating to the Merging Pattern. 135
The Origins of the Merging Pattern. 137
The Gifts to the Merging Pattern. 143
Communicating with Someone Caught in the Pattern. 147
How to Relate to Them Successfully 148
Questions 161

- 8 - Relating to the Enduring Pattern 167
The Origins of the Enduring Pattern. 169
The Gifts of the Enduring Pattern. 172

  Communicating with Someone Caught in the Pattern 176
  How to Relate to Them Successfully 177
  Questions 192

- 9 - Relating to the Aggressive Pattern 203
  The Origins of the Aggressive Pattern 205
  The Gifts of the Aggressive Pattern 208
  Communicating with Someone Caught in the Pattern 212
  How to Relate to Them Successfully 215
  Questions 227

- 10 - Relating to the Rigid Pattern 237
  The Origins of the Rigid Pattern 240
  The Gifts of the Rigid Pattern 244
  Communicating with Someone Caught in the Pattern 248
  How to Relate to Them Successfully 249
  Questions 263

- 11 - The Personality Patterns in Romantic Relationships . 270
  How the Patterns Interact in Romantic Relationships 271
  Same-Pattern Relationships 273
  Questions 279
  Different-Pattern Relationships 282
  Questions 292

- 12 - How to Create Healthy Relationships 296

- 13 - Moving from Me to Us 301

- 14 - Conclusion 303

  Endnotes 304
  Bibliography 305
  Index 307
  About the Author 311

Acknowledgments

I first want to profoundly thank Lynda Caesara, who first introduced me to both energy work and the personality patterns and has been my primary teacher of them for over twenty years. Much of the material in this book comes from her teaching, extended by my own observations and insights. I have also drawn on material from the writings of Helen Palmer, A. H. Almaas, Laurence Heller, Wilhelm Reich, Alexander Lowen, John Pierrakos, Stephen M. Johnson, Barbara Brennan, Linda Kohanov, Wendy Palmer, and Anodea Judith.

My clients and my fellow students have fleshed out those teachings by providing hundreds of real life examples of the personality patterns in action. They have been a continual source of insight and inspiration, and I want to thank each and every one of them. I especially thank the entire community of students studying the personality patterns for their support of both my books. As with my first book, the creation of this book has become a labor of love for me.

I also want to thank Christine Hassler, who first suggested that I teach a course on how to use this way of understanding others to help people create better relationships.

And lastly, for their support with proofreading, I want to thank Sally Boden-O'Sullivan, Jean Selkirk, and Connie Habash.

Introduction

The Origins of This Book

THIS WAY OF UNDERSTANDING PEOPLE was originated in the 1930's by Wilhelm Reich, a star student of Sigmund Freud who began his career as a Freudian psychoanalyst. But Reich saw things that Freud had not, because he was paying more attention to the body, and he was able to perceive how life energy moves through the body. Using his talents, Reich saw that his patients displayed certain patterns of defense mechanisms and muscular tension, which he called "character structures." Over time, he began to develop a whole new way of understanding personality.

But Reich was also apparently a hard person to get along with. Because he wanted the life energy in every person to be free, he rebelled against all constraints, including the authorities and laws of every country he lived in. In response, the mainstream psychoanalysts in those countries saw him as a threat and got him thrown out of two countries and then imprisoned in a third. As a result, his way of understanding people was championed by only a few of his students and never entered the mainstream. For decades, it remained hidden in the backwaters of Freudian psychotherapy and energy healing. Others clarified and refined his map of the character structures, but it never got out to the general public.

I first encountered this teaching in a class devoted to working with energy, and as I used it with my own clients, I realized how incredibly accurate and valuable it is. Eventually, I decided to gather the different threads of this lineage and weave them together with my own discoveries in a book written for the general public, not just psychotherapists. That book is called *The 5 Personality Patterns*, and it describes how the patterns show up in individuals.

This new book includes more about the personal and interpersonal skills each of us needs to learn to become an emotionally mature adult and introduces new material on how you can use your understanding of the personality patterns to guide you in relating to others. However, it does not include nearly as much detail on each of the personality patterns. For a more complete understanding of each pattern, please see my earlier book.

Learning to See the Patterns

As you read this book, you may recognize which patterns you go into. You may have epiphanies and see yourself more clearly. In fact, I hope that you do. When attempting to figure out which personality patterns you go into, look especially at what you do when you're upset and overwhelmed. That's when your safety strategies are the most obvious. You may also want to ask your family and friends for feedback on how you behave when you're upset. However, don't lose sight of the fact that your patterns are safety strategies — they are not who you are and not your essence. They prevent your essence from shining through and manifesting as presence.

Your personality patterns are also not a way to justify your behavior. Identifying them will help you understand what's behind your behavior and how to change it, but they're not an excuse for mistreating anyone, including yourself. I often suggest that clients let themselves be guided by this maxim: "Treat yourself at least as well as you have ever treated your dearest love."

Similarly, understanding another person's personality patterns will help you understand what's behind their behavior, but it does not obligate you to accept mistreatment from them. You may feel compassion for them and want to help them feel safer, but you still need to protect yourself and keep yourself safe. Managing their behavior is their responsibility, not yours. Being upset is not a license to mistreat anyone.

When Seeing the Patterns in Others

However, be aware that, if misapplied, your knowledge of the personality patterns can also be used as a weapon against those around you, even those you love. As you read this book, you will probably recognize which personality patterns your friends and family go into, and you may be tempted to turn your understandings into accusations, such as *"You're so rigid!"* or *"You're just leaving!"* I urge you not to impose your insights on others or put them in a box this way. If you label people, they will feel judged, and they won't like the idea that your new understanding gives you power over them.

Introduction

Instead, use your new understanding to see their needs and fears more clearly and interact with them more skillfully. Use it to get yourself out of your patterned reactions so that you can treat them in a kinder and more compassionate way. Instead of expressing your discoveries in words, try expressing them in new behaviors that work better for the other person, as well as for you.

When you do talk about your insights, instead of telling others what you've discovered about *them*, tell them what you've discovered about *yourself* and how that has helped you. If they seem interested, give them this book and invite them to explore it with you.

Use your new knowledge to act more skillfully and lovingly toward both yourself and others. Don't use it to judge yourself or others or to justify your own patterned, unhealthy ways of acting. And don't use it to attack yourself for being stuck in your patterns or others for being stuck in theirs. Remember, we're all doing the best we can.

This Book Includes Three Main Ideas:

- To navigate through life skillfully, you need to let go of two big beliefs that we all mistakenly hold about ourselves and others.
- To become a mature, healthy adult, you need to develop multiple sets of personal and interpersonal skills.
- To relate successfully to others, you need to learn how to approach and interact with them in ways that fit with their personality patterns.

This book helps you see through those mistaken beliefs, teaches you the skills you need to become a healthy adult, and shows you how to approach and interact with others in ways that will work better for them. In short, it shows you how to have better relationships.

People Are Not Their Patterns

Whether you're relating to others or yourself, here's the main thing to remember. People are not their patterns, but their presence. Your patterns are what you *do*, not who you *are*. To remind you of that, I will speak of people being in pattern, doing a pattern, or caught in a pattern, but I will never say someone *is* a pattern.

Your presence is who you really are, and your patterns tend to block your presence from shining out into the world. Each of the patterns starts out as a safety strategy, as a way to feel safer, but it becomes a mask covering the person's presence. So your goal is not to be in pattern more efficiently. Your goal is to get out of your patterns and be present as much as you can.

- 1 -

Our Two Big Mistakes

We live with two big mistaken beliefs:
- We think everyone experiences the same world that we do.
- We think we're seeing the whole picture, fully and accurately.

Big Mistake #1 — Everyone experiences the same world I do

We think that we're all the same. Since each of us has experienced only one way of perceiving the world, that is, our own particular way, we think that everyone else's way of perceiving is the same way as ours. For instance, if our main channel for perceiving the world is the visual one, we assume that everyone's main channel is the visual one. If our main channel is auditory, we assume that everyone's main channel is auditory. If our main channel is kinesthetic, we assume that everyone's main channel is kinesthetic. What else can we think? Our own way is the only way we have ever experienced.

Similarly, if we are head-centered and focused on ideas, we assume that everyone is focused on ideas. If we are heart-centered and focused on connection, we assume that everyone is focused on connection. If we are belly-centered and focused on action, we assume that everyone is focused on action. Again, what else can we assume? Our own way is the only way we have ever experienced.

And our assumption that everyone else perceives the same world we do leads us to think that they should naturally agree with us as we describe what we perceive. And when they don't, we're often surprised and confused, and we start telling ourselves some sort of story, a story that boils down to either, *"There's something wrong with them"* or *"There's something wrong with me."* That misunderstanding is the source of much of our suffering in the world, not to mention many, many fights.

Big Mistake #2 — I see the whole picture, fully and accurately

We think that we perceive the world clearly, accurately, and in its entirety. Again, we have no way to compare our own perceptions to the perceptions of others. So we have no way of knowing that we're not perceiving in all the ways that humans can perceive, and therefore not taking in the complete experience of what is before us. In reality, we are perceiving only a slice of the whole experience: the slice that comes to us via our habitual sensory channels and in the forms that we expect.

And even that slice is distorted. Our unconscious beliefs are filtering and distorting our raw perceptions according to what we believe is more or less important. Some parts of the picture have been shifted to the foreground, brought into clear focus with vivid colors, while other parts of the picture have been moved to the background, dimmed and dulled until we hardly notice them at all. But we aren't aware of these distortions, so we think that what we see is an accurate picture of the world. This is how our unconscious beliefs shape our experience of reality. Reality doesn't change, but what we perceive is shaped and distorted according to what our unconscious beliefs say we should either attend to or disregard.

Again, we don't notice these unconscious distortions of our raw perception, because this is the only way we've ever perceived the world, so we have nothing to compare it to. But another person's unconscious distortions of the same scene may be showing them something very different, and that invisible difference is often what confuses us and causes us to sputter, *"But it's obvious!"* Needless to say, this misunderstanding is the source of many fights, too.

What's Your Habitual View?

Think of it this way: imagine that you live your entire life in a small room. The walls, floor, and ceiling of this room are made of TV screens — screens so big that they fill the entire wall, ceiling, and floor. Wherever you look, there are only screens. Everything you know about the world — everything that you see, hear, feel, touch, smell, taste, or perceive in any way — comes to you through the screens. Even how you perceive yourself comes through the screens.

Now ask yourself, *"What channel are my TV screens habitually tuned to?"* Are you watching The Fear Channel, the channel which highlights all the dangers surrounding you? Are you watching The Love Channel, the channel devoted to feeling connected to others and pleasing them? Do you spend most of your time watching The Winning Channel, the channel which shows you who's up and who's down and how you can fight your way to the top? Are you watching The Avoid Losing Channel, the channel focused on how to stay small and hidden and avoid getting run over by those fighter types? Are you watching The Correctness Channel, the channel focused on keeping things ordered and correct, on doing it the right way and making sure that others do it the right way, too?

Obviously, which channel you habitually watch will make a huge difference in how you perceive the world and how you perceive yourself. And if you watch the same channel all day, every day, you will have nothing to compare it to, no way to know that it is just a small fraction of the whole picture. You won't even know that there is a whole picture, a bigger, fuller world that you have never experienced. You won't know what you're missing.

You may notice that some people refer to things that you don't experience, or that they focus on things that don't make sense or don't seem important to you. But you'll usually explain it by telling yourself a story, like *"They're stupid"* or *"I'm stupid"* or *"They're wrong"* or *"I'm wrong"* or *"They're mean"* or *"I'm not good enough"* — a story that boils down to either *"They're deficient"* or *"I'm deficient."* But, whatever you tell yourself, your stories won't challenge your belief that your view of the world is accurate and complete. In fact, they'll usually reinforce it.

So we go through life seeing a filtered, distorted picture of the world and interacting with others based on incomplete and distorted information. Then we wonder why life is such a struggle and why it is often so hard to get others to agree with us and cooperate with us.

Safety

During my 40 years as a psychotherapist, I have come to believe that feeling safe is the first need for everyone, the need that comes before all other needs. Everyone needs to feel safe. Some people say that our need to feel loved is equal to our need to feel safe. That may be, but all my work with people suggests that safety comes first and is probably stronger. Stephen Porges, author of *The Polyvagal Theory*, says, *"If you want to improve the world, start by making people feel safer"* and I agree.

So ask yourself this question: *How do you try to feel safer? When you're in distress, what do you do to make yourself feel safer?*

Before you continue reading, take a moment and jot down some answers. Naming your main safety strategies will help you recognize not only when you've gone into distress, but will also be important clues as to which personality patterns you habitually go into to try to feel safer.

Everyone wants to feel safe.

Don't judge yourself for what you do. Just notice that by doing those things, you're trying to feel safer, and it's okay that you're trying to feel safer. This is what we all do. Maybe you try to feel safer by being alone. Or by being everyone's friend. Or by being big and tough. Whatever you do, for right now, just notice it.

And if you often judge others for how they behave, try shifting your attention to just noticing the fact that they are also trying to feel safer. Then notice *how* they are trying to feel safer.

So how can we ever truly find safety? How can we ever learn to see the world as it really is and navigate skillfully through it? How can we get what we want, especially in our interactions with other people?

This book is about answering those questions.

- 2 -

The Skills You Need to Manage Yourself

Develop Your Inner Witness

When you start doing therapy or any sort of self-reflective work, your first task is to develop the Inner Witness (also known as the Observing Self). The inner witness does not judge or comment on your experience. Its job is simply to record what you think, feel, say, and do — moment by moment — so that afterwards you can go back and walk through the experience again to see how you got from point A to point B.

For instance, suppose you're remarried after a bitter divorce, and you're going out for the evening with your new husband. It's time to go, but you're not quite ready yet, and your husband calmly says, *"Come on, honey, we'll be late"* and you suddenly find yourself enraged and screaming at him. What happened? How did you get from "not quite ready yet" to enraged and screaming? You can ask your inner witness to very slowly play back all the steps in between. As you review the steps, you can begin to see the connections. Before your husband spoke, maybe your inner dialogue went something like this:

Uh-oh, it's getting late. But I still have this one more thing to do to get ready. If I don't do it, I won't feel fully dressed for this party.

But if I take the time to do it, I'll be late again. I hate that. What's wrong with me? Why can't I be on time? [attacking self]

He'll probably complain about it again. I really hate that. He's got no right! [attacking the other]

My first husband used to complain about my lateness, and then, when he left me, he pretended that it was because I was late so often. [now furious and lost in the past] *Damn him! It wasn't my fault!*

At this point, your hapless second husband says, *"Come on honey, we'll be late"* and you bite his head off, not distinguishing between him and your first husband.

If you have not developed your inner witness, you may believe that your anger must have been caused by something your new husband did, and your mind will get busy looking for evidence to justify that belief. But if you have the ability to go back through your own experience second by second, you'll realize that what angered you was a hurt from the past and that the present situation only reminded you of it.

Now you know some important things:

1. You are still hurt and angry about the past situation.
2. You are not being hurt right now.
3. You are caught in a reaction based on your past.
4. Your new husband did not cause your upset.

Your inner witness has helped you learn something about yourself and come back to being more present in the here and now.

Developing the inner witness is the first step for all inner work. It is the mirror you look into to see yourself more clearly. Its job is simply to show you a clear reflection of yourself. It does not judge. It does not comment in any way. It just plays back the movie of everything that was going on, both inside you and outside you.

Learn to Attend to Your Raw Sensory Experience

Along with developing the Inner Witness, each of us needs to be able to perceive our own raw sensory experience, and to do that, we need to learn to tell the difference between our sensory experience and our mind's interpretation of it. Many of us spend most of our lives up in our heads — commenting on our sensory experience, deciding what it means, and telling ourselves stories about it. Those of us who disregard the sensory experiences in our bodies, and those who dissociate so that we don't feel them, may live our entire lives with very little direct experience of our own lives, that is, of our raw perceptions.

This leaves us with an impoverished experience of life. While our minds have great value, they are not where real life takes place. We live in a physical world, and our lives happen at the interface between our awareness and the physical world. It is in our raw sensory experience of the world that we are most alive. That is where real life happens, not in our thoughts about it. And the only way to be present with our raw sensory experience is to take the mind off its throne and put it aside for the moment.

Let's clarify the distinction between experiencing life through the mind and experiencing it directly, through raw sensory perceptions. The mind is the place of thinking: of reasoning, evaluating, understanding, drawing conclusions, and making decisions. It is the place where we deal with concepts like up and down, in and out, and cause and effect. It is where we

> *It is in your raw sensory experience that you are most alive.*

make judgments, like good and bad, right and wrong, and true and false. And it is in the mind that we create the beliefs and stories that define for us who we are and how we interact with the world. All of these activities share one important quality — they are not the raw data, but things we do with the raw data. They are derived from the raw data, and so they are one step removed from it.

The raw data exist only in the present moment and only in our own direct experience: in our experiences of texture, pressure, movement, size, shape, weight, temperature, location, taste, smell, color, brightness, sound, pitch, vibration, prickliness, tension, pain, pleasure, and the like. In these experiences, there is an aliveness, a freshness and immediacy. They are happening right now, right here, to you.

When you are lost in your inner commentary, you have left your felt-sense experience of the moment, and while you're gone, you are missing the Now. The only time real life is happening is Now. And the only place it is happening is Here. So the only way to fully engage real life is to be present in the Here and Now. That means putting your attention on your five senses — on your raw sensory experience — rather than on your thoughts, beliefs, and stories. It means putting your attention especially on feeling the core of your own body. It is in your inner felt-sense of your core that you can find your self most vividly. And it is there that you can discover the self that you may have been looking for in your mind.

Practicing this skill

As an example, let's consider the difference between thinking about a strawberry and actually eating one. In your mind, you probably have a lot of information about strawberries — like their typical size and color, how much they cost, how long they stay fresh, where and how they're grown, how you feel about the pesticides used in growing them, and so on. You may have years of accumulated information, beliefs, and judgments about them.

All of this knowledge has value, but it is not the direct experience of tasting a strawberry. To get that experience, you must put aside the thoughts and focus your attention on the sensations of a real strawberry in your mouth, right now. The easiest way to do that is to put an actual strawberry in your mouth and bite into it. Try this, if you have a strawberry (or any fruit) handy. Bite into it slowly and notice how focusing on the taste and texture and juiciness tends to turn off your thoughts. Notice how, if you love the taste, your whole body relaxes in order to just take it in. And notice how you are experiencing *this particular strawberry right now*, not strawberries in general. You are getting the experience of *this strawberry* first-hand, as raw sensory perceptions.

Practice attending to your raw sensory experience frequently and notice how easy or difficult it is for you. You may need to practice this skill repeatedly for months to become skillful at it. Begin with simple forms, like tasting the strawberry, feeling the pressure on the soles of your feet as you walk, or inhaling deeply and noticing what you smell. Throughout your day, just practice for a moment wherever you are find yourself. Then gradually add more complexity, like staying with your raw perceptions when you're upset or while also doing a task.

As you practice attending to your raw sensory experience, you will notice that all of life becomes more vivid, fresh, and immediate for you.

Disidentify from Your Inner Critic

Inside each of us, there is a voice that criticizes us whenever we do something wrong. This voice is called the inner critic, and it is an amalgamation of all the commands we heard as a child to *"Be good," "Tell the truth," "Stand up straight," "Don't hit your brother," "Don't draw on the walls," "Don't talk with your mouth full," "Don't run with scissors," "Don't talk back,"* etc., etc., etc. Every time whoever raised us told us what to do or not do, our little brain recorded it. Over time, we built up a library of their voices and mixed them together into one voice that tells us Who We Should Be.

The Job of the Superego

The inner critic is part of something larger that Freud called the superego. It develops in early childhood, roughly between two and five years of age. The superego's job is to stop you from doing things that will get you in trouble with your parents and caregivers. It tries to keep you inside the Good Boy/Good Girl box they have defined, where you are loved and safe. The inner critic becomes a kind of inner policeman, interrupting you the moment you have an impulse to do something bad, and scolding you to stop you from actually doing it.

Of course, to stop you, it has to beat down an awful lot of your impulses and desires. After all, you *want* that cookie, dinnertime or not. To make you obey, it criticizes and shames you. Anything you've seen others do, it copies and uses against you. Its tone can range from being merely devaluing to being outright vicious. The development of this counter-force inside you changes you from a free, spontaneous, uninhibited child into an internally censored, well-behaved child. Your parents like this, of course, and praise you for being such a good boy or girl.

Developing a superego is an important and necessary step for every child. Now you have an internal mechanism that can regulate your behavior, something you did not have before. For the first time, something is able to intervene between having an impulse and acting on it. For the first time, how others will respond to your action enters your decision-making process. This is a real step forward, although ideally it would not include self-hatred.

The superego is composed of three parts:

- the ideal self-image
- the inner praiser
- the inner critic

The ideal self-image holds all your internalized images of the perfect you — the one that Mom and Dad want you to be, the one they love best. These are your images of the Good Boy or Good Girl, of *Who I Should Be.*

Each time you have an impulse to do something, your superego compares your impulse to your ideal self-image. If the impulse fits with Who I Should Be, your inner praiser speaks up and says *"Good boy!"* or *"Good girl!"* In response, you feel proud and worthy. You like the praise, so you act like that more often.

Every time your impulse or action does not fit with Who I Should Be, your inner critic attacks you. It says *"Bad boy!"* or *"Bad girl!"* In response, you feel ashamed and unworthy. You don't like those feelings, so you try to avoid acting on those impulses.

The voice of your inner critic is not your own voice.

But the voice of your inner critic is not your own voice. It is not the voice of your heart or your essence. It is only the voices of the people who raised you. For some people, this inner voice is so clear in their head that they can tell you which parent is speaking. For most people, all the voices have been mixed together into one voice, which they think is their own. And for some, there isn't a voice at all, but only a bad feeling in the body, as if the voice is speaking in their unconscious and only the bad feeling rises into awareness.

It's also important to distinguish here between the inner critic and your conscience. Your conscience is based more on empathy and compassion for others, so it develops later, when those abilities come online. It matures along with you as you mature. The inner critic, however, doesn't mature much after it is formed, so for the rest of your life it operates with the understanding and maturity of a five-year-old. New situations are measured only against *"Will Mom and Dad like this? Will I get in trouble for this?"* It is a young part of you, trying to protect you in its 5-year-old way. And the inner critic doesn't advise you, it attacks you in order to control your behavior. A critic attack always devalues you in some way. It makes you feel small or stupid or bad. That devaluing is the hallmark of the inner critic and the way you can recognize it every time.

The superego's purpose is to maintain homeostasis in your psyche, which means keeping you within the Good Boy/Good Girl box and not letting you go outside it. Obviously, it is not a fan of inner work. It will attack you for exploring outside the known territory. In effect, the superego is an internalized parent. It holds your parents' image of who you're supposed to be, compares your current state to that, and then corrects any difference. It tries to keep you out of trouble. It helps you learn manners and all of the other norms that you need to learn to get along in society. It gives you your first ability to regulate your own behavior and conform to social norms, which is good. But there is one last major step that needs to happen for the formation of a healthy, mature ego structure.

Separating from the Superego

After your superego forms, it is supposed to separate from your central ego and its voice. You will then disidentify from your inner praiser and inner critic, and begin to hear them as separate voices in your head. You will still hear what your inner critic and inner praiser have to say about your impulses, but you will also be able to hear your own inner voice and feel your own feelings as you make your own decision. It will be an informed decision, not the impulsive act of a two-year-old, and not just a slavish obedience to the standards set by Mom and Dad. It will be your own decision. Now you are beginning to form a healthy ego and an authentic self.

But what if this last major step doesn't happen? What if your superego does not separate from your central ego? Then the voices of your superego do not just praise or criticize you; they drown out your own voice. Then the voice of your inner critic is loud and constant in your head, and when it speaks, you think it's your own voice. You do not question it. You think it speaks the Truth. When your inner critic attacks you, you don't realize that something separate from you is attacking you, or that you can defend yourself against its attacks. And you don't realize that your inner critic cannot praise you, but only criticize, so its words are not a fair assessment of your actions and your worth.

How to Have Better Relationships

Unfortunately, this last developmental step does not happen for most people. Their inner critic stays fused with the voice of their self, and they can't tell the two apart. So they think that the critical voice in their head — the voice that is shaming them and calling them names — is their own voice.

If you listen closely as they talk aloud, you can almost hear what their inner critic is saying inside their head. It's like listening to one side of a phone call and guessing from the side you hear what the other side must be saying. For example, if they are telling you about finding the bathroom flooded when they arrived, they will say something like, *"The bathroom was already flooded when I got here at 10 . . . well, it wasn't right at 10 . . . it was five minutes after 10."* Did you catch that? During each of those pauses, their inner critic was correcting them about the time, even though the exact time was not important to the story.

Failing to disidentify from your inner critic is a real problem. It will leave you unable to defend yourself when your inner critic attacks you. And it will leave you with very little internal space to experience anything new. As soon as a new impulse or feeling arises within you, your inner critic will attack it and try to push you back into the Good Boy/Good Girl box that will guarantee Mom and Dad's approval. Its attacks can be quite savage and leave you feeling ashamed and worthless.

The failure to complete this developmental step is just that — an incomplete developmental step — it is not a personal failure. And it is not a personality pattern.

A critic attack doesn't just correct a mistake, it devalues you. It makes you feel bad about yourself for having made the mistake.

To complete the process of disidentifying from their inner critic, most people need training in how to recognize its voice and defend themselves from its attacks. Once they can perceive the voice of their inner critic as separate from their own voice, they can start to recognize its attacks.

The distinguishing characteristic of a critic attack is that it attacks your value as a person. It doesn't just correct a mistake, it makes you feel bad about yourself for having made the mistake. It is not the voice that says, *"Hey, you're driving too fast. Better slow down."* It's the voice that says, *"You idiot!*

You're screwing up again! You always do this!" It makes you feel small and ashamed of yourself.

Bottom line: disidentifying from the inner critic is a crucial step in everyone's inner work. If you haven't already, you need to find a way to stop your inner critic from beating you up and running your life. To become your authentic self, you need to learn to hear your own inner voice and feel your own inner experience and desires.

Defending Yourself Against a Critic Attack

Once you can recognize a critic attack, you are ready to learn how to defend yourself against it. You do this by using your own life energy to push back against it, instead of letting it use *your* life energy to squash you. Over time, this practice will profoundly change your relationship with your inner critic.

Even though your inner critic may seem at first like an 800 pound gorilla that stomps freely on your small, helpless self, as you practice pushing back against it, the life force that used to feed your inner critic will be redirected into feeding your self. Your inner critic will begin to shrink and your self will begin to grow. Eventually, your self will become bigger and stronger than your inner critic. It will be able to feel an incoming attack and either hold your inner critic off at arms length or just tell it to *"Sit!"*

As you change your relationship with your inner critic, there is one more thing that you may need to do, and that is to stop it from using your mouth to attack others. Just as your inner critic tries to make you behave according to Mom and Dad's Rules, it often tries to make others behave according to those rules as well. It does this by criticizing and correcting their performance. The extent of this outward criticizing varies from person to person, depending on how much outward aggression their personality patterns allow.

In some people, most critic attacks are directed inward, toward the self. In other people, most critic attacks are directed outward, toward others. Some people start with an inner critic directed almost entirely inward, but as they find their inner strength, their inner critic turns outward and begins to attack others. If your inner critic attacks others, you must learn to control it. You can still express anger, but you must learn to do it cleanly, rather than as an attack on their value.

Once you have disidentified from your inner critic and learned how to defend yourself against its attacks, your inner exploration and growth can proceed much more rapidly. You will have cleared a space inside you, within which you will be able to try out new experiences and find your own voice. While it is unlikely that your inner critic will ever disappear completely, your relationship to it will have been turned upside down. Instead of your inner critic being in charge and running your life, now you will be in charge.

Whenever you open the door to some new experience, especially one outside the Good Boy/Good Girl box mandated by your parents, your inner critic is still likely to squawk and try to stop you. But it won't get to make the decisions any more. In time, you will even come to recognize this kind of critic attack as a sign that you are growing and entering new territory, not a sign that you are in trouble.

The Basic Energy Skills

In addition to the psychological skills discussed above, learning to manage yourself requires that you also learn certain basic energy skills. The good news is that developing these energetic skills is good for you. All of these skills are needed for developing emotional maturity and becoming a healthy adult.

You can also get audio recordings and a whole video course at www.the5personalitypatterns.com to support you in your practice.

The Centering Breath – the doorway to Core

Introduction

Let's start with one of the most basic skills, the Centering Breath. Its purpose is to bring you back to your core, which means to bring your attention back to the center of your own body. Your core is a column that includes your spine and extends from the crown of your head straight down through your torso to your perineum.

First, sit forward in your chair. If you're slouched, with your back rounded and your pelvis tipped back, instead sit forward so that your knees are a bit lower than your pelvis, which will make your pelvis tilt forward just a little bit. That will support your spine in a more easy, relaxed way. What we want is a relaxed but erect spine, an easy spine with your head floating easily on top of it.

Now, some of us have a tendency to tip our heads back. So to find out if you do that, first try dropping your chin a little bit. And then slowly rock your head backward and forward. You may notice there is a place where you feel a sense of connection up through your spine and into your head — a place that feels easier, like this is where your head can sit without you having to hold it. Let your head stay there.

Practice

Again, sit forward in your chair and let your knees be just a bit lower than your hips so your pelvis tilts forward a little. That will facilitate a relaxed erectness in your spine and allow your head to float easily on top of it. If you find you have a tendency to tilt your head back, just let your chin drop a little bit, and let the back of your head rise a little bit.

And now, bring your awareness to the column in the core of your body, and imagine that you can breathe in through the very bottom of the column and fill your core with breath, all the way up. And then send it all the way back down and out the bottom. Breathing in through your nose and out through pursed lips.

So it goes like this:

- breathe in through your nose and fill the column all the way up,
  then all the way down and out through pursed lips;
- breathe in through the bottom and all the way up,
  and all the way down and out through pursed lips;
- breathe in through your nose and all the way up to the top of your head,
  then all the way down and out through the bottom.

Do the in-and-out cycle at least three or four times. You may find that you want to continue doing it for a while, which is just fine.

And notice, how do you feel now, compared to the way you felt a moment ago? Perhaps you feel a little more centered or focused. Perhaps a little more relaxed. If you feel some tingles, you're probably feeling more energy moving through your body, which is a good thing. You want to have a strong flow of life energy through your body so that you can do things with it. In order to act in life, you need to have a current of life energy flowing through your body so that you can channel that energy into actions.

If you feel anxious, like maybe you're not doing it the right way, don't worry about that. First of all, you can't hurt yourself. And secondly, you're just beginning this practice. Remember that it's okay to be a beginner. It's always okay to be a beginner and to just be learning.

Whatever your inner critic says about that, just tell it to shut up and sit down. It's trying to help you, but it has the perspective of a five-year-old. So it's trying to help you stay in the Good Girl / Good Boy box that Mom and Dad wanted. But they probably never learned energy skills, so you've ventured out of their box. In fact, whenever you're growing and experiencing something new in life, you will be out of their Good Boy / Good Girl box, so you may feel a little scared, and you may have an inner critic attack. That's just a sign that you're growing and exploring new territory.

Doing the Centering Breath will gradually give you a felt-sense of the core of your body and open the doorway to the next energy skill, which is called Core.

Core – how to know your Self

Introduction

Core is the energetic skill of holding your attention on your core.

First, where is your core? It is that column from the crown of your head straight down through your body to your perineum. Your perineum is that little patch of skin at the very bottom of your torso, between your genitals and your anus. So imagine a column in the middle of your torso, which goes all the way from the crown of your head down to the bottom of your torso.

The Skills You Need to Manage Yourself

Now, what is your core? It is the place in your body where you are the most you. If you want to find yourself, this is the place to look. If you want to know how you feel, this is the place to put your attention. Your thoughts happen in your head, but your sensations and feelings are in your body, and most of them are in your core. You certainly have sensations in your arms and legs, but the more important feelings are in your core.

Your core is the place in your body where you are the most you.

So how does feeling your core help you? What's important about it? Well, feeling your core allows you to reference your self. If you want to strengthen your felt-sense of self, this is the place to put your attention. It is the place to sense into in order to discover what you feel right now. *Happy, unhappy, scared, angry, sad, ashamed, joyful, peaceful?* All of those feelings are going to be here, in your core. It is also the place to feel into to discover *What do I need? What do I want?*

You need to be able feel your core in order to self-reference. And that is important because you need to self-reference in order to make choices in life that are good for you. Choices that are based on real, accurate information about what you feel and want. Not choices based on what someone else wants you to feel, or on what the rules say you should feel. When you have accurate information about your own needs and wants, you can practice good self care and navigate through life more skillfully.

If you've been trained by your family or your culture to never put your attention on this part of your body, you likely don't know what you feel. And this has happened for many, many people. There are many families and cultures that teach their children, *"No, you should not put your attention on your core, and you shouldn't know what you want. When you reference yourself and speak what you want, you're being selfish."* This is taught much more often to girls than to boys, but it's bad for everybody.

Many people are taught that they should not know who they are, but only who other people want them to be. And if that happened to you, you may have been living your whole life for other people — being who they want you to be, doing what they want you to do, and trying to feel what they want you to feel. But, no matter how hard you try, you still have a self inside, a self who's not happy with this project and who may be feeling something very different than they want you to feel.

In fact, developing a strong felt-sense of your core is the source of authentic self confidence. Perhaps you wonder, *What is self confidence?* Think of it as 'self confide-ance'. It is confiding in yourself. And confiding in yourself means telling yourself the truth — the truth about, *How do I feel? What do I want? What do I need? What's going on inside me? Do I like this? Do I not like this? Do I want to move toward that person, or do I want to pull away?*

> *A strong felt-sense of your core is the source of authentic self confidence.*

One of the great benefits of having a strong felt-sense of your core is that you can feel yourself directly and know that you exist, right here and right now. You literally feel full of yourself. It's just wonderful. You do not need anyone else to validate you because you can feel yourself directly. And that's the source of authentic self confidence.

Developing a strong felt-sense of your core is also the foundation of your personal power, because your core is the foundation of your strength and will. Without a felt-sense of your own core, it's very hard to accomplish big things in life because you don't have a center to operate from. You don't have that sense of personal will, of strength and ability, that having a strong core gives you, so you can easily get exhausted.

Without a felt-sense of your core, you may feel hollow and empty inside. You may feel like you're not enough and be constantly looking for validation and help from others. If you always look to others for direction, you may have become very good at reading other people, and that is a very useful skill to have in life. The good news is that developing a strong felt-sense of your own core and learning to self-reference will not diminish that. You'll still be able to reference other people and read what they want and feel. But you will have more choice about whether to put them first or put you first, because you'll actually have a you.

Practice

As you practice sensing your core, keep in mind that it's a very subtle experience. Initially, you may not feel anything at all. Over time, it will become more vivid, and you'll be more able to feel it. So calibrate your attention to notice subtle experiences, because it is initially faint for most

The Skills You Need to Manage Yourself

people. If you're looking for something intense, it's easy to miss it and think, *Oh, nothing's happening*, and then get distracted by an inner critic attack, and that's not useful.

We'll start with the Centering Breath, just to help you find that area of your body. Then we'll shift to simply putting your attention on your core. They're two slightly different practices. The Centering Breath is easier because it gives you something active to do. You're breathing in and filling up your core and then breathing out and emptying it. In contrast, just sensing your core is a quieter, more subtle practice.

Again, sit forward in your chair. Let your pelvis tilt down a little to support a relaxed erectness in your spine, with your head just floating easily on top. If you have a tendency to tilt your head back, just let your chin drop a little, and let the back of your head rise a little.

Once again imagine that you can breathe in through the bottom of your torso and fill your core all the way up. Then breathe down and out as you empty it. In and up through your nose, and out and down through pursed lips. In and up all the way to the top. Then down and all the way out. Then in and up once more, then down and all the way out.

Now just let your body breathe itself. And, in whatever way you can, put your attention on that column in the center of your torso and gently sense into it. As you breathe in, imagine you're breathing into that column. Let your attention follow your breath and gently sense into it. However you experience your core is okay. You may feel it as a kinesthetic sensation in your body, maybe a vibration, an aliveness, or just an awareness of presence. If you're more visual, there may be an image in your mind's eye. Or, if you're more attuned to sound and the auditory channel, there may be a faint hum, a vibration, or a note. However it is for you is just fine.

If you're wondering, *Am I really doing anything? Am I perceiving anything, or am I just imagining it?* be aware that, at the beginning, it's often difficult to tell the difference. Don't let yourself get sidetracked or discouraged by that. As you practice, your perception will gradually get stronger, and that distinction will become clearer to you.

As you practice this, you are also strengthening your attention. Simply by exercising your attention, you are causing your attention to grow stronger. It works the same way that exercising a muscle causes the muscle to grow stronger. So for right now, don't get caught up in the question of whether you're actually perceiving something or just imagining it. Either way is fine.

Also be aware that emotions may surface as you do this. If they do, just notice them and gently bring your attention back to sensing your core. Don't try to pretend that you're not feeling whatever you're feeling. But at the same time, don't let the emotion hijack your attention. Just notice it, bring your attention back to your core, and let the experience of your core unfold within you gradually over time.

Today we're spending only a few minutes sensing your core. As you spend more time with it in the days ahead, you'll be able to explore it more deeply. And since your experience of your core will probably be subtle, any emotions that arise from feeling it will probably be subtle, also. That will give you time to work through whatever feelings come up.

As your felt-sense of your core gradually becomes stronger over the coming weeks and months, several different things may happen. As you begin to reference your own feelings, needs, and wants more clearly, you may want to say out loud what you're discovering about yourself. You may begin to find your own voice, even if you've never had a voice before. If you've been focused only on others and not able to focus on yourself, it may feel like you're speaking in your own voice for the first time in your life.

You may begin to find your own voice.

If that happens to you, you're probably going to want other people to listen to you more than they used to. It may be that you've had a habit of not speaking for yourself and they've had a habit of not really listening to you. You'll probably want to change that. You may find that you assert yourself more, that you say what you feel and what you want. Changes like that are a natural outgrowth of feeling your core and knowing yourself more directly.

This is not a problem — it's a sign that you're growing. However, it may require some adjustments in your relations with some people. They are used to the way you were when you didn't really know what you felt and you would just automatically do whatever they wanted. Now, you may not want to do whatever they want. You may want something different. So that change may require some adjustment and renegotiation between the two of you.

Again, I want to emphasize that you will not lose whatever skills you already have in referencing other people and their needs and feelings. What you're doing now is developing more skill in referencing yourself. So you'll still be able to take care of other people, if you want to, and as you want to. But now you'll also be able to take care of yourself.

Your goal with this skill is to make it second nature — to practice it so much that it becomes something that your body does automatically, all the time, without having to think about it. When that happens, you have embodied it. Just like you did with the skill of balance. When you were a toddler and learning to walk, you learned about balance. You practiced it over and over and over again, day in and day out. You practiced it until you embodied it, and now it's something your body does automatically, without your conscious mind having to think about it at all.

Notice for instance, that during all the time you've been reading this, you have not fallen over once. And you didn't even have to think about not falling over. Without you putting your conscious attention on it, your body has been maintaining your balance in the background.

When we talk about a skill being embodied, we mean that level of unconscious competence. And that is what you want to achieve with all of these energy skills. It takes a lot of practice, but as you practice, you'll find that each skill gets easier and easier. That's because practicing these skills also strengthens your control over your attention. So, as you practice each of these skills, your attention also gets stronger, and that will make your entire life easier.

Grounding – your source of support

Introduction

Have you ever wondered what gives your body a felt-sense of support? What gives you the feeling that there is firm ground under your feet and you have a solid place to stand in the world? Or what gives your body a sense of connection, a sense of belonging here?

Have you wondered how to fill your body with strength, or alertness, or courage? And is there a way to do that intentionally? Yes, you can learn to bring all of those energies up into your body. All of them come from your connection to the earth. Your grounding is the key to bringing all of these energies up into your body.

So what is grounding? It's your connection to the earth below you. And it's your connection to the entire physical plane, the whole world of time and space. Your connection to all of this is called *grounding*.

How to Have Better Relationships

Holding your attention on your connection to the earth gives you a felt-sense of connection and belonging here. It gives you a felt-sense of safety and of support. We often talk about support as an emotional thing, like people approving of you, admiring you, understanding you, but there's also a more fundamental kind of support. It's the support of physically feeling the earth under you, holding you up.

If you've ever been in an earthquake, you've experienced this on a visceral level. I live in California and I was here for the big earthquake in 1989. Everyone here was shaken to their core. For weeks, it was the first thing everyone had to talk about. The idea that the earth could move under us was deeply upsetting. If you've ever been in an earthquake, you, too, have a felt-sense of this. Our need to feel the earth as solid and stable under us is profound. But to fully feel its support, we have to be energetically connected to it. It is energetically feeling the support of the earth under you that gives you a felt-sense of support.

Being grounded is the key to feeling supported.

How do you develop this? You put your awareness on this connection. You practice connecting from the bottom of your core down into the earth. Think of it as extending your own core down into the earth. You can go as far down as you like — into the soil, into the bedrock, or even all the way down to the center of the earth itself.

Without it, you may feel like you're not supported here. A lot of people come into therapy and say they don't feel supported in life. They're thinking about it psychologically, but usually the source of the problem is the fact that they don't have a strong energetic connection down into the earth. The psychological part may be true, too, but if you address only the psychological level, you're missing the deeper fundamental cause. Over and over, I've seen that many of the issues that seem intractable in therapy can be solved by learning the basic energetic skills of Core, Ground, Edge, and Me/Not Me.

If you don't have a connection to the earth, you will likely feel unsupported and unsteady, both emotionally and physically. You will feel like you have no place to stand and no firm ground under your feet. You may be a pushover because, without a solid foundation, it's easy for someone to knock you over. You may not feel safe here in the physical world. If any of those things are happening to you, it's time to practice grounding.

The Skills You Need to Manage Yourself

Similarly, without grounding, you may feel weak, like there's no energy or strength flowing up into you. You may also feel overwhelmed by other people's energy coming into your space. When you have a firm grounding connection, you can send all of their energy down into the ground.

I also want to note that I'm speaking of being grounded or not grounded as if it's black and white, and it's not. Like everything else in the world, it's shades of gray. A person can be completely ungrounded — with no connection to the earth plane at all — or a little bit grounded, or more grounded, or even very deeply grounded. But whatever your situation is, practice will improve it.

Practice

We're going to start with a brief Centering Breath and Core, and then we'll add Ground.

Once again, sit forward in your chair with an easy, relaxed erectness in your spine. Your pelvis tilted just slightly forward, maybe your knees a little lower than your hips. Your head floating easily on your spine.

And start with breathing in through the bottom of your torso and filling your core all the way up. Then all the way down and out again. Breathing in through your nose and out through pursed lips. Again, all the way up, and then down and out. Once more, all the way up, and then down and out.

Now, gently put your awareness on your core, on that column from the crown of your head down to your perineum. The whole column, not just part of it.

And now let yourself gently imagine that your core is extending downward into the earth. Different people have different ways that they like to imagine this. Some people imagine it as a root, like the root of a tree. For them, it's more brown and woody, and as it grows down, smaller roots grow out from it in all directions.

Some people imagine it as a steel cable, a really strong, shiny, beautiful steel cable that goes down deep into the earth.

Some people prefer a massive anchor with a big anchor chain like they have on an aircraft carrier or a supertanker. A chain made of enormous links of cast iron that weigh hundreds of kilos a piece, and they go all the way down, deep into the earth, to a huge anchor at the bottom.

How to Have Better Relationships

Some people like to imagine their connection more as an underground stream. It could be a flow of some kind of fluid, or a stream of liquid light. Maybe the stream glows blue, or green, or yellow, or any color you like. And maybe the light has little bubbles in it that sparkle in different colors. You can even imagine them as little sparkly bubbles of consciousness, bubbles of awareness.

Or you can imagine your connection down deep into the earth as a flow of love, with your love flowing down and out the bottom of your core, all the way down into the heart of the earth.

It can be anything you like. There is no right way or wrong way. There is no normal way. It can be any color or texture or material. For you, the experience may be more visual, so you see it in your mind. Or it may be more auditory, like a sound you hear inside. Or it may be more kinesthetic, like a felt sensation inside your body.

Take some time to play with it and try out some different ways. Ask your body what kind of grounding it wants, what would make it happy. Just let your imagination explore and find whatever it finds. Remember, you can change this anytime you want. You can do it a different way the next time. There's no right way and no wrong way. And no one's going to judge you.

Whatever form you're imagining, let it grow downwards. If it's only down 10 feet into the ground below you, let it go down further. Maybe let it go 100 feet down through the soil and the layers of clay. Gradually, gently, let it go all the way down into the bedrock, and maybe eventually, all the way down into the heart of the earth.

And as you do this, notice what you're finding. No judgment, just noticing. As your core extends downward, let your awareness go with it and see what you find. You might be expecting that the earth below you will be dead and uncaring. Is that what you find? You might be expecting that it will somehow be alive. Is that what you find? Do you find some sort of intelligence?

What if the earth is an intelligent being? And what if the earth is happy to connect with you? Ask yourself, *"Does the earth seem friendly? Does it like me?"* You can also ask it, *"Do you like me? Am I safe here?"* Then pause and notice what you experience after you ask. The response often comes in a form you're not expecting, so let your awareness open out to receive any sort of response.

The Skills You Need to Manage Yourself

Many tribal cultures relate to the earth as Mother or Grandmother. Now, my personal grandmother wasn't that much fun. She was old and strange and smelled bad. Maybe yours was, too. So think of this as your ideal grandmother, the one who opens the door and says, *"Oh, I'm so glad you're here."* And she hugs you and gives you hot chocolate and cookies. She's happy to have you sit on her lap and tell her everything you think and feel, and she's just happy that you're here and that you're you. She loves you just the way you are, and you don't have to be any different.

Let yourself feel into the possibility — "What if the earth likes me?"

Don't try to force anything. Just let yourself feel into the possibility — *"What if the earth likes me?"* What might your experience be then? Again, just notice your inner experience. No judgment, just noticing. What are you finding?

Make it a two way flow

Now let's add something. Notice whether there's any energy or emotion in your body that you would like to get rid of — maybe anger, fear, or shame. The fact is, you can send that energy or emotion down and into the earth. The earth is huge, so no matter what you send, it will never be too much for the earth. In fact, any energy you send is welcome. It feeds the plants. It feeds all the living creatures that draw their energy from the earth. It's all life energy, so it's food for them, and they like it.

Similarly, the connection you have with the earth is a two-way street. Just as energy can flow down from your body into the earth, it can also flow up from the earth and into your body. And you can ask the earth to send you any kind of energy you need. You can ask it for aliveness. You can ask it for strength or courage or will. You can ask it for love or safety. You can ask it for a feeling of belonging. You can ask for qualities, or abilities, or colors. You can say, *"Send me some yellow light"* or *"Send me pink light."* Whatever you want.

Let yourself play with it. Ask it to send whatever you want up into you. Maybe it fills your legs and your pelvis first and then gradually fills up your torso and spills down your arms. Maybe it fills your fingers, your hands, and your arms. And then gradually fills your neck, and your head, and even fills your face. There might be so much that it spouts out the top of your head like a fountain.

Again, notice your experience now, allowing whatever sort of connection you have to just be there. Let your awareness include your physical body, your emotional body, and your connection with the earth. And just notice what's happening for you now. Again, no judgment, just noticing.

Now, begin to gently expand your awareness to include the room you're sitting in, but don't abandon your energetic connection with the earth. Keep part of your attention on that connection. Keep part of your attention on that flow, or root, or whatever it is, so that you maintain your relationship with the earth. Maybe there's a flow coming up, or a flow going down, or maybe both at once. Let that continue, even when you're not consciously aware of it.

A second version of Grounding

Once again, let yourself start with the Centering Breath. An easy, relaxed sense of core. Relaxed erectness, head floating easily, pelvis tilted down a little. And let yourself breathe in the bottom and fill all the way up. Then down and all the way out. In once more and all the way up; then down and out. In and up, down and out. Do it at least three times, but also try doing it 10 or 20 times. Let these practices become your own. Explore them, have fun with them, play with them. See what happens if you do the Centering Breath 20 times.

The Centering Breath has probably highlighted your core. If not, just bring your attention to it. Notice that column from the crown of your head down to your perineum. Maybe it feels like a column of awareness or aliveness. Or maybe it feels like flesh and bone.

And now we'll do a different kind of Grounding. Last time, you extended your core downward and sent your energy down deep into the earth. This time, imagine that the bottom of your core can open and you can invite the earth's energy to come up into you and fill you. Simply ask the earth to send up into you whatever kind of energy you would like, in whatever form you would like — colors, qualities, a stream of bubbles — and let that begin to fill your whole body.

You may experience it coming up into the bottom of your torso, filling your pelvis first, and then spilling down into your legs and gradually filling them up. Or maybe you imagine it coming in through the soles of your

The Skills You Need to Manage Yourself

feet and filling your legs from the bottom up, and then filling your pelvis. Either way, let it gradually come up to your waist, and then up further, filling your back and your chest all the way up to your shoulders, and then spilling down your arms. Filling your arms with this lovely energy from the earth. All the way down into your hands and fingers. Maybe there's so much that it leaks out of your palms and fingertips.

Allow it to continue filling your neck and your head — the sides of your head, the back of your head and your face, all the way up to the very top of your head. There may be so much that it fountains out the top of your head and begins filling your personal bubble, filling it with whatever kind of energy you have invited the earth to send you.

Now remember, this is still a two-way street. So if there's any kind of energy or emotion in your body that you don't want, you can also send that down into the earth, where it will become compost for the plants. If you'd like to get to know that feeling better first, you can do that — you can sit with it and have a conversation with it. You can do whatever you like. There is no right or wrong way. You get to explore everything.

So now just notice what's happening in your experience. Right this moment, what's happening? No judgment, just noticing. And how is this version of Grounding different for you than the first version we did, the one where you start by sending your energy down into the earth? How is it different when you start with inviting the earth to come up into you instead? Again, just notice.

As you're ready, let your awareness begin coming back out to the room around you. But keep part of your attention on your core, on this connection, and on the earth below you. Let all of that continue, to whatever degree it does. And remember, you're new at this, and it's okay to be a beginner. As you keep practicing, you will gradually get more skillful with it.

How is this version different from the first one we did? Well, the first one, where you send your energy down, and you penetrate the earth, is a more masculine energy. This one, where you invite the earth to penetrate you, is a more feminine energy. And the best part is, you don't have to choose. You can do both of them at the same time: you can send your awareness down, penetrating the earth, and you can invite the earth to come up and penetrate you. You can do both at once.

Edge – your protection & shield

Introduction

The field of psychology has produced many books on the importance of *psychological boundaries.* These books show you the difference between living with healthy boundaries and living without them. They help you distinguish *my feeling* from *your feeling, my responsibility* from *your responsibility.* They teach you how to say "no" when you need to, even though you may disappoint someone else. And they show you how to deal with the long list of objections that often arise — both in you and in others — when you first begin to assert your psychological boundaries.

But those books rarely even mention the importance of developing strong *energetic boundaries.* To develop your energetic boundaries, you first have to put your attention on your own space and your edge. As you may already know, you have an egg-shaped bubble that surrounds you. It extends out about an arms length beyond your body in all directions, including above and below you. This is your own space, and it contains much of your own energy field.

To get a sense of your edge, imagine that your bubble is surrounded by a membrane, like the membrane that surrounds a cell. The cell membrane separates 'inside' from 'outside' for the cell. It regulates what enters the cell and what leaves the cell. The membrane you have at the edge of your personal bubble does the same for you. It regulates what goes in and out of your personal space.

Without a strong energetic boundary around your bubble, other people's thoughts, feelings, and energies can easily get into your space and mix with your own thoughts, feelings, and energies. This will confuse you and make it hard for you to sort out what you think, feel, and want.

Now your edge has a second function that's equally important. It creates a container that actually holds your energy within your space and your body. It works like a jar full of water. Your energetic container forms the jar and your energy is the water. If the jar is big and strong, it can hold a lot of water. If the jar is small and weak, it can't hold very much. If it's big and weak, it can start to hold a lot, but when it gets too full, it just bursts. And if it leaks, it never gets full.

You want a big, strong container because it can hold more energy. The bigger and stronger your container is, the more energetic charge you can hold in your space, and with more charge, you literally have more power. When we talk about empowerment, we mean more than just shifting your attitude. We mean literally filling your container with energy, because with energy, you can make things happen in the physical world. With energy, you can accomplish things in life. And that's important.

A big, strong container is the key to empowerment.

The good news is that, by putting your attention on this membrane, you can strengthen it. Your edge has intelligence, just like a cell membrane does, so you can communicate with it. You can instruct it to allow into your space only what is good for you.

Practice

Start by centering yourself in your Core. Then hold in your mind an image of your bubble, which extends out about an arm's length from your body in all directions. In your mind, highlight the membrane at its edge, and then reach out to communicate with it. Tell it how you want it to protect you and help you, thank it in advance for its help, and listen for any response. You can tell your boundary to allow in only what is good for you, or any words that feel right to you. Then, over time, notice what effect strengthening your energetic Edge in this way has on your experience of yourself and the world.

Because our culture is so unaware of the energy world, this idea of holding an energetic boundary around yourself may sound strange to you, but don't let that discourage you or keep you from practicing this exercise. The results can be dramatic, especially if your energetic boundary has previously been weak or leaky. I recommend spending 5-10 minutes a day on this practice until it becomes second nature, that is, until your body does it automatically, even when you're not consciously focused on it.

Me / Not Me – how to differentiate yourself

Introduction

Along with learning to differentiate what is *me* from *you* in the psychological sense (my needs vs. your needs, my responsibility vs. your responsibility), you also need to learn how to clear out foreign energies — energies that do not belong to you — that have gotten into your space. This is basic energetic hygiene, and it's just as important as the physical hygiene of washing your body. It's especially important for anyone who has a weak energetic boundary, since their weak boundary doesn't stop foreign energies from getting into their space. Having other people's energies and feelings inside your space will make you feel overwhelmed and confused. You will feel much safer and clearer when you have only your own energies and feelings inside your space.

Practice

In order to keep your space clean, you need to learn and practice this skill. The practice goes like this:

1. Say your own name or the name that most resonates with you as your own. Notice the frequency of that name: that is your personal frequency. If the idea of frequency doesn't make sense to you, think of it as your note, your taste, your scent, your feeling tone, your is-ness, or whatever works for you.
2. Look for that same frequency in your torso, in the core of your body.
3. Use one of the following methods to clear out of your body and your bubble anything that doesn't match your own frequency.
    a. Ask your core, the column in the center of your body, to expand and push out ahead of it anything that doesn't match your frequency. Imagine it gradually expanding in diameter and pushing everything that is "not me" out ahead of it, the way a glacier pushes rocks ahead of it. This method seems to work better for people who are more kinesthetic.
    b. If you're more visual, try this: tell everything that is "not me" within your space to light up so you can see it. Then imagine using a vacuum cleaner to vacuum out all the lit up stuff. Or

The Skills You Need to Manage Yourself

highlight and delete each one just as you would on a computer. Or you can blow up each foreign piece, if that appeals to you.

c. Or, since each piece that is "not me" came from someone else and really should be there instead of here in you, imagine that there is still a thread that connects each piece to wherever it came from. Then just instruct all the threads to become elastic and pull their pieces out of you and back to wherever they belong. Many people like the "putting everything back in order" feeling of this one.

d. Or, invent some other method for clearing all the foreign energies and feelings out of your space. Let your imagination go and be as creative as you like. Your method can be anything that gets the job done.

Wrapping up

So we've practiced the Centering Breath, Core, Ground, Edge, and Me/Not Me. To develop these energy skills, do each one at least every day, and preferably several times a day.

With each of these practices, your goal is to do it so often that you embody it — until your body learns to do it automatically, without you having to think about it, just the same way that your body regulates your heartbeat and blood pressure and digestion and everything else that is going on in the background. Your body is already holding attention on each of these tasks, without your conscious awareness. In fact, you're already holding many different attentions at once, without even realizing it.

Your goal with each skill is to embody it.

And as you do these practices, day by day, notice:

- *How do you feel after each practice, compared to how you were feeling before?*
- *What effect does it have on your overall inner state?*
- *What effect does it have on how well the day goes for you?*
- *Does it change how you behave toward others?*
- *Does it change how others behave toward you?*

How to Have Better Relationships

The more you develop these energy skills, the more likely it is that other people will regard you as safe. That may change how they behave toward you, so notice how others behave toward you as you develop these skills.

And lastly, I want to encourage you to continue experimenting and playing with these practices. Approach them in an easy and lighthearted way and have fun with them.

Learn to Manage Your Own Inner State

Children vs Adults

Take a moment to ask yourself: what's the difference, emotionally, between being a child and being an adult? Here's a clue: when someone says, *"He's such a child"* about another adult, what do they mean?

The main emotional difference between being a child and being an adult is your ability to manage your own internal state. A mature adult is able to manage their own internal state; a child is not. We expect children to frequently need help managing their emotions, but we expect more from adults. We might even say that the ability to manage your internal state is one of the main traits of a mature, healthy adult.

> *The main emotional difference between being a child and being an adult is your ability to manage your own internal state.*

In psychology, we talk a lot about the difference between a regulated nervous system and a dysregulated nervous system. Emotionally mature adults are able to self-soothe and self-regulate, while children are not. Learning to self-soothe and self-regulate is the doorway to becoming functionally an adult. Just getting older and bigger isn't enough. You need to learn how to manage your own inner state.

So how do you learn to manage your inner state? Practicing and developing all the skills we've already discussed will give you a strong foundation, but there are a few more skills needed for self-regulation, which I describe below.

The Skills You Need to Manage Yourself

Learn How to Soothe Yourself

There are many, many ways to calm and soothe your body, and you probably already have some favorites, so I won't try to list them all. But here are two very effective methods that you may not have heard about. I learned them when studying Applied Kinesiology during the 1970's and EFT (Emotional Freedom Techniques) more recently.

The AK 4-Point Rubbing Technique

Here's a simple self-soothing technique you can use to calm your body down. I call it the AK 4-Point Rubbing Technique because I first learned it when I was studying Applied Kinesiology.

To do it, you simply rub 4 points on the front of your body, all at the same time. The first 2 points are at the edges of your sternum, just under your collarbones. They're called the collarbone points in EFT and K-27 on acupuncture charts. To find them, start at the notch in your neck and come down an inch (2cm) and then out an inch (2cm) to the left and right. The two points are about two inches (5cm) apart, just under your collarbones. You'll use the thumb and first two fingers of one hand to rub these two points.

To find the other 2 points, imagine a small clock face centered on your belly button, with the numbers on the clock face arranged in a circle about 2 inches (5cm) wide. The points you want are at 4 and 8 on the clock face, so they're about an inch (2cm) to each side of your belly button and down about half an inch (1cm). You'll use the thumb and first two fingers of the other hand to rub these two points.

To keep your hand muscles from getting tired, keep your hands still and use your arm muscles to move your hands back and forth. Your arm muscles are much bigger and stronger, so they won't tire so easily. If you use your finger muscles to do the rubbing motion, you'll probably find that they get tired quickly.

When you first notice that you're upset and before you start the rubbing, focus on your body and try to locate the sensations of your upset. Notice where they're located and what the sensations are in that area. Then keep your attention on those sensations as you do the rubbing.

How long you do the rubbing is up to you. You may want to continue for several minutes as you feel the intensity of the sensations gradually diminish. Or you may feel the sensations diminish rapidly and feel like you're done more quickly. Often the reduction in intensity is remarkable. Remember to breathe while you're rubbing.

You can use the AK 4-point rubbing technique on yourself anytime you want to shift your inner state. It's free and easy and always with you, and there are no side effects. Some people tend to stop breathing while they focus on the rubbing, so remind yourself to keep breathing as you do it.

You can do this technique as much as you want, any time you want. Over time, you may notice that you generally feel less anxious than you used to. And knowing that you have a tool to soothe yourself will probably make you less prone to feeling anxious in the first place.

<u>The Fingertip Squeeze</u>

This is another simple self-soothing technique you can use to calm your body. All you do is squeeze the tip of each finger, side to side, while you take in a slow, full breath and then slowly let it out.

If you feel the fingertip area, you'll notice that there's a little dip on each side, about even with the base of the fingernail, and that squeezing there just feels right. Take a long, slow inhale and exhale while you squeeze and hold each one. If you want to stay for more than one breath before moving on, do so. After doing one hand, switch and do the other hand. As you move slowly from finger to finger, you'll notice your breathing slows and deepens as your entire body calms down.

The Fingertip Squeeze has the advantage of being discrete. If you leave your hands in your lap while you do it, no one will notice. While sitting around a conference table at work, you can do it under the table, completely out of sight. While sitting in the dentist's chair, you can do it in your lap. You can do it almost anywhere without attracting attention and without anyone noticing. Again, remember to breathe.

Pause before acting

It's also important to learn to pause before acting because, as the old saying goes, "Speed kills feeling". This is what's behind the popular advice to "count to 10" or "take 3 deep breaths." The pause gives your heart and mind a chance to catch up with your impulse and consider it. Instead of letting your unconscious, automatic reaction dictate what you do next, you're giving yourself a moment to feel, think, and make a conscious choice.

Training yourself to pause before acting may be difficult, and you may need to practice it many times before pausing becomes automatic, but giving yourself this time will pay you back many times over. Your conscious choice will almost always be wiser than your first impulse.

Consider the consequences

As you pause, consider the consequences of each option. *If I do A, then B will happen. If B happens, then C will follow,* and so on. Take a moment to notice where each option leads and how you will feel about winding up there. Then ask yourself, *"Is this who I want to be?"* Your answer to that question will show you the larger, long-term effects of each path and probably make your choice clear and easy.

What is Needed to be a Healthy Adult

Here is some of what a person needs to do to become a healthy adult and be ready to create a healthy, adult relationship. This list may not be complete, but it gives you a start.

Developing self-awareness skills

1. Develop the Inner Witness
2. Learn to track your own inner state
3. Learn to shift your attention from the stories you're telling yourself to your raw experience
4. Discover that your reactions are an opportunity to learn about yourself
5. Shift your relationship with your Inner Critic:
   a. recognize that it is not your own voice and disidentify from it
   b. recognize its attacks
   c. learn to defend yourself against its attacks
   d. reclaim for yourself the energy that has been feeding it
6. Make "the Turn" from avoiding pain to seeking truth
7. Learn to accept your current inner state and inquire into it with lighthearted curiosity

8. Practice being deeply intimate with your own experience, no matter what it is, so that you can learn from it
9. Learn how to use this deep awareness of yourself in negotiating to get what you want

Healing the past and growing up

1. Develop the basic energy skills: Ground, Core, Edge, Me/Not Me
2. Develop healthy psychological boundaries
3. Learn to self-reference without self-judgment
4. Heal the core traumas that have shaped and organized you. Recognize your own conditioning, contradict it, and heal/clear out of your body what drives it. Learn to look forward to the increased sense of freedom and power you will feel each time you reclaim a disowned piece of yourself.
5. Learn to recognize when you shift from an adult state to a child state
6. Learn how to shift yourself back to an adult state
7. Develop a relationship with your own inner child, listen to its needs, and be the parent who makes arrangements to get those needs met
8. Learn healthy skills for communication, disagreement, inquiry, and joint decision-making
9. Learn to measure and anticipate your own needs and limitations
10. Learn to measure and anticipate the needs and limitations of others

Questions

Learning Core

"Once we learn Core, do we need to continue practicing it?"

Think of it this way. You probably don't have to practice maintaining your balance all day, every day, because, by practicing it for years as a little kid, you embodied it. So now, your body does it automatically, even while you're consciously focusing on something else.

You went through the same process when you learned to ride a bicycle. You learned how to ride a bicycle by doing it. And the more you did it, the better your body got at doing it, until eventually you got to the place where you had embodied it and you didn't need to consciously practice it anymore. But while you're riding a bicycle, your body still has to be attending to it in the background so it can alert you if something is going wrong and you need to pay attention to it.

Once you've really embodied a skill, you don't need to consciously pay attention to it so much anymore. But you do have to practice it consciously, often for years, until you have embodied it. And even then, part of you still has to monitor it and alert you if you are losing your sense of Core. I still tune in to my core most mornings as I'm waking up, even though I've been practicing it for 20 years.

More energy from doing Core

"I've been practicing Core intensely in the past week and a half and I'm already noticing that I'm not exhausted at the end of the day any more. I had thought that my exhaustion was normal. It's great to know I can control and manage my own energy."

Well, hurray for you! Yes, developing a felt-sensation of your own core will help you run more energy, develop a stronger energetic container, and keep your body more full of your own life energy. And those are just some of the benefits of developing the basic energy skills.

Handling anger

> "What is the first thing you personally do when you get upset or angry? Do you immediately turn to a centering process?"

There are many ways to handle getting angry. I want to encourage you to try them all and see what works best for you. They at least interrupt your automatic, unconscious reaction in some way, which gives you a moment to think before you act. I find doing the Centering Breath very helpful. I also find that wiggling my butt really, really helps, because when I get upset or angry, I'm often assuming that whatever I wanted is somehow very important, and wiggling my butt feels so foolish that it shakes me out of my assumption of preeminence, if you know what I mean.

- 3 -

The Skills You Need when Interacting with Others

The 6 Levels of Relationship

How do you even know when you're in a "Relationship?" How is a capital-R Relationship different from all the other relationships of life?

Let's start by looking at relationships in general: acquaintances, friends, lovers. If we put these on a spectrum according to the amount of emotional investment in the relationship, we discover that they fall into six fairly discrete groups, the six levels of relationship.*

1. **Acquaintanceship** – Acquaintances are the people that we don't really know; we just happen to bump into them in the course of daily life: bus drivers, store clerks, most co-workers. What distinguishes this group is that we don't choose them in any way. We choose something else that causes us to be in that place at that time (the bus, the store, the job) and we meet these people along the

---

* This model is based on one presented by Terry Gorski in a talk on relationships. I have modified it somewhat, but I am indebted to him for the majority of it. I do not know whether it was original to him or based on someone else's work.

way. We have contact with them by chance, not by choice. Acquaintanceship is by far the largest of the six groups, and this is where all our relationships start. If we particularly like someone in this group, we may choose to invite them into the next level.

2. **Companionship** – A companion is someone we seek out in order to share an activity with them. At this level, the activity is still more important than the person. For instance, suppose that you're a tennis buff. When you want to play tennis, you start calling up your tennis friends. If the first one can't play, you say "thanks" and move on to the second one. You go down the list until you find someone who has time to play tennis. The people are interchangeable; it is the activity that is primary. This is not an insult to anyone. We all know that our relationship centers around tennis because that's the only time we see each other. If you come to like one of your tennis buddies particularly, you may want to invite them into a friendship.

3. **Friendship** – Now the priorities are reversed: the person is more important than the activity. Suppose you want to see your friend Bob. You call him up and say *"Can you get together today?"* If he says "yes", then you negotiate what you want to do together. Maybe you'll see a movie, or take a walk, or eat dinner, or even play tennis. What makes you friends is that you are getting together to enjoy each other's company, rather than for a particular activity.

Notice that in these first three levels, there is no commitment to any further contact in the future. These levels are based on choices you make for the present moment only: accidental contact (no choice), choosing the activity, and choosing the person. The next three levels are based on your priorities over time and reflect deepening degrees of commitment.

4. **Committed Friendship** – Time is the new feature here. Now there is an agreement to continue to be available to each other in the future. This is not an exclusive relationship. It is expected that you will each have other committed friends as well, but there is a commitment to continue this friendship for the foreseeable future.

5. **Primary Friendship** – This is your "best friend". This person is not only a committed friend, but the most important one, the one you

put first when you have to choose. Priority is the new feature here. You may change best friends from time to time, but there can be only one person at a time who has priority over all others.

6. **Life Partner** – To priority we now add permanence. Your life partner is assured that they are not only the most important person in your life, but that they can depend on holding that office for life. Otherwise, we're back to level 5. This is why the marriage vow is "until death do us part" instead of "until we change our minds."

These two conditions (priority & permanence) make this level of relationship uniquely powerful for us emotionally. It is this relationship which most stimulates our unconscious hopes and fears and fantasies. What makes this level of relationship so powerful is its resonance with our first love affair, the one we had with our mother when we were an infant. She was our first "one and only love" and that relationship remains in our unconscious as the prototype of all future love affairs. Each new love stirs those old hopes and fears and shapes our feelings in the present. This level of relationship touches our deepest wounds, offering us both the hope of healing them and the fear of being hurt anew.

Having sex does not determine what level of relationship you have with someone.

And, of course, this is typically the relationship we are referring to when we say we are "looking for a Relationship." We already have a "small-r relationship" with the friend or acquaintance we are talking to, but it is the "big-R Relationship" we mean when we say we are looking for one.

Notice that having sex does not determine what level of relationship you have with someone. A person can have or not have sex at any of these levels. For instance, at an orgy a person might have sex with someone simply because they happen to be within reach. This is sex at the acquaintance level. When someone goes to a bar to find a partner for a one-night stand, they are having sex at the companion level. Sex can also take place within the context of a friendship or a committed friendship or a primary friendship.

However, adding sex to a relationship can be confusing, because the touching and tenderness and pleasure of sex also recreate the infant-mother experience and stir up our unconscious hopes of once again finding that one-and-only love connection. So adding sex can easily skew our perception of the relationship and make us feel like we are now in level 6, when in fact we're not.

The various relationships within a person's birth family, tribe, and clan aren't included in this model, since they're governed more by the person's culture, ethnicity, religion, tribe, and the like, but I hope that having this model of non-family relationships will help you navigate more skillfully through life.

Relationship is Voluntary

Outside of family and beyond the level of acquaintances, all adult relationships are voluntary. We have said "yes" to the connection, and we can always say no to it.

Some of us forget this simple fact and are surprised when someone announces that they're ending their connection with us. For instance, if you grew up in an intact family (no divorce, no one died or left), you may have unconsciously assumed that no one ever leaves, since no one left during your childhood. So being suddenly left by a lover or best friend may be a shock to you. Conversely, if your childhood included someone important leaving, perhaps via divorce or death, you may have unconsciously assumed that no relationship is permanent, and you may now be unable to believe that anyone will stay, no matter what they promise.

Since whatever family you grew up in was your first experience of human connection, it usually shapes what you expect from relationships for the rest of your life. If your early experiences of relationship were good enough, you probably approach relationships believing that you belong, you are safe and loved, and you can say 'yes' and 'no' to others without losing the relationship.

On the other hand, if your early experiences of relationship were more wounding, you may approach relationships believing that you do not belong, you are not safe and loved, whatever you say may lead to trauma, and you are always in danger of losing the relationship.

Because of their childhood wounds, some people have a hard time saying a real, full-hearted 'yes' to a relationship. They believe that such a 'yes' leaves them vulnerable to a repeat of the old heartbreak, so they try to protect themselves by controlling their relationships and avoiding deep emotional attachments.

Other people believe that, in order to keep a relationship, they must always say 'yes'. To do that, they learn to abandon themselves inside and instead focus only on what the other person wants. This allows them to say 'yes', even when their real answer would be 'no'. They become experts at pleasing others, but feel empty inside.

Similarly, some people believe that they can't say a real 'no' without losing the connection. So they believe that in order to say 'no', they must end the connection. Often they do that by fleeing. If they cannot flee, they may outwardly say 'yes', but then passively avoid their 'yes' by not following through on it.

Some people simply cannot reference their own core enough to find their own 'yes' and 'no' inside, so they either follow an external set of rules, or follow the other person's lead.

These difficulties with knowing your own true responses and speaking them clearly can create many problems in relationships. That's why we went into so much detail in the previous chapter about the skills you need to learn in order to authentically know yourself and manage your own inner state. In this chapter and the next one, we're building on that foundation by adding the knowledge and skills you need to communicate and relate successfully with others.

The 4 Levels of Communication

This map of the levels of communication is a way of assessing the depth of intimacy in any given exchange. Many people are already unconsciously aware of these levels because whatever social skills training they had was good enough that they're able to automatically sense what level of intimacy is appropriate in a given situation and shift into that. However, not all of us were so fortunate, so you may find that having an explicit map of these levels of communication is a big help.

How to Have Better Relationships

1. Small Talk – (Talking About Nothing)

We call this small talk because you are not really talking about anything of importance. These are conversation openers (or even entire conversations) about the weather, the time, or anything in the immediate surroundings.

Sometimes those of us who are more focused on being intimate and open dislike this level of contact. We may get judgmental about it and call it boring or dishonest. I think that when we do that, we're missing the function of this level of contact. This is the opening level of contact, the one used when striking up a conversation with a stranger. The overt communication here is free of content because the real communication is not about content, but about whether we're going to communicate at all.

For example, if you're sitting on a park bench and you say to the stranger next to you, *"Nice day today, huh?"* your real question is not the one about the weather, but the one beneath it, in which you're asking *"Are you open to talking with me?"* The stranger's reply might range from a smile and an agreeing comment to an icy stare or turning away and leaving. Clearly the first response means *"yes"* and the last means *"no,"* but those answers were only implied, not stated.

The indirectness of this form of communication makes it safer for both people. A direct query, such as *"Are you open to talking with me?"* would have been more intimate and confronting. As we will see in a minute, it would have been a leap to the fourth level of communication, to talking about *us*. That would be too big a leap and would probably make the other person uncomfortable. But by talking about the weather, we can negotiate that question non-verbally and then gradually consider whether we want to move to communicating on a deeper level.

2. Talking About Something

Here the content begins to be important. We have already established that we have permission to talk with each other, so now we can proceed to talking about something we care about, but not yet to talking about ourselves. The subject could be anything — it could be sports, science, politics, or even the weather, as long as we care about it. Here *what* we are saying is the foreground, and *how* we are saying it is more in the background. We might be agreeing or disagreeing, but our focus is on the content of our communication, more than on the subtext.

The Skills You Need when Interacting with Others

This is more intimate than the first level because we care about this subject. The fact that it matters to us is what moves this communication up to level two. But we are still focused mostly on the facts of a subject outside of ourselves. Most public communication falls into this category, as well as many conversations among men.

3. Talking About Me or Talking About You

Now the subject is personal. I am telling you about me and my thoughts and feelings, or you are telling me about you and your thoughts and feelings. We are now talking explicitly about ourselves and our own inner experience.

The shift to personal disclosure is what marks this as a deeper level of communication than the second level. If in-ti-ma-cy means into-me-you-see, then we are now letting that happen. We are revealing ourselves to each other.

Notice that only one of us may be revealing themselves, while the other just listens. All the focus may be on only one person, as they explore and put into words their inner experience, while the other person just holds space for them.

Or the two people may be trading personal disclosures as a way to get to know each other at a deeper level. This level of communication is more common among women and usually happens in private conversations.

4. Talking About Us

At the fourth level, the subject is not you or me, but us: how we feel about each other, how we treat each other, what we want from each other, and what our hopes are for the relationship in the future. This is 'talking about the relationship'. It is the most tender and vulnerable level of communication and is almost always reserved for private conversations. When a woman says to her lover, *"We need to talk,"* she is probably saying *"I want us to talk on level 4."*

Using this map to communicate more skillfully

Notice that the shifting of a conversation from level 1 to level 2 to level 3 is a process of deepening intimacy between the participants. As they

49

negotiate and establish a sense of connection at one level, they may feel safe enough to progress to the next level.

Notice also that a conversation doesn't necessarily stay on one level, but may move from level to level, either up or down, often depending on how safe the participants feel. For example, two strangers may meet at a party, begin with level 1 and progress to level 2, or even to level 3. But if a new person joins the conversation, they will probably drop back a level because they no longer feel safe enough to stay where they were. As they get to know the new person a little more, they may again shift to a more intimate level or they may not, depending on how safe each person feels.

Within one conversation, people may be talking on different levels.

You may also notice that, within one conversation, different people may be communicating on different levels. Each will unconsciously move to the level where they feel most at home. And often, they will then attempt to get the others to join them at their preferred level. This difference in preferred levels is frequently a source of friction within a male-female couple, with the man wanting to talk on level 2 while the woman wants to talk on level 3 or level 4.

Clearly, there is much more that we could explore about these different levels and how people use them in various situations, but I trust that this brief overview at least gets you thinking and helps you more skillfully navigate your communications with others.

The Basic Communication Skills

The Steps of Communicating[*]

1. Show up, meaning be present in your body, here and now. If you're not present in your body, you can't get any information from it about what it feels and wants.

---

[*] I first learned this schema from Angeles Arrien as "4 Steps for Living". I have expanded it somewhat.

The Skills You Need when Interacting with Others

2. Feel into your core. Remember, this is the place where you are the most you, so this is the place to put your attention to get a direct felt-sense of what's going on with you.

3. Translate what you feel and think into words so you can communicate it to others. Don't expect them to read your mind or feel your feelings. It's your job to put it into words.

4. Say what you feel and think without blame or judgment of yourself or anyone. Tell them what you feel and think and want, but use 'I statements', not 'you statements'. Attacking them will likely only cause them to stop listening to you and get defensive.

5. Be open to their response. Notice how others respond to you. There is information in their responses. Be open enough to take it in and learn from it.

This process is simple, but also profound. Don't expect yourself to be perfect at it right away. You may have grown up in a family or culture that punished anyone who was open and vulnerable in this way. You may have seen others insulted and humiliated for expressing themselves this openly, and you may have been hurt that way yourself. If so, doing these steps may bring up many old fears, hurts, and angers. That's okay. That's part of your healing. But find or create for yourself some safe situations in which you can practice this and be supported in staying with and digesting whatever comes up for you. Anyone who can hold space for you may be able to help. Good friends are one possibility; supportive therapy is another.

Doing this well takes some skill, especially since it requires developing a felt-sense of your own core. That is another reason that developing a felt-sense of your core is so valuable.

Be Honest

Years ago, I was told that the English word 'honest' comes from *un est*, the Latin words for 'one' and 'to be', so to be honest means 'to be one with what is'. Further research has shown that this is not the actual derivation of the word, but I still like the idea that honesty arises from being one with what is, in other words, from being one with what is true for you.

Tell the truth

This means saying what is true for you. Doing so creates an inner clarity and integrity that's good for you and strengthens you over time. Conversely, saying something that is not true confuses and weakens you, as well as your relationships with others. As a psychotherapist, I've often seen the internal havoc caused by parents that lie and teach their children to lie. I recommend telling the truth.

However, telling the truth does not require you to say out loud everything you think and feel. Sometimes what is true for you is that you don't want to reveal something or you've promised not to reveal it, so you want to stay silent. When questioned about it, *"I'd rather not say"* can be an honest answer. Similarly, *"I don't want to talk about that"* and *"You know I can't talk about that"* can also be honest answers. So telling the truth does not obligate you to say what you don't want to say, but only to avoid lying about why.

Keep your word

That is, do what you say you will do. If you later find that you can't or no longer want to do it, say so and renegotiate your original commitment. Don't just ignore it or pretend that you never said it. Own your original statement and renegotiate it. Doing this will build a sense of integrity within you and show you more clearly who you are. Again, this practice is fundamentally good for you and for your relationships.

Use 'I Statements' Instead of 'You Statements'

The difference between 'I statements' and 'you statements' is simple: an 'I statement' is a statement about yourself, while a 'you statement' is a statement about the other person. Most 'I statements' will start with *"I think"* or *"I feel"* or *"I want"* or something similar and then continue with the details about what you think, feel, want, etc. Most 'you statements' will start with the word "You", as in *"You think,"* *"You just,"* *"You always"* or something similar and then continue with whatever it is that you're saying about the other person. Again, an 'I statement' is a statement about yourself, and a 'you statement' is a statement about the other person.

The Skills You Need when Interacting with Others

One thing to watch out for: don't try to sneak in a 'you statement' by putting *"I think"* or *"I feel"* in front of it, as in *"I think you're a jerk"* or *"I feel like you're hurting me."* Those are not 'I statements'. They're 'you statements' disguised as 'I statements'. The messages embedded within those two examples are *"you're a jerk"* and *"you're hurting me."*

Many of us grew up in families or cultures where talking in 'you statements' was what everyone did, and we learned to do it just to fit in. It was a way of emotionally protecting ourselves. But the protection comes from not revealing anything about yourself, so if your desire now is to communicate something about yourself, it is time to learn to speak in 'I statements.'

> *Don't try to sneak in a 'you statement' by putting "I think" or "I feel" in front of it.*

Think of it this way — the whole point of most communication is to reveal something about yourself. That is the essence of your message to the other person, whether it is *"I love you"* or *"I want you to take out the garbage."* And if you want to create more connection and intimacy in the relationship, revealing something about yourself is a good way to do it.

This is especially important when your agenda includes discussing something about the other person or their behavior. Even if what you're saying about them is true and they know it is true, they may see your assertion of it as an attack and automatically deny it just to protect themselves. Again, your assertion may provoke a needless fight and derail your larger agenda.

Similarly, unless it's a compliment, none of us like it when someone else tries to tell us who we are or what we feel. And this is especially true if their comment is a complaint or a criticism. Even if we agree with their statement, we usually want to define ourselves, rather than let someone else define us, because being defined by someone else diminishes our sense of our own autonomy.

So, if you're unhappy with someone's behavior, instead of criticizing or complaining about their behavior, use 'I statements' to tell them how it affects you. For instance, instead of saying, *"You scare me,"* say, *"I feel scared of you."* Instead of saying, *"You always do that,"* say, *"I don't like it when you do that."* Instead of saying, *"You hurt me,"* say, *"I feel hurt."* Even the phrase *"I feel abandoned"* will be heard by most people as *"You abandoned me,"* so instead say *"I feel lonely for you"* or *"I miss you."* In working with couples, I have found that the phrase "I miss you" often goes straight to the partner's heart and stops the fight.

When you use 'I statements' and talk only about your own feelings, the other person is less likely to argue with you, and if they try to minimize your feelings, you are on stronger ground. You can ask if they think they know your inner experience more accurately than you do. On the other hand, if you start claiming to know about their feelings and inner experience, you are the one who is on shaky ground. And you're intruding on their autonomy, so they may need to disagree just to reassert their autonomy. So don't do that. Talk only about your own inner experience and your own feelings. Avoid 'you statements' and use only 'I statements'.

Using only 'I statements' also requires that you stop and feel into what is really going on inside you. You may have been skipping this step completely, and doing this may be totally new for you. That's alright. You can learn this skill. All you need is practice.

If you want to improve your communication with your romantic partner, the steps are exactly the same: come back into your body and feel into your core. Find some words to describe your own inner experience, and then say those words to your partner, without blame or judgment of yourself or them. Doing this shifts both of you into being more open and vulnerable, and that may well start to change your habitual attack-defend-counterattack dance into a mutual curiosity about each other's experience. And perhaps into a desire to give your partner what they want.

Using only 'I statements' also requires that you stop and feel into what is really going on inside you.

As a couple's therapist, I have often given this 'I statements only' assignment to a couple. First, we practice it in my office, and then I ask them to continue this practice at home until our next session. When they return, they're often amazed at the results. They didn't know that they were frequently using 'you statements' to attack each other. They didn't realize that they were using them to hide their own needs and fears. And they are often amazed at how using 'I statements' and revealing themselves has taken the fuel out of their fights and drawn them closer emotionally.

Changing the way you talk to others will likely do the same for you. The more you avoid 'you statements' and instead use 'I statements', the

The Skills You Need when Interacting with Others

less you will provoke defend-counterattack responses from others, and the more you will invite them into an exploration of how the two of you feel when you interact. If things between you are difficult, that will bring the real problems to the surface so that the two of you can solve them, instead of just attacking and defending all the time. If things between you are fairly smooth, it will deepen the connection between you and create the conditions for a deeper emotional intimacy.

Listen for the Embedded Statements

When you're listening to someone, pay attention not only to what they're saying on the surface, but also to the statements embedded within their words. What do we mean by embedded statements? We mean statements that are contained within a larger statement and may be true if the larger statement is true. They're not stated directly, so we often don't notice them, but they're often the essence of the larger statement.

Here are some examples:

Larger statement	Embedded statement
"I'm afraid I will disappoint you."	"I will disappoint you"
"What if I don't want to?"	"I don't want to"
"Mom says I can't do it."	"I can't do it"
"I can't do anything right around here."	"I can't do anything right"
"I'm afraid you don't love me."	"You don't love me"
"Sometimes I think we'll never get there."	"We'll never get there"
"Do you think we should just give up?"	"We should just give up"
"What if you're wrong?"	"You're wrong"

55

Hearing the statement hidden within a longer sentence gives you a clue to what is going on with the other person below the surface. They may be consciously aware of it, or they may not. If they are not consciously aware of it, you can help them become aware of it by asking them about it. You don't know whether they believe it or not, so don't assert that. Just ask them about it. You might say something like, *"Are you saying that _____?"* and then listen to their answer.

Hearing your question will help them check internally to see if it is true. They may find that it is true. If so, now they know something more about themselves.

Or they may find that it is not true. Again, now they know something more about themselves.

They may deny it so fiercely that you think maybe it is true, and they're just being defensive. If this happens, remember that it's not your job to uncover what's going on in their unconscious. They also heard their fierce denial, and they may already be wondering about it. Given time, they may discover whatever the truth of it is, without your help.

The Skill of Negotiating

In my 40 years as a Marriage and Family Therapist, I have noticed that nearly all the couples who seek my help share one common trait: they do not have a way to negotiate differences and make shared decisions. In other words, they have not developed a way to express to each other what each of them wants, why they want it, and how important it is (or isn't), and then negotiate some mutually agreeable solution, some way for each of them to get enough of what they want that they both feel good about it.

Nearly all unhappy couples lack this skill.

In every case, their couples therapy included helping them develop a method for doing that — for exploring a difference, negotiating with each other, and reaching a mutually agreeable solution. The particular method that they use can vary widely from one couple to another, but as long as they each feel that it works well enough for them personally, it will work for them as a couple.

The Skills You Need when Interacting with Others

Some couples do the exploration and negotiation entirely verbally. Perhaps they sit down and talk it over until they agree on a solution. Or perhaps, instead of facing each other, they give each other more space by walking side by side while they talk it over. Some couples do it in writing, either by writing letters to each other or by taking turns writing in a shared journal. Often those couples like having some time to read and consider what the other has written before responding. And some couples don't use words at all; they communicate with each other entirely through their behaviors. For instance, if he has offended her, she might show her upset by disconnecting from him in some way, such as going silent or cold toward him. If he wants to apologize, he might show that by doing something for her, such as washing her car. If she accepts his apology, she resumes her connection with him. The obvious downside of this method is that it is harder for each of them to learn about the other's inner life — their wants, needs, hopes, and dreams — not to mention fears left over from their childhood traumas. But some couples do use this method, perhaps because they learned it by watching their parents do it.

Some heterosexual couples narrow the areas of potential dispute by giving each other sovereignty over certain territories. Often she handles the inside of the house (furnishings and decorating), and he handles the yard and the garage (landscaping, mowing the lawn, fixing the cars). When painting is needed, it's her job if it's the inside of the house and his job if it's the outside. Same-sex couples may divide up their responsibilities in a similar way, based on who runs more feminine energy and who runs more masculine energy. If there is a garden, one of them may claim it as their own territory, and the other may be glad to be free of it. Sometimes one of them brings in all the money, and the other takes care of the children or contributes in some other way. These divisions of labor and responsibility can simplify their lives enormously by reducing the number of shared decisions that they need to make.

The point here is simply that every couple needs some way to negotiate differences and make shared decisions, including the decisions about who will be responsible for what. As long as their method gives each of them enough of what they want, it will work for them as a couple. The mechanism they use doesn't really matter, as long as they both find it satisfactory.

In my experience, this is the biggest single factor in determining the couple's happiness with each other and the likelihood that they will stay together. One of the things that makes a 'healthy couple' healthy is that they have an agreed upon way to negotiate differences and make decisions together, and one of the things that lands other couples in therapy or divorce is that they don't. I'm not saying that having such a method is a guarantee of happiness, but I am saying that not having it leads to trouble, because there are always going to be differences that must be negotiated and shared decisions that must be made.

This skill is needed in many sorts of relationships, not only in romantic ones. It is needed in any relationship that includes shared responsibilities or decisions, such as collaborations, partnerships, and friendships.

Communication 101

These are some guidelines you may want to use when having important conversations, especially if the topic is emotionally charged for either of you. Throughout the process, whether you're speaking or listening, it is your responsibility to manage your own feeling state.

Asking for what you want

1. Deal with only 1 issue at a time
2. Be specific and personal
3. State clearly what *behavior* you want from the other person, that is, what you want them to do and say
4. End with "Would you do that for me?"

When talking

1. State facts
2. State your personal feelings / experience
3. Talk only about yourself, not about the other person
4. Use 'I statements'
    - no 'you statements'
    - no blaming
    - no name-calling
    - no attacking the other person
    - no interpretations of their actions

The Skills You Need when Interacting with Others

When listening

1. Invite them to tell you about it
2. Clarify what is unclear to you by asking questions
3. Take time to let what they are saying to you sink in. You may need to ask them to slow down or pause for a minute while you take it in.
4. On important points, restate what they said, ending with "Is that right?"
    - do not minimize or discount their feelings; this is *their* experience
    - for the moment, put aside agreeing or disagreeing
    - your purpose is to understand and *show* that you understand
    - feeling understood will calm your partner's fear and anger
5. Do not attempt to respond until they agree that they have finished their statement, at least for the moment, and they want to hear your response

Notice Their Ways of Thinking and Perceiving

The 3 Centers of Intelligence

This is an old teaching, but it's fundamental to understanding people, so I want to make sure you're aware of it. The basic idea is simple: we have three centers of intelligence in our bodies, not just one. These three centers are the Head Center, the Heart Center, and the Belly Center. Each one has its own kind of intelligence, and their areas of expertise do not overlap. They are actually organs in our energy body, but because we cannot see our energy body, we name them according to areas of our physical bodies.

<u>The Head Center</u> is concerned with thinking, with logic and reason and facts and all that we commonly think of as the mind. It is the place of words, numbers, and maps. This is where we divide one thing from another and notice patterns, rules, and systems. The head center compares things to each other and establishes ranks and hierarchies. It tries to put things in order. It perceives the world mostly through concepts, and since concepts generally arise in opposing pairs (up and down, right and wrong, now and then), our minds also tend to emphasize differences and oppositions. This is useful and natural. It is the nature of the intelligence of the head center.

How to Have Better Relationships

The Heart Center has a very different king of intelligence. It knows the world through love, connection, and feeling. It wants to be closer to what it loves, immersed in what it loves. If you love a person, you want to be closer to them. If you love singing, you want to sing. If you love mathematics, you want to do mathematics. The heart center does not care about good and bad or right and wrong. It does not care about rules and forms. It simply feels the pull of love and wants to move closer to whatever it loves. There is a flowing quality to the heart and a softness to the heart's intelligence, as opposed to the sharp, dividing clarity of the head's intelligence. The heart center is not the heart muscle that pumps blood through your body, but rather the energetic organ located in the center of your chest.

The Belly Center has a third kind of intelligence, the intelligence of the body. It is the intelligence of the physical world, the world of space and time, of motion and action. Sports, dancing, martial arts, and even driving a car all engage the intelligence of the belly center, because those actions require that you put your attention on where you and others are in space, how everyone is moving, and what will happen next. Just throwing a ball back and forth engages your belly center. Just standing up from your chair does it. When athletes speak of being 'in the zone', they mean times when they are not thinking or feeling, but just doing — times when the mind and heart are quiet and the belly center is running the show. The belly center is located about 2 inches (5 cm) below your navel.

We often use the wrong kind of intelligence for the task at hand.

So our three centers of intelligence each have their own domain, and in their own domain, they are very competent. Their kind of intelligence is the best kind of intelligence for navigating that domain. However, they are not good at navigating the other domains. For instance, when driving down a crowded street, counting the other cars will not help you avoid an accident. Loving them and admiring their beauty will not help, either. Similarly, when filling out your tax forms, just entering whatever number "feels right" won't work — you have to do the math.

How things can go wrong

When we apply the wrong kind of intelligence to a task, things can go wrong. But because we have favorites, we often do that — we often use the wrong kind of intelligence for the task at hand. Our first favorite is the one we trust the most and use the most. We've practiced this one a lot, and we're pretty skillful at it. Then we have our second favorite. We may be pretty good at it, too, but it's not quite as developed as the first. And then there is our least favorite, the one we have practiced the least and where we may not be skilled at all.

So take a minute and ask yourself, which is your favorite?

- Do you trust your head and try to think your way through life?
- Do you trust your heart and try to feel your way through life?
- Do you trust your belly and try to move through life?

None of these are right or wrong; each has its place. The problem is only in being so wedded to one kind of intelligence that you apply it to every problem, even when it's not the best one for the task.

Now ask yourself the same questions to determine your second favorite. Which one do you do second? Is it a close second or a distant second? How much skill have you developed in this area, compared to your first choice?

And what about your third? Many people don't really like their third one. They don't trust it, and they don't use it much, so they have never developed much skill with it. It may be like an orphan child in your psyche, ignored and undeveloped.

As you get used to thinking about people in this way, you may be able to see pretty quickly who in your life is primarily head-centered, who is primarily heart-centered, and who is primarily belly-centered. Does this help you understand them better? Does it help you understand how they are different from you and why the two of you sometimes see things differently? Can you use this awareness to interact with them more skillfully?

How the 3 centers shape groups and cultures

Now let's shift our attention from individuals to groups of people. If you think back to high school, most of the star athletes were probably belly-centered, right? And most of the kids in the Math Honor Society were probably head-centered. And what about the kids who were heart-centered? A little harder to find their niche, right?

To see why, let's look at the effect of culture as a whole. I live in the USA, which is a head- and belly-centered culture. Your culture may be different, but here in the US, we acknowledge and value head center and belly center skills more than heart center skills. Most of the high-paying jobs require head-centered skills, like analysis, planning, and design. Some of the belly-centered jobs do pay well, such as major league sports, but most don't, like physical labor. And heart-centered jobs, like caregiver and nursery school teacher, don't pay well, either. There are exceptions, of course, but these observations are generally true.

So we see that our culture here in the USA generally uses the head center first, the belly center second, and the heart center is a distant third. How does that affect individuals living here? Well, if you also favor your head center, then your belly center, then your heart center, you fit right in. You feel at home here, because you and the culture are aligned in this.

What if you're more belly-centered? Life here may be a struggle. You may be able to find a belly-centered way to shine or you may not, but you will probably always feel that you're not smart enough.

And what if you're more heart-centered? You probably feel that you don't fit in, but you don't know why and think you're somehow deficient. But in fact, it is not that *you* lack value. It is just that you live in a culture that doesn't value your heart-centeredness. If you were to move to a more heart-centered culture, like Italy, you might find that you fit right in. In my therapy practice, I have seen this problem repeatedly. Heart-centered clients who don't feel at home here in the US often feel much more comfortable after moving to a heart-centered culture.

The same problem arises any time you join a group or take a job that requires the skills of a center that you have not yet developed. In order to function well in that situation, you need to develop that center of intelligence.

How do you develop a neglected center of intelligence?

You use it. You intentionally move your attention to that part of your body and you do things that require you to practice those skills.

To develop your Head Center, intentionally move your attention to your head and practice thinking about things, putting them in categories, seeing differences, seeing patterns, analyzing trends, putting things in

The Skills You Need when Interacting with Others

order, and so on. Focus on logic and reason, cause and effect, mathematics, maps, charts, and graphs.

To develop your Heart Center, intentionally move your attention to the center of your chest and do things that focus on love, connection, beauty, harmony, and the like. Things like poetry, singing, dancing, painting, or sculpture. Things like music, stories, and creating in general. Anything that focuses on feelings and expressing those feelings, especially feelings about beauty and love.

Becoming a healthy, mature adult requires developing all three centers and integrating them into your core.

To develop your Belly Center, intentionally move your attention to your belly and practice activities that involve moving through time and space, activities like running, swimming, dancing, playing catch, and sports or martial arts in general. Doing these activities competitively will push you even further in developing your skills.

Integrating the 3 centers of intelligence

You may have noticed that all three of these centers are located within the core of the body. One of the great benefits of developing a felt-sense of your core is that it helps you integrate the three centers. Doing the core practice will help you see where along the column your attention is strongest and where it is weakest, and it will help you strengthen your attention where it is weaker. Becoming a healthy, mature adult requires developing all three centers and integrating them into a single core.

The Channels of Perception

This is about which senses we favor as we take in and process our experience, not which centers of intelligence we use to understand it. You're probably familiar with the idea that we perceive the world through our five senses: seeing, hearing, touch, taste, and smell. What you may not have heard is that we tend to use only three channels to process our perceptions:

- the visual (seeing)
- the auditory (hearing)
- the kinesthetic (touch and all internal sensations, including smell and taste)

And we all have a favorite. We tend to perceive and process our perceptions more through one of those channels than the others. Some people experience the world mostly through the visual channel, that is, by seeing it. When you ask them to recall a previous experience, their eyes will look up as they internally view the memory of the experience. In their home, they will likely want things to be beautiful and clean, or at least neat. When they talk, they will often use visual words, like *"I can see that," "That's clear,"* and *"That looks right."* People who experience the world this way will naturally be more skillful at visual tasks, like drawing, fashion design, and learning by reading.

Other people experience the world mostly through the auditory channel, that is, by hearing it. When you ask them to recall a previous experience, their eyes will often move horizontally left or right as they internally listen to the remembered experience. In their home, they may be especially annoyed by stray sounds, like a dripping faucet, or the TV in the next apartment. When they talk, they will often use auditory words, like *"I hear you," "That sounds right,"* and *"Clear as a bell."* People who experience the world this way will naturally be more skillful at auditory tasks, like playing and composing music, speaking a new language, and learning by listening.

Lastly, some people experience the world mostly through the kinesthetic channel, that is, through sensations. When you ask them to recall a previous experience, their eyes will look down as they internally feel their way through the remembered experience. In their home, they may want things to be convenient and easy to reach, rather than beautiful or neat. When they talk, they will often use kinesthetic words, like *"I get that," "That fits,"* and *"That feels right."* People who experience the world this way will naturally be more skillful at kinesthetic tasks, like sports, choreography, and learning by doing. They will also likely need to move as they learn, which will often get them into trouble during grade school with visually-oriented teachers who insist that they *"Sit still!"*

In addition to our favorite way of perceiving the world, we also have a second favorite and a least favorite. We have our main channel, then a close or distant second channel, and then one that we may not use at all. Many people use only two of the three channels most of the time. So their ways of perceiving the world can be abbreviated as V/A, A/V, V/K, K/V, A/K, or K/A.

The fact that different people perceive and process their experience through such different combinations of channels creates many of the differences that we see from one person to another, and it is the source of many disagreements and misunderstandings.

The psychic/energetic channel

But the situation is actually even more complicated than that. While all of the above is well known in psychology, there is an additional channel of perception that is less well known, and that is the psychic channel. It is available to everyone, but often not developed or consciously used. People tend to become more or less aware of this channel — and skilled in it — depending on their needs during childhood and their personality patterns.

Those who are aware of this channel are more able to perceive the energy world that underlies our physical world. This may include seeing or feeling the energy fields around people and the energetic cords connecting them. They may also be able to communicate by sending and receiving pictures, feelings, and even thoughts psychically. There are many teachers and schools that specialize in helping students develop their psychic and energetic skills, and if you look for them, you will probably be able to find some near you.

These differences in how we perceive and process our experience are the source of many disagreements and misunderstandings.

While many people are not consciously aware of the psychic/energetic channel, their bodies are nonetheless perceiving and processing that data, so when the knowledge gained from it rises into their conscious awareness, they think of it as 'intuition' or a 'gut feeling'.

Correlations with the Head, Heart, and Belly Centers

You may be wondering if there is a direct correlation between the three centers of intelligence and the various channels of perception. In my experience, there are tendencies, but not strict correlations. And since each of us has most- and least-favorites among both the centers and the channels of perception, looking for correlations can quickly get complicated. Instead, I encourage you to explore this in yourself and those around you and see what you can find. And, in the chapters on each of the personality patterns, we will discuss the tendencies of that pattern.

Respect Their Autonomy

Everyone values their own autonomy. That is, they want to make their own decisions about what they do and what happens to them. This is a natural result of developing a self and an ego structure. We all do this. We want our own way.

If you've ever parented a two-year-old, you've seen this in action. A two-year-old is just developing their sense of autonomy, so it is fragile and easily wounded. And because of that, they will often defend it fiercely.

If a person's autonomy is challenged, they will often fight for it.

For instance, being given orange juice when they wanted milk may precipitate a tantrum, even if they like both orange juice and milk. Their tantrum is not over the difference between orange juice and milk. It is over the fact that they were not given a choice.

We all care about our autonomy so much that, if it's challenged, we will often fight for it. And many of us will fight for it even in situations where the difference between what we wanted and what we got is trivial. What matters to us in those situations is not the outcome, but the fact that we were not allowed to choose for ourselves. We want others to respect our autonomy.

So, in order to interact successfully with others, you will need to respect their autonomy. Fortunately, you can do that easily by observing a few simple steps.

The Skills You Need when Interacting with Others

Ask permission

As you begin your interaction with them, ask if it is okay. Say something like,

> "Can I ask you a question?"
> "I have a question. Is this a good time?"
> "I need your help. Are you available?"

By asking their permission, you are acknowledging that they have a choice. It's wise to do this even when you're pretty sure their answer will be 'yes', because by asking, you are showing respect for their autonomy. That will help them feel safer around you and make them more likely to agree to whatever it is that you're asking of them.

Asking permission also alerts them to the fact that you want something from them and helps them prepare internally to listen to your request. This may seem trivial to you, but for some people, it matters a lot, as we'll see in the following chapters.

You may feel impatient to get on with making your request, and to you, stopping to ask permission may seem like a waste of time, but try it out for a few weeks and see if it makes a difference in how others respond to you. Even if it's a small thing to you, it is a big thing for some people. And why not tilt the odds in your favor, right from the start?

Avoid declaring something about them

Avoid declaring that such-and-such is objectively true about them. Many people don't like being told by someone else what they think and feel, and when you declare something about them, you're giving them an opportunity to disagree with you and start a fight over whether it's true or not. The fight will derail your agenda and may create so much turmoil that you're never able to get back to what you wanted to talk about.

Instead, *ask them* if such-and-such is true. For instance, instead of declaring *"I know you like solving problems,"* ask *"You like solving problems, right?"* Or instead of declaring *"You probably don't care about this,"* ask *"Do you care about this?"*

If they say yes, you can use that as a starting point for whatever it is that you want to say or request. If they say no, you can ask them to tell you more about why they say that. By doing that, you're expressing interest in them and inviting them to tell you more about themselves. Most people like that, and it will make them more inclined to listen to you and give you what you want.

Adjust Your Approach to Suit Them

Respect their space

Some people will want you to move closer to them, while others will want you to keep your distance. And often, they will want you to know what they want without having to tell you. Of course, their preferences on this will depend partly on what sort of relationship they have with you — for instance, whether you're co-workers, family, or lovers. But a big part of it will also depend on which personality patterns they do and how much they trust you to respect their preferences. The more you respect their preferences for distance or closeness, the more they will trust you. We will discuss this more in the chapters concerning individual patterns, particularly the enduring pattern.

Respect their pace and timing

Similarly, some people have a very rapid inner pace, which causes them to speak and act rapidly, while others have a much slower inner pace, which causes them to speak and act much more slowly. Some people speak in one continuous stream, while others pause — even within a single sentence — while they find the next part of their thought. Before you respond to them, you need to figure out whether they're finished speaking, or they're just pausing, but not finished yet. The more you can read and respect their pace and timing, the more they will trust you. Again, we will discuss this more in the chapters concerning individual patterns, particularly the enduring pattern.

Respect their norms

Different cultures have different norms concerning the use of formal versus informal forms of address, greeting rituals, personal distance, eye contact, and so on. Those norms are beyond the scope of this book, but

The Skills You Need when Interacting with Others

you would be wise to notice and respect the norms used by anyone with whom you want to have a better relationship. In international diplomacy, these details of ceremony and etiquette are referred to as protocol, and they are considered so necessary to maintaining good relationships that each country employs protocol officers who are responsible for making sure that their representatives respect the norms of the other country. In personal relations, I suggest that you also notice and respect the norms of others.

Holding Space for Someone

"Holding space" is a term that we use often in the healing professions, but sometimes without clearly explaining it. Since your own ability to hold space for others is so valuable in creating better relationships, I want to explain more clearly what it takes to "hold space" for someone.

When you're interacting with someone else, there are three basic stances you can take regarding the purpose and focus of this interaction. They are:

1. It's about me

2. It's about them

3. It's about us

Let's take a look at each one in more detail.

1. It's about me. This interaction is about me. It is about my agenda and me getting what I want, and the other person's job is to help me get what I want. It is not about them or their agenda. It's just about me. Right now, only my needs are important.

Typically, this is the kind of interaction you'll have when you go to see a therapist or other healer. You have hired them to help you get what you want. It is their job to put all their attention on you and help you get what you want.

2. It's about them. This is the same type of interaction, but now the roles are reversed. Now you are in the position of the helper. Your job is to make the interaction about them and their agenda, not about you and your agenda. For right now, your needs aren't important, only their needs are important. You have to leave your agenda out of it and focus on them and their needs.

In order to do this, you must be capable of tracking your own needs and your own agenda well enough to perceive how they are influencing your responses. This requires a high level of self-awareness and skill in tracking your own inner experience. In addition, your needs must already be addressed well enough so that you are okay, at least for the moment, and you don't need to get anything for yourself.

3. It's about us. This kind of interaction is much more complicated, because now the wants and needs of both people are important. It's about both people's agendas at the same time. And those two agendas aren't always similar. They may be so different that they're in conflict. So the two of you have to do something entirely new: you have to negotiate with each other. You have to explore what each of you wants and how to get it until the two of you find some sort of compromise that is good enough for both of you.

This process of negotiation and compromise introduces a whole new level of complexity into the interaction. Both of you must use communication skills that you didn't need in the first or second types of interaction.

By now, you've probably noticed several things about these three ways of interacting. For instance, #1 is pretty much the way a child sees the world, and rightly so. When we are very young, our attention is usually limited to our own needs and wants. A big part of growing up is learning to shift our attention to include other people's needs and make them important, too. You may also have noticed that being a good parent often calls on you to shift into stance #2 to help your child discover what they feel and want. And #3, of course, is the stance needed most of the time in adult-to-adult relationships, especially in personal ones, like friendship and romance.

Holding space for someone requires that you shift into stance #2 and stay there.

Holding space for someone requires that you shift into stance #2 and stay there for the entire time you are holding space for them. For many of us, this can be very difficult to do, since we always have our own needs and wants waiting in the background, and they may say or do

The Skills You Need when Interacting with Others

something that triggers one of our needs and brings it into the foreground. Managing that internally without losing focus on supporting the other person is the key to successfully holding space for them.

In order to succeed in managing your own inner state during this interaction, you must be grounded, centered, okay enough for the moment, and skillful in self-awareness. And since you probably do have an agenda concerning what the other person should do (most of us do), you must be able to truly put it aside in order to be present for them and support them in pursuing their agenda.

If you think that you already know what would be best for them, this is a very hard thing to do. If you believe that you see the big picture and know where they're going and the best route for them to take, it is difficult to resist trying to steer them toward that route. Personally, I find it very helpful to take a more modest view of my own vision and understanding, and instead to hold a deep conviction that I *don't* already know what is best for them, but that there is something wise in them that does know where they are going and how to get there, so that, even though I don't see how this is all going to work out for them, I can relax, trust the process, and just support them in their agenda.

Holding space becomes even more difficult when you're trying to do it for someone who is personally important to you and has a big effect on you, like your lover. What direction they are going may have a huge impact on you and on the fulfillment of your own needs and wants. So you are that much more vulnerable to getting triggered and reactive while trying to hold space for them. This means that you have to be that much more grounded, centered, and able to put your own agenda aside for the moment.

This is a very big task. Over the years, I've noticed that, when couples come in for couple's counseling, this is usually where their connection and communication is breaking down. If they can't hold space and listen to each other at all, their relationship may be an unending fight over who gets to go first. Or the situation may be that they are able to start to hold space and listen to each other, but the listener quickly gets triggered, goes into a reaction, and again, it turns into a fight.

Typically, the conversation in my office goes something like this: one of them starts describing what upsets them in the relationship, but they get only a few sentences into it before the other can't hold their internal distress any longer and interrupts them, either to defend themselves or to launch into describing what upsets *them* in the relationship. Within a few minutes, they're once again into their usual fight.

The secret is in being able to internally hold space for yourself at the same time.

So what's the secret to being able to hold space for someone else, even when you get triggered? The secret is in developing the capacity to internally *hold space for yourself* at the same time, that is, to have an internal adult that can notice when the child inside you gets triggered and can step in to soothe the child inside, even while you continue holding space for someone else on the outside. This doesn't mean that you can tolerate an unlimited amount of internal upset. It only means that the adult inside can monitor the internal situation, measure your own limits, and gracefully call a time out while there is still some slack inside — before things inside you go off the cliff and you go into a reaction. In real life, that might mean saying something like this: *"What you're saying is important to me, and I want to be able to listen to all of it and help you sort it out, but I just hit a reaction inside that's more than I can hold and still give you the attention you deserve, so I need to take a time out and go take care of this upset inside of me. I will come back and continue holding space for you as soon as I can. Is that okay?"*

This is a tall order, to be sure, but it is possible. The key, I think, is accurately measuring how much slack you still have inside so that you can predict, *before you get there,* when you will likely run out of internal resources and go into a reaction. This means that you need to know yourself well and have done some of your own healing. You need to have cleared enough of the charge out of your own usual automatic reactions that you can at least see them coming before they swamp you. You need to be able to perceive the small signals inside that indicate you're going into distress and a big wave of emotion might be coming. And you need to pay attention to those small signals — ignoring your own inner experience and pretending that you're okay won't help. When the wave hits, it will still swamp you.

Accurately measuring your own internal reserves requires a clear-eyed assessment of yourself, one that recognizes your limits as well as your talents. Noticing those small signals gives you some warning about your own internal distress so you can gracefully call a time out and disengage before you go into overwhelm and reaction. It forewarns you so that you can both

The Skills You Need when Interacting with Others

disengage from the other person in a caring way and take care of yourself. It lets you be proactive in managing the problem, instead of reactive. And it helps you take responsibility for yourself and your distress, rather than dumping it on the other person, the one you were trying to hold space for.

In summary, in order to hold space skillfully for someone else, you must:

- know whether this interaction, in this moment, is about me, you, or us
- know the difference between stances #1, #2, and #3
- be able to shift into stance #2 at will
- track and manage your own internal state
- notice the small signals that you are going into distress
- proactively disengage before you go into reaction

I hope this helps you assess your own skills in holding space for others and provides some ideas about how you can improve your skills and become good at it.

- 4 -

About the Personality Patterns

Your experience of life is determined mostly by your habits of attention and the patterned flow of your life energy.
— Steven Kessler

Pattern vs Presence

Almost all of us have noticed the difference between being present and being in pattern, although we usually call the two states by other names. Being *present* means that all of our attention is here, in this time and place. Usually, this happens only when we're feeling relatively safe. At these times, our bodies are not in a state of alarm conditioned into them by past traumas, and our perceptions are not filtered or distorted by thoughts and feelings from the past. This allows us to perceive the real situation happening right now and respond to it in a healthy and effective way.

Being *in pattern* means that our perceptions are being filtered and distorted by a personality pattern. A personality pattern is an automatic, body-based reaction that we go into to try to buffer ourselves from feeling overwhelmed. But it's a reaction that was conditioned into us by traumas in the past. It is not a response to the present situation. Sometime in the

About the Personality Patterns

past, it was the best strategy we could find to deal with a difficult, ongoing situation, so we adopted it and repeated it. Over time, it was so deeply conditioned into our bodies that now it automatically kicks in whenever we feel distressed, making us react as if the past distress is still happening to us, even when it is not.

Being present means that all of your attention is here, in this time and place.

While in a pattern, we usually feel that our reaction is completely justified. This happens because our mind and body are filled with the feelings and perceptions of the past situations. It's as if an old tape recording is playing and drowning out our perception of the present situation. At some level we believe that the old trauma is happening all over again. Often this makes the present threat seem much larger than it really is, causing us to overreact to the current situation. Overreacting is one of the major indicators of being in pattern.

A friend who is practicing noticing when she is in pattern and getting herself out of pattern described the two states this way:

> *On Tuesday afternoon I had a brief sense of happiness and satisfaction after a meeting with my manager and updating her on my projects. I checked off some major activities and felt good about my work.*
>
> *About an hour later everything changed. All of a sudden a flood of To Do items overwhelmed me: a charge to my dad's credit card of $1000, insurance claim forms waiting to be completed, my daughter's tuition challenges, being behind on paying my own bills. My office was messy and I couldn't find things I needed. I was late leaving for my dentist appointment. I experienced a huge deluge of everything I had blocked out of my mind because of work priorities.*
>
> *Instead of taking time to ground myself and address the fact that I was now in pattern, I rushed out of the house to my dentist appointment, forgetting my wallet and that I needed gas. From the moment I left the house, everything became a struggle. People were driving like lunatics. I didn't have any money to buy gas. My dentist's office had over-billed me for a cleaning and couldn't see it even though it was OBVIOUS! Every human encounter was difficult, frustrating, awkward, maddening, and tiring.*

> *Later, when I took time to ground myself and come out of pattern, I felt this rush of what I can best describe as ease. Relief. A wave of harmony and relaxation. I didn't need to fight or struggle. I do think that deep down I felt safer, but that is so primal I often don't recognize it.*

This description paints a vivid picture of how feeling threatened and overwhelmed tends to throw a person into pattern and how different that is from being present. However, going into pattern is not the only possible response to a threat. It is possible to stay present while dealing with a real danger in the here and now. The difference is that, when you're present, you're seeing and hearing the real situation around you and responding to the particulars of the actual current threat, not to something from your past. You are composing a new, flexible response based on this particular situation. Because your response is tailored to the current situation, it works better than an automatic, fixed reaction. And, because you are present in the moment, you can monitor how well your response is working and adjust it as needed. Your response is calibrated to this situation; it is not an overreaction based on past situations.

For many of us, however, staying present when we're upset is nearly impossible. Our bodies are so deeply conditioned by the traumas still stuck in them that we go into pattern the instant we feel uncomfortable. In fact, many of us stay in pattern nearly all the time. Our unconscious personality patterns have become so strong that they rule our lives, coloring our every thought and feeling and determining our actions. When asked why we behave that way, our only answer is often, *"That's just who I am."*

However, things don't have to remain this way. Your wounds can be healed. Your old conditioning can be softened. You can learn now the skills that you didn't learn earlier. And you can live most of your life in the present, rather than from inside your personality patterns.

You Are Not Your Personality Patterns

As you learn about the personality patterns, the most important thing to remember is that *a personality pattern is not who you really are*. It is what *blocks* who you really are. It buffers you from feeling overwhelmed, but it also

About the Personality Patterns

stops you from directly experiencing yourself in the moment and expressing that in the world. When you were distressed as a child, you naturally used whatever capacities you had to buffer and protect yourself. This was needed. It was the best you could do at the time. Gradually, the buffering strategies that you used were conditioned into your body and mind. Over time, those buffering strategies developed their own internal logic and structure and became your personality patterns. But they are *not* who you are.

So who are you? You are Presence. You are the awareness, in this moment, of this moment. You are not your thoughts, emotions, or behaviors. You are not even your body. You are just a simple, open awareness. In many spiritual teachings, this awareness is called Essence or Spirit. Often, it is called the True Self, and that term is used to distinguish it from the False Self or personality. In this book, I will refer to it simply as *presence*, or as *being present*. Presence is who you are underneath all the conditioning, armoring, beliefs, and identities that you carry. You are the experiencer, pure and simple.

It is also important to remember that your personality patterns are not some sort of failing for which you should be punished. You developed them to try to keep yourself safe in difficult situations. And since making your personality patterns work requires that you employ some of your best skills, such as creativity, love, strength, and will, you've also been practicing and developing those skills, even while lost in a pattern. Adopting a particular personality pattern is a way of practicing and sharpening a particular set of skills — perhaps the skills you need to accomplish something important in your life.

The 5 Safety Strategies

Each of the five personality patterns begins as a simple safety strategy, a way to buffer yourself from fully feeling your distress. Each safety strategy works by moving your attention and life energy away from feeling your distress, but they do it in five different ways:

- moving your attention away from the person or thing that's upsetting you

- moving your attention away from yourself and toward the other person to get them to fix your problem

- pulling in and sending your attention and energy down into the ground to help you hunker down and endure it

- pulling your energy up and throwing it at people to feel big and strong and intimidate them into doing what you want

- contracting inside so you don't feel your inner distress as much and focusing instead on performing better

Now, the best choice is actually being present. But when you feel unsafe, being present with your experience does not necessarily make you feel safer. In fact, it will make your distress more specific and more vivid. So in order to stay present in a distressing situation, you have to be able to hold self, even as you are vividly aware of how scared, ashamed, angry, sad, or heartbroken you feel in the moment.

The best choice is being present.

But when you are overwhelmed, you cannot do that. By definition, being overwhelmed means that your experience in the moment is more than your system can handle, so you need some way to buffer yourself from fully feeling all of it. And that is what these safety strategies do for you. Each one protects you by buffering you in some way from feeling your own experience fully.

In essence, the five safety strategies are five different buffering strategies — leaving, connecting, hiding, dominating, and being good. And they are the source of the five personality patterns. When a person uses any of these safety strategies over and over and over again, they are honing the skills needed to make that particular safety strategy work. And gradually, it gets conditioned into their body so deeply that it becomes an automatic, self-sustaining, self-reinforcing personality pattern.

How Do Kids Choose?

We know that a kid doesn't develop all five personality patterns, so how do kids choose which ones to use and which ones to ignore? It's very

About the Personality Patterns

simple and practical. They try out all five of these safety strategies, see which ones work and which ones fail, and keep using only the ones that work for them.

They will try to physically or energetically leave and get away. That's the leaving safety strategy. They will try to move toward whoever is upsetting them, create a connection with them, and get them to solve their problem. That's the merging safety strategy. They will try to just hunker down and wait for the storm to blow over. That's the enduring safety strategy. They will try to intimidate others in order to force them into compliance. That's the aggressive safety strategy. And they will try to be good boys and girls by focusing on performing better. That's the rigid safety strategy.

You can watch a kid as they try out all five. And you'll notice that some of the safety strategies work better than others for that particular kid in their particular situation. And one or two strategies may not work at all, because that kid just doesn't have the talents needed to make it work, or something about their family situation stops it from working.

So which of the five safety strategies will work for a given kid depends on two different factors. One factor is, what inborn skills and talents does this kid have? And the other factor is, what's their family situation? Are they an only child, or do they have siblings? Where are they in terms of birth order? What gender are they? What are their parents like? And what image do their parents have of a good boy or a good girl? They're also embedded in a community, which may include a religious or political world view, and all of those larger social structures have their own ideas about what is permitted and how a child should behave.

As the child tries to deal with their daily problems and find ways to feel safer, they find that some, but not all, of these five safety strategies work for them. Usually it's two of the safety strategies, sometimes three. So what does the kid do? Well, kids are pragmatic. They do whatever works. If they try out one of these safety strategies, and it works pretty well for them, they will try it again. If it keeps working, they will do it over and over and over. Each time they use it, they are practicing the skills that make it work, so they're likely getting better at it. Or, if it doesn't work for them, they'll give up

Kids will try out all five safety strategies and use the ones that work for them.

on it and try something else. Gradually, they sort out the few that do work for them, and those few become their habitual safety strategies.

As you repeat a safety strategy over and over, it grows into a personality pattern.

As with any habit, repeating a safety strategy over and over again gradually conditions it into your body and it changes from something that you consciously choose into something that your body just does automatically whenever you feel distressed enough. And that's how a safety strategy grows into a personality pattern.

And as you grow, your personality patterns become so much a part of your self-image and your overall personality that, if someone asks you why you do that particular safety strategy, you'll probably say something like, *"Oh, that's just me. That's just how I am."*

A Brief Overview of the Personality Patterns

As we said above, each personality pattern grows out of a safety strategy that a child employs to buffer itself from the sense of overwhelm it feels when its needs are not being met. With repeated use, the safety strategy gets conditioned into the child's body and becomes a personality pattern. What defines a personality pattern is the particular strategy it uses to manage the sense of overwhelm, not the age when the pattern first appears or the wounding that happened at that time.

People go into their personality patterns to varying degrees of intensity. Some people are caught in their patterns nearly all the time. For them, those personality patterns rule their life. They identify with them deeply and they shape every aspect of their reality and behavior. Conversely, other people wear their personality patterns so lightly that their behavior is influenced only in moments of extreme distress, while the rest of the time they are able to stay present. Most people fall somewhere in between these two extremes.

This variation is partly due to the fact that early childhood environments also exist on a spectrum, ranging from the nearly ideal to the unspeakably horrible. A milder, more ideal early environment tends to

About the Personality Patterns

produce lighter patterning in a child, depending, of course, on the child's sensitivity to that particular kind of wounding. A more extreme early environment tends to produce more deeply entrenched patterning in a child, again depending on that particular child's sensitivity to that kind of wounding. While the severity of the wounding influences whether and how deeply the child goes into the pattern, there is a great deal of variation from person to person in the amount of wounding needed to induce a particular personality pattern. What one child finds intolerable, another may hardly notice. This seems to depend on the sensitivities and talents that we bring with us and, perhaps, on what we came here to do and learn.

Let's look at each of the five personality patterns in developmental order.

Leaving – Here, the wounding happened very early, most likely during pregnancy, when the baby's incoming spirit did not experience the safety that it needed to complete its transition into the physical world. During this time, the developmental task is embodiment, the process by which the spirit reorients itself from the spirit world to the physical world and bonds with the physical world and the physical body. Ideally, the physical body and the physical world feel safe enough for the baby's spirit to settle into the body and claim it. Then her* spirit can use the body as a reference point, a center to return to if it gets lost or shattered. As time goes on, her physical body then develops an energetic boundary that keeps out foreign energies and increases her felt-sense of safety.

In the formation of the leaving pattern, however, something in the physical world repeatedly shocks the incoming spirit so badly that its attention fragments, causing it to flee back to the spirit world to protect itself. Being shocked out of the body this way interferes with the spirit's process of orienting itself to the physical world and rooting itself in the physical body. These shocks leave the newborn baby's delicate self so vulnerable that any intense energy directed at her can cause her self to once again shatter into fragments. And without a felt reference point in the body to return to, she finds it difficult to reassemble her self.

---

* To avoid the cumbersomeness of having to continually say "he or she," I will say "he" in some parts of this chapter and "she" in others. In this section, I will assume the child is a girl. However, everything said about her could just as easily be said about a boy. When "he" is used, everything said about him could just as easily be said about a girl.

81

How to Have Better Relationships

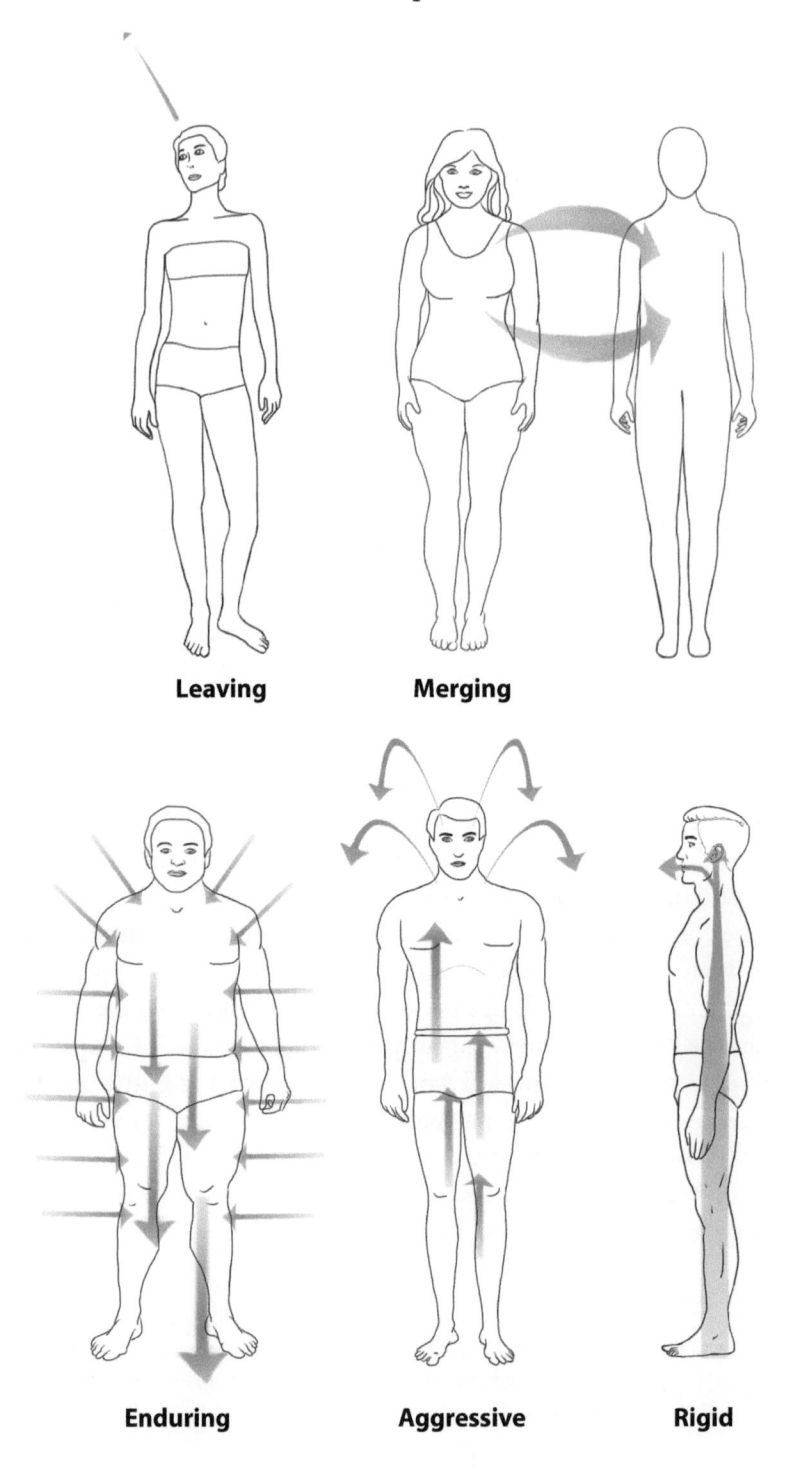

Leaving **Merging**

Enduring **Aggressive** **Rigid**

82

About the Personality Patterns

Such repeated shattering prevents the child from ever coalescing a strong sense of self, firmly anchoring it in the body, and creating the strong energetic boundary around her body that will make her less vulnerable to future shocks. This means that, even as an adult, she will be easily overwhelmed. Her self will tend to fragment under pressure, which may leave her unable to function because she cannot find a center from which to operate. Most likely she will maintain a strong connection to the spirit world and will be highly creative, sensitive, and aware of energetic phenomena. But she will doubt her right to exist in the physical world and will have trouble functioning here.

Merging & Compensated Merging – Here the unfulfilled need was for nurturance. The deprivation happened during the first few years of life, usually in relation to nursing and/or bottle feeding. The child didn't get or couldn't take in the nourishment and soothing she needed, so she never felt full and satisfied. The tension of being hungry or otherwise upset was not fully released, so some anxiety always remained in her system. This anxiety further inhibited her ability to take in and metabolize nourishment and she got stuck in a cycle of needing, not being able to effectively receive, and never getting full. This left her feeling hollow and empty inside.

There are two ways that she can handle this situation. She can identify with the need and wait for rescue, or she can project her need onto others and then try to fulfill their needs. The first method leads to the pure merging pattern, the second to the compensated merging pattern. These are fundamentally the same personality pattern, but in the compensated merging pattern the feelings of need and helplessness are covered over by a pretense of self reliance and power.

A child in the pure merging pattern will be clingy, fragile, and need a lot of attention. A child in the compensated merging pattern will act self-reliant too soon by rejecting her own needs and focusing on helping others instead. While the second child looks more functional, the compensation is only a mask covering the unfinished work of this stage of development. In both situations, she practices referencing others, but avoids referencing herself. The gift of this strategy is that she then becomes skillful at sensing the needs of others and providing what's needed.

Enduring – At around the age of two, a new need arises in the child. He is now walking and talking and grappling with the discovery that he is separate from his mother. This discovery of separateness brings with it the need for autonomy — the need to be in charge of his own body and actions. He begins to say "No!" and to oppose attempts to control him.

While this assertion of his autonomy is exactly what he needs to do to complete this developmental stage, this is also a distinctly new behavior, something a baby doesn't do. If a parent or caregiver cannot tolerate his budding autonomy, a conflict will arise. As the parent tries to suppress his autonomy by controlling and punishing him, he will feel humiliated and enraged.

He will actively resist the parent's domination for as long as he can, but will eventually conclude that he cannot win and will switch to resisting passively. He will withdraw deep inside himself to protect his last shred of sovereign territory and, in a last act of autonomy, turn his will against himself to suppress his own desire to act and even to express himself. He will hunker down and limit his opposition to *"You can't make me."* This method of relating to the world is the core of the enduring personality pattern.

To make this safety strategy work, a child must have the will and strength required to silently persevere, even while enduring hardship and mistreatment. He does this by sending his life energy, even his very self, down into the ground and hiding it there. The difficulty is that he gets stuck down there, unable to move and act in the world. The benefit is that people who do this personality pattern are typically more grounded than others and often have great stamina.

Aggressive – Here, the unmet need was the need to feel contained and protected by something larger and stronger. This child won the battle for autonomy and felt proud of his strength and will. But then, in what felt to him like a life or death situation, he discovered that what he loved and trusted was not there to protect him. So he faced his fear alone and survived by summoning all his internal resources and willing himself through it. He felt betrayed, and it was his trust in others that was shattered. The unfulfilled need was once again safety, but here the focus was on the interpersonal, emotional safety of being able to depend on others.

This feeling of being failed or betrayed by what he thought was protecting him can be created in several different ways. In one scenario, the

About the Personality Patterns

child simply has such a big energy that his parents are not able to energetically contain him. He wins all the battles, but discovers that he faces the world alone. Conversely, the parent may be authoritarian and dominating, but this child refuses to give in, even though he loses most of the fights.

In a third scenario, one parent seduces him into a coalition against the other. In doing this, the seducing parent is ignoring the child's needs and using the child to meet his or her own needs. The seduction may include sexuality, but it is often purely emotional. When he realizes that his love for the parent was used to manipulate him, the child concludes that loving is dangerous and that it opens the door to being used and betrayed. He closes his heart and unconsciously resolves, "You will *never* do that to me again."

The child who develops the aggressive pattern has developed a cohesive sense of self, a strong will, and the ability to defend his own personal space, but he is always a little guarded. He finds it hard to trust or depend on others, or even to let them have their own space — space that he does not control. He still harbors a deep, unconscious terror that he will once again be used and betrayed.

Dominating every situation becomes his only way of creating a sense of safety for himself. He does, however, become skillful at making things happen in the world, and this becomes one of the gifts of the aggressive pattern.

Rigid – The injury here was that the parents could not value the child's inner experience. Having lost contact with their own inner life, they could not nurture their child's inner life. Instead, they focused on the child's appearance and performance, on things like manners, posture, correctness, and grades. They taught her to follow the rules they followed, and to obey the authority they obeyed. They could love their child for her achievements and performance, but not for her feelings and beingness.

Each of us needs our inner self, our being, to be seen and valued. If our parents see only our appearance and performance, we tend to lose contact with our inner experience and come to believe that our surface — our performance — is all that we are. Without contact with our inner self, we are unable to find our own inner guidance, so we have to rely on an outer form of guidance to help us make decisions.

A child who suffers this injury becomes focused on the forms and rules of life and loses touch with life's essence and substance. She tends to experience the world indirectly, through words, rather than directly through sensations and feelings. Rules replace personal feelings in her decision-making process. She may use language well and become a terrific performer, but for her, doing has replaced being, and the map has replaced the territory. In new situations, her plea will be *"Tell me the rules,"* because without the rules, she has no way to navigate.

When extra energy hits her system, she will attempt to contain it so that it doesn't really affect her and interfere with her performance. Instead of allowing it to emotionally move her, she will shunt the energy into activity — she will get busy and do something. While people who go into this personality pattern may not have much feeling, creativity, or color in their lives, they are often very successful on the outside, living in model homes with perfect lawns.

Primary and Secondary Patterns

Now that we've had a brief first look at the five personality patterns, it's important to also notice that people typically do more than one pattern. When they feel overwhelmed, they first go into their primary pattern. If that pattern is not solving the problem at hand, they will shift into their secondary, or backup, pattern. Some people even go into a third pattern, although this is rare. So, as you read through the descriptions of the personality patterns, be aware that you probably do two of them, not just one. You may go into one much more often than the other, or you may do them about equally.

This observation that each person does two patterns, arranged as a primary and a backup, came to me through the oral teachings of Lynda Caesara. She received it as an oral teaching from Harley SwiftDeer Reagan. I have not seen this insight from any other source. Lacking this piece of the puzzle, some writers have suggested that each of us does all of the patterns to varying degrees. I believe that is a mistake, which arises out of defining the personality patterns as collections of behaviors, rather than as safety strategies that a person habitually employs to buffer himself from feelings of overwhelm. In my opinion, the thing to watch for is what strategy a person employs first when distressed and, if that one fails, what strategy the person switches to next. These are the person's primary and secondary patterns.

About the Personality Patterns

Simply exhibiting some of the behaviors of a given pattern is not the same as adopting those behaviors as a safety strategy. You may have taken on the behavior of a certain pattern because that was what was expected in your family or community, even though you couldn't make the behavior work as a buffer against your distress. Similarly, if your parents did a particular pattern and trained you in its skills, you may have learned that pattern's skills, even though you don't use them as a safety strategy. Or you may have been blessed with the talents of a particular pattern, but never developed those talents into a safety strategy. To determine whether you do a particular pattern, notice how you try to protect yourself when you feel overwhelmed. That's the key.

People in Different Patterns Live in Different Worlds

Now let's consider how being in different personality patterns affects how we communicate with each other. Have you ever been in a disagreement with someone and been completely baffled by their description of the situation? Maybe you said to yourself, *"They must be blind,"* or *"They must be crazy,"* or even *"What an idiot!"* Most likely, what was happening was that both of you were in pattern, but in different patterns.

Your perception of reality was distorted by your personality pattern in one direction, and their perception of reality was distorted by their personality pattern in a different direction. *So the two of you were actually perceiving different realities.* And all the while, each of you was convinced that your own view was accurate, because it matched the way you usually see the world. What neither of you realized was that your usual views are distorted.

That means that people who are caught in different patterns are actually living in different worlds. Let's go back to the analogy of watching different channels on TV, channels that focus on different things and evoke different emotions. Here in the US, there is a TV channel that shows only horror movies, one after the other, all day long. I would call that the Fear Channel. And a person who watches only the Fear Channel, all day, every day, would soon believe that the world really is a terrifying place, and they'd better be ready to run, because that would be their main experience of the world. And that is the flavor of being caught in the leaving pattern.

Now let's compare that to a different person who watches only the Hallmark channel, which I would call the Love Channel. That channel shows mostly love stories, movies where, at first, there are obstacles to their connection and love, but by the end of the movie the obstacles have been removed, and they can happily fall in love. And a person who watches only that channel, all day, every day, would believe that Love Solves Everything and Love Conquers All. They wouldn't think there's anything to be afraid of or that they need to be ready to run. They'd think, *I just need to love them more, because love will solve everything.* That is the flavor of being caught in the merging pattern. Notice that these two people are living in completely different worlds.

> *People who are caught in different patterns are actually living in different worlds.*

Now let's compare them to another person who watches only TV channels that focus on competing and winning, channels with shows about sports, fighting, or wars. They're watching the Winning Channel, the channel that emphasizes winning and gets you emotionally invested in winning. And they learn that having bigger energy and more power is the way to win. So in their world, winning is everything, and they become one of the kids who wins most of the fights. That is the flavor of being caught in the aggressive pattern.

Now let's look at the opposite of that experience: the Avoid Losing Channel. Let's look at the kids who lost most of the fights, the kids who may have tried as hard as they could, but Mom or Dad would not let them win and even punished them for trying to win. Those kids decided, *"I give up. I can't win. I'll never win. I'll just keep my head down and try to avoid losing."*

Now, the only way to avoid losing is to avoid competing, which means don't participate and don't take a position. Don't say, *"Oh yeah, this is my team and I want us to win."* No, don't let yourself care that much. Maintain an attitude of, *"I don't care who wins. It's not important to me."* Or later, while in college, an attitude of, *"Yeah, it'd be nice to graduate from college, but you know, maybe I will and maybe I won't. It's not important."* Because the key to not losing is *Don't play the game or invest in it.*

About the Personality Patterns

And also, *Don't let the game finish*, because it's when the game ends that you either win or lose. So interrupt the game somehow. If you're playing checkers, just accidentally knock over the board. If you're in college, somehow fail to complete some courses. Or if you're just about to graduate, somehow forget to do the final exam, so they give you an incomplete. Because if you succeed, everyone's attention will turn to you, and back when you were young, that's when you would get attacked. That's when Dad or Mom would turn on you and humiliate you, so don't let that happen. Don't stand up and draw attention to yourself. Don't stick your head up, because it'll just get blown off again. Sabotage yourself just enough to keep yourself safe. And that is often the purpose of self-sabotage: it allows you to avoid drawing attention to yourself and therefore avoid getting attacked.

This is the safety strategy of the enduring pattern. It's actually a very adaptive response to a situation in which you cannot win. But to do it, you have to shift your attention away from *How do I win?* to *How do I avoid losing?* And when you do that, you've started watching the Avoid Losing Channel.

But the way you watch this channel is different from the others. You don't pick up the TV remote control and actively select the channel yourself. You stay passive. You just sit there while someone else selects the channel they want to watch, and then you silently resent it while you watch their channel with them. At most, you quietly leave the room. Maybe you complain about it days later, or maybe not, but you don't ever confront them directly about it. That is the flavor of being caught in the enduring pattern.

Finally, let's go to the fifth personality pattern, the rigid pattern and watching the Correctness Channel. Here, rather than competing against each other, everyone is competing against a standard, and their goal is to meet that standard. On this channel, there is One Right Way, and everyone is focused on performing perfectly, according to that One Right Way. In these competitions, there are judges rather than referees, and you win by getting the highest score from the judges, not by directly defeating your opponents. As an example, consider Olympic figure skating. I would bet that everyone who is an Olympic figure skating champion does the rigid pattern, because you would have to do the rigid pattern to want to spend so much of your life practicing the same routine over and over again in the hope of someday performing it flawlessly for the judges. That is very difficult to do. And it's not about having fun. It's about performing perfectly. Watching the Correctness Channel gives you the flavor of being caught in the rigid pattern.

Again, notice that, because they are caught in different patterns, each of these people are living in completely different worlds.

Seeing the same reality

So, is there any way that two people can see the same reality and agree on what they're seeing? Yes, there are two ways this can happen. First, this can occur when both people are in the same personality pattern. Second, it can occur when both people are present, that is, not in any pattern.

When both people are in the same personality pattern, their views of reality are distorted in similar ways, so they are seeing similar realities. Neither reality is accurate, but they won't notice that, because they have no accurate view for comparison. Instead, they feel reassured by their agreement. They interpret it as proof that they are seeing the whole truth of the situation.

We all like this feeling. It makes us feel safe and tells us that we are right, so we seek it out. We choose friends who run the same personality patterns we do, and we join groups that validate our patterns. Those who fear that danger lurks around every corner feel safer in the company of others who also see danger (both are watching the Fear Channel). Those who value connection are happiest in the company of others who also value connection (both are watching the Love Channel). And those who believe in following the rules find comfort in the company of others who also value the rules (as long as they value the *same* rules, whether those rules are libertarianism or communism, "law and order" or "free love").

The second situation in which two people can see the same reality occurs when they are both present, that is, when neither of them is in pattern. Now their views of the situation are much closer to reality and are therefore similar. Obviously, this is a much better situation. It is also the only path to actually resolving disagreements that are based on being in different patterns.

This is why it is so important for each of us to recognize when we have gone into pattern and take steps to get ourselves out of pattern.

How to Discern Your Own and Others' Patterns

When you first heard about personality patterns, your first question was probably, *"Which one am I?"* So what did you do? Maybe you read about the personality traits of each pattern, and you compared them to your own experience of yourself, looking for a match.

Approaching the question this way is natural, but it's based on the idea that this is a set of types and that a person *is* a type. And it's based on thinking that each type is a collection of traits and attributes, just like they are in other maps of personality.

But that is not what the personality patterns are. It's not how they are created or what defines them. They are not collections of traits. They are safety strategies. Each one arises out of a safety strategy, out of a way of trying to feel safer. And you are not a type. You are a person who habitually *uses* a particular set of these safety strategies to try to buffer yourself from distress.

The best way to discern your patterns is to watch what you do when you get distressed.

So the best way to discern which patterns you go into is *not* to look at your personality traits. The best way is to watch what you *do* as you get distressed. Watch what happens in your body when you first feel a little uncomfortable with a situation. Watch where your attention goes and what becomes important to you. Then watch what you do as your distress builds.

Here are the five safety strategies and the actions that follow from each. Notice which one you go into when you *first* get upset or distressed:

- **You want to leave.** Your attention and energy move away from whatever is distressing you. You feel scared. You think "*I gotta get away.*" You move away from them physically or you leave your body to get away.

- **You want to connect.** Your attention and energy move toward others. You're nice to them so they'll like you and help you. You agree, appease, or compliment them. You try to give them what they need, even if it's not what you need. You think they are the solution to your problem.

- **You want to hide.** Your attention and energy pull in and go downward to help you hide, or at least hunker down and endure whatever is coming. You might agree on the outside, but on the inside you think, *"You can't make me."* On the inside, everything starts to feel heavy and stuck. You don't take action; you just endure.

- **You want to fight.** Your attention and energy flow up and out to push against whatever and whoever is bothering you. You get big, intimidating, or angry to coerce their compliance with your will. Or maybe you get charming, but your intention is still to control and dominate them. You get bigger and more aggressive.

- **You want to do it the right way.** Your attention and energy go to performing correctly in this situation. Your chest and belly tense to dampen the flow of life energy and feeling through you, and your attention goes to how well you're performing. You get tight and rigid. You feel anxious. You focus on correctness.

If you monitor your body and attention carefully, you'll probably notice that you almost always go into the same safety strategy when you first get upset. This is your *primary* pattern. As your distress builds, you may stay with that strategy for a short time or a long time, but sooner or later, if things get bad enough, you switch into a different safety strategy. This is your *backup* pattern.

As you monitor yourself in more and more situations, you'll see yourself doing this same sequence again and again: primary pattern, then backup pattern. A few people use a third safety strategy, but most people use only two. I've never known anyone to use four or all five.

So this is the way to discern which patterns you go into: watch the sequence of safety strategies you use as you go from feeling safe and happy into a little distress, and then more distress, and then a lot of distress, and then overwhelmed.

This method is much more accurate than trying to match your personality traits and talents with those of the patterns. This is true for several reasons. First, you do two patterns, not just one, so trying to fit yourself into one category will just be confusing. Second, you may have some of the traits or talents of a particular pattern, but not actually use that pattern to feel safer. You may have learned those behaviors from your parents or just been born with those talents. In that case, we can say that you have the gifts of that pattern, but you don't *do* the pattern, i.e., when in distress, you don't automatically use that safety strategy to try to feel safer.

About the Personality Patterns

When you want to figure out which patterns someone else goes into, use the same method:

- Look at which safety strategies they use, not their personality traits or talents.
- Watch what they do and say when they seem to be feeling safe and happy.
- Notice what they do and say as they get a little annoyed or upset.
- Notice how what they do and say changes as they get more and more upset.
- Notice how what they do and say changes as they go into overwhelm.

Just practice watching people's behavior relative to their level of distress, and you'll begin to figure this out. As you practice it, you'll get better at it. It's often easier to see patterned behavior in others than in yourself, because you have some distance and probably feel safer in the moment.

Also, when you're watching a movie or TV show, ask yourself what patterns the characters are exhibiting. I don't watch a lot of TV shows, but I have watched The Big Bang Theory. And it didn't take very long for me to think, *"Oh, so Sheldon, the main character, is probably caught in the leaving and rigid patterns, and his roommate Leonard is probably caught in the enduring and rigid patterns, and Penny, the girl across the hall, is probably caught in the merging and aggressive patterns."* By doing it this way, you can turn discerning patterns into something fun that you can share with your friends.

Also, don't confuse a behavior with being caught in a pattern. Just because a person feels angry doesn't mean they're doing the aggressive pattern. Anyone can feel legitimately angry, no matter what patterns they do. Just because a person wants to get away from danger doesn't mean they're caught in the leaving pattern. Getting away from danger may be exactly what's needed in the moment, no matter what patterns you do.

Here's the difference: when you're caught in a pattern, you feel compelled to do its behavior, whether that behavior fits the situation or not. It's what you automatically do when you get distressed, as if it's the only tool in your toolbox. If the only tool in your toolbox is a hammer, every problem looks to you like a nail. That doesn't mean every problem *is* a nail, or that hitting it with your hammer will solve it.

So don't confuse having a feeling or a behavioral response with being caught in the pattern that you associate with that behavior. The question is, when you get distressed, what do you do automatically? To discover this, practice watching yourself as you go from feeling safe to feeling a little upset, to feeling more and more upset, and see what behaviors you go into and what safety strategies you habitually employ. It's not about personality traits. It's about the safety strategies.

Questions

Examples of distressing situations

> *"You said we get into pattern when we're distressed or overwhelmed. What would be some examples of distressing situations that might put a person into pattern?"*

Any situations which upset you: conflict at work, disappointment in a romance, times when you feel hurt, angry, scared, mistreated. Any of those could put a person into pattern. And there are many people who actually live in one or in both of their patterns nearly all the time and hardly ever come out into being present.

Two versus three patterns

> *"You mentioned that sometimes people have three patterns. What circumstances allow for a person to have two versus three?"*

I'm not sure about that, and few people actually do three patterns. But a person who does the compensated merging pattern may appear to do three patterns, because the compensation will have the flavor of one of the other patterns: the leaving pattern, the enduring pattern, the aggressive pattern, or the rigid pattern. So a person who does the compensated merging pattern may seem to do three patterns, but the one that they're using as the compensation is just a flavor. They don't really do that pattern, and under pressure, it will collapse.

About the Personality Patterns

Pattern development

"Is it possible to have an experience that typically causes a pattern without developing that pattern?"

Yes, two children with the same difficult experience can develop different safety strategies to handle the situation. It depends on the child's inborn talents and preferences, as well as the environment. And on their life purpose, if you think in terms of having a life purpose. So whether a person develops a particular pattern is a combination of many factors. And the environment is one factor, but not the only one.

Discerning patterns

"I've noticed that with some people, it's difficult to see what patterns they may have. Any suggestions on how to help determine this efficiently?"

In order to really see somebody's patterns, you need to see them in a time when they're distressed enough that they are in pattern. If they're not in pattern right now, you can't see their patterns in action. You may be able to pick up some clues from their body shape, attitude, speech patterns, skills, and gifts, but those don't actually tell you what they do when they're distressed. The patterns are safety strategies we go into when we get distressed. So the only way you can tell what safety strategies a person uses when they're distressed is to watch them when they're distressed.

Old defense patterns

"I find I'm using old defense patterns whenever the situation triggers how I felt in earlier environments. So we go into old patterns, even when people are absent?"

You bet we do. Lots of people, even at 60 or 80 years old, are still very stuck in their patterns from childhood, even though those patterns were a response to people and situations that are now long gone. The patterns get conditioned into the body, and they become automatic unless you take action to clear out the old traumas that are fueling them and practice energy skills to get yourself out of pattern.

Do we change patterns

"Do we change patterns over time?"

I have not seen that. It seems that the patterns generally get conditioned into a person's body during childhood, and they typically don't change in adulthood. However, a traumatic event can shift how much time a person spends in one of their patterns versus the other. I've seen traumatic events that caused such ongoing distress that the person shifted from living mostly in their primary pattern to living mostly in their backup pattern. And then later in life, as that trauma was gradually healed and cleared out of their body, their ongoing distress decreased enough that they returned to living mostly in their primary pattern, or even mostly in presence.

People without patterns

"Can someone not have one of these patterns at all? If they had an easy childhood and do secure attachment?"

I don't know of anyone who doesn't do any patterns, but there are people who wear their patterns lightly. They feel securely attached and emotionally safe, so they're able to be present most of the time, and it takes a lot of distress to put them into pattern. But, if they get distressed enough, they will still go into their patterns. I haven't met anyone who doesn't ever go into pattern.

Feeling to heal

"In addition to coming back to your self, don't you need to allow yourself to feel the emotions and release them, too?"

Yes, that is part of the process of healing. But that requires that you have the ability to come back, because each of the personality patterns moves your attention away from your distress in its own particular way. That's how it buffers you from feeling your distress fully. For instance, people who do the leaving pattern move their attention away from their body in order to feel their distress less vividly. But then, in order to come back into their body, they have to face that distress. The emotions are still there, and if there was trauma, it's still there. It's hard to come back, so they tend

About the Personality Patterns

to stay in their head and not really live in their body. And that stops them from fully embodying, which creates many other problems. That's why getting out of pattern is such an important part of growth and healing.

Developmental order and pattern order

"Since the rigid pattern usually develops later than the others, does it tend to be the backup pattern for people versus the first?"

It's a very reasonable question, but no, not necessarily. The developmental order doesn't seem to dictate which pattern a person goes into first and which they go into second when they're feeling distressed.

Aging

"Do these patterns tend to become more prominent as a person ages? How bad can this become?"

Well, as we get older, some of us do inner work to heal our core wounds, and since the patterns are fueled by the traumas still stuck in our bodies, that makes our patterns get lighter. But other people don't do inner work; they just get more stuck and crotchety as they age, so they go farther into their patterns. And sometimes, just before dying, all the person's patterns and defense mechanisms dissolve as the their heart finally comes to the fore. So, many paths are possible as we age.

Patterns and chakras

"Do these patterns correlate with the chakras?"

I don't think so. I know lots of people have tried to make that correlation, but I don't see it. It's easy to correlate the first two patterns with the first two chakras, but after that, the correlation gets more and more difficult. Our minds instinctively look for patterns and correlations, so we have a tendency to see them, even when they aren't really there. I suspect that people get hooked by the apparent correlation of the first two patterns with the first two chakras, and then can't let go of the idea when it doesn't work out. That has produced some very tortured models, in my experience.

- 5 -

How to Understand and Interact with Each Pattern

How to Understand and Interact with Each Pattern

PATTERN	FEELS SCARED BY . . .	TRIES TO FEEL SAFER BY . . .	HOW TO INTERACT WITH THEM
Leaving	• big, strong emotions or energies • aggression, conflict • personal unhappy feelings • lack of an exit path • living in a cold, unloving world • needing or depending on others • feeling attached to others	• leaving or dissociating to limit contact • avoiding conflict • avoiding inhabiting the body • staying up in their head • keeping it abstract and general • keeping it light, playful, impersonal	• keep your contact light • keep it head or heart centered • make it fun & playful, not too personal, with a warm, kind flavor • more about ideas than feelings • avoid talk of needs, hurt, anger, shame • avoid any intense feelings
Merging	• loss of the heart connection • abandonment, rejection • feeling empty or alone • having needs • conflict with others • disappointing others • not being enough • having to struggle to do a task	• merging and sending feelers into others • maintaining a heart connection with others • appeasing, accommodating, flattering • manipulating, giving-to-get • focusing on and expressing feelings **Simple Merging** • getting others to take care of them • crying out for help **Compensated Merging** • ignoring own needs & taking care of others	• keep your contact personal • speak from your heart to their heart • stay heart centered, connected, kind • focus on feelings, not ideas • strong personal feelings are okay • avoid attacking them **Simple Merging** • take care of them, as needed • support their self-care and self-action **Compensated Merging** • support their own self-care

How to Have Better Relationships

PATTERN	FEELS SCARED BY . . .	TRIES TO FEEL SAFER BY . . .	HOW TO INTERACT WITH THEM
Enduring	<ul><li>being invaded or controlled</li><li>loss of a buffering space around them</li><li>being found, exposed, humiliated</li><li>attempts to find or control them</li><li>feeling messed with</li><li>obligations, deadlines, tests</li><li>others' desires and needs</li></ul>	<ul><li>retreating into their own space, hiding</li><li>being unreachable, unmovable, passive</li><li>enduring; not responding or sharing feelings</li><li>no self-expression, no self-action</li><li>not initiating or taking a position on anything</li><li>automatically saying "No" at first</li><li>resisting all attempts to move or control them</li></ul>	<ul><li>always stay aware of their space</li><li>respect their space and boundaries</li><li>do not invade their space at all, ever</li><li>do not attempt to move or control them</li><li>reassure them: "you're not in trouble"</li><li>place your request at the edge of their space</li><li>leave them alone to process it</li></ul>
Aggressive	<ul><li>abandonment by others</li><li>betrayal by others</li><li>any deception or manipulation</li><li>any loss of control</li><li>any challenge to their dominance</li><li>feeling weak, needy, or scared</li><li>having to trust and surrender</li><li>depending on others</li></ul>	<ul><li>dominating self and others</li><li>controlling the situation</li><li>assessing who has power & how much</li><li>energetically tracking others</li><li>manipulating and charming others</li><li>intimidating and scaring others into compliance</li><li>distrusting others, trusting only self</li><li>detecting any untruthfulness</li></ul>	<ul><li>develop a strong felt-sense of your core</li><li>always speak and act from your core</li><li>stay in your core, even if they blast you</li><li>reassure them: "I'm here" and "I care about you"</li><li>match their energy, but don't escalate</li><li>tell them the truth, no matter how bad</li><li>set and enforce your own boundaries and expect them to be tested repeatedly</li></ul>

How to Understand and Interact with Each Pattern

PATTERN	FEELS SCARED BY . . .	TRIES TO FEEL SAFER BY . . .	HOW TO INTERACT WITH THEM
Rigid	<ul><li>deviations from the Rules</li><li>chaos and disorder</li><li>broken agreements</li><li>loss of control</li><li>changes in plans</li><li>imperfection, making a mistake</li><li>being wrong, blamed or guilty</li><li>uncontrolled play or spontaneity</li><li>surrendering into feelings</li></ul>	<ul><li>performing well, according to the Rules</li><li>enforcing the Rules & Forms on others</li><li>maintaining Standards and Order</li><li>keeping agreements</li><li>keeping everything under control</li><li>planning each step before starting</li><li>executing the plan exactly</li><li>being right and doing right</li><li>being and doing what is expected</li></ul>	<ul><li>learn about their particular Rules</li><li>interact with them within those Rules</li><li>keep your agreements with them</li><li>keep things in order</li><li>avoid causing chaos</li><li>avoid surprising them or changing plans</li><li>gently support them in having feelings</li><li>ask about their feelings, hopes & dreams</li><li>help them manage their Inner Critic</li></ul>

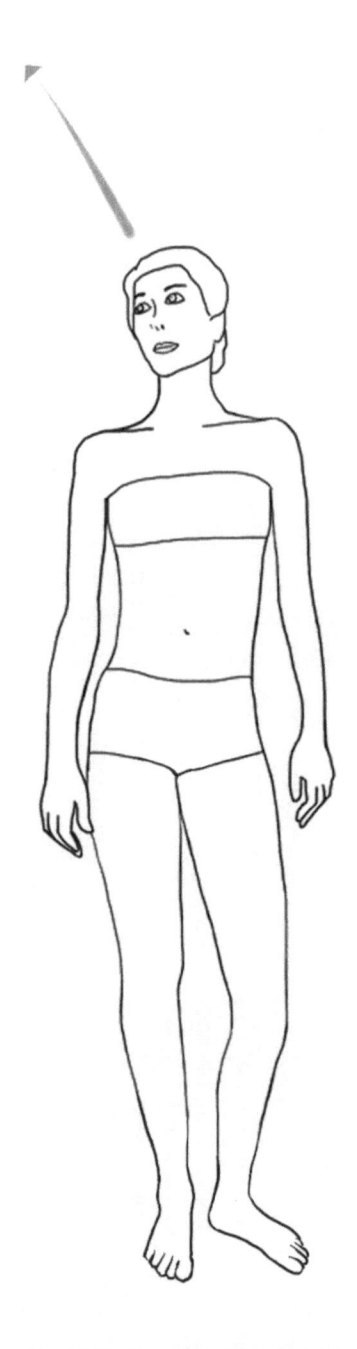

The Leaving Pattern – body and energy flow

- 6 -

Relating to the Leaving Pattern

Like all the survival patterns, the leaving pattern is a way to buffer the self from feelings of overwhelm. It is a habit of attention, fueled by trauma held in the body. The original trauma is the shattering of the incoming spirit's attention, usually before birth. We're going to focus on one pattern at a time because that's the clearest way to study them, but keep in mind that people do more than one pattern.

Centering Yourself

Before we get into the chapter, let's do the Centering Breath to help you be more present in your body.

Imagine a column inside your body, from the crown of your head down to the bottom of your torso, and imagine that you can breathe in through the bottom of that column and fill it up. Begin by breathing in through your nose and filling the whole column with breath, from the bottom all the way up to the top. And then, breathing out through pursed lips, send all that breath down and out the bottom of the column. Do that again several more times: in and all the way up, then out and all the way down. Again, in and up, and out and down. And up once more, all the way up to the top, and then back down and all the way out.

> And just notice, how do you feel inside now? Did something shift? Do you find yourself somehow coming more into your body and feeling more centered in yourself?
>
> That's what we want. I encourage you to do this repeatedly, throughout the day. You can do the whole practice in 20 or 30 seconds, so it's no big deal. And you can do it in any moment that's free. While you're on hold on the phone, or waiting at a stoplight, or waiting in line, do the Centering Breath. If you're feeling upset or off balance, do the Centering Breath, and it will bring you back to yourself.

What would your life be like now if . . . ?

What if, for as long as you could remember, your awareness was not always located inside your physical body? What if your awareness could hover above you and look down at things? And even leave our physical dimension and go to other dimensions and have all kinds of adventures?

What if you discovered that every time you get scared, you actually do leave your body? And you can't help it, or stop it. What if you discovered that you're actually kind of scared of this place and these people? What if being all by yourself feels safer to you than cuddling up with someone?

If all that were true for you, how would you experience the world? Maybe you'd be more of an observer than a participant in your life, as if you're watching it happen from a distance. You might feel like a person standing outside a house and looking in through the window at a party going on inside. The people inside might seem happy. They might be laughing and having fun, and you might feel lonely, out there by yourself. But you also might feel safer out there, looking in.

And this would probably seem normal for you, because whatever we usually experience, we think of as normal. So we make the classic mistake of thinking that it must be this way for everybody. That's why the first discovery that everyone makes when they study a map of personality is that what's normal for them isn't necessarily normal for everyone.

But this is what a person who is caught in the leaving pattern experiences much of the time. I use the phrase "caught in the leaving pattern" because I want to remind you that you are not your patterns. You are your essence. Your natural state is to simply be present in the here and now.

Your personality patterns are defenses that you go into when you're distressed as a way to feel safer. But they are not who you really are.

The five personality patterns are five different ways that people try to feel safer and less distressed. When a person who's caught in the leaving pattern feels scared, they automatically think, *"I've gotta get away."* And they move away from other people because that helps them feel safer. It's normal for them, but not for everyone.

The Origins of The Leaving Pattern

To understand how and why such a defense mechanism gets created, we need to go back to the very beginning of life, to the womb. While the baby's body is growing in the womb, there is a consciousness that comes into it. You might call it the spirit, the soul, or something else.

The Problem: the womb did not feel safe enough

Ideally, that spirit settles into the physical body and claims it. Gradually, it attaches to the physical body and begins the process of developing a strong felt-sense of self in the core of the body. This process is called embodiment, and it is the main task of the first stage of a person's psychological development.

That is the ideal, the process that unfolds when the incoming spirit feels held by a warm, holding love and everything goes well enough. But for people who develop the leaving pattern, that did not happen. For them, the womb and the world did not feel safe and loving enough, and their spirit did not settle into the body. The lack of safety may have started with the mother's personal situation or with larger, external circumstances. Perhaps the mother is ill, poor, or alone, or she is in a violent relationship or environment. Suppose she's living in a war zone, with explosions every night. Whatever the cause, if the mother's body is in distress, her distress is communicated into the womb space, and the incoming spirit feels that distress.

The Solution: flee

So what does the incoming spirit do to feel safer? It flees the womb and goes back to the field of divinity, the place of oneness and love and safety. Later, it will come back to the body, but if it again finds distress, it flees again. Some of this coming and going of the spirit is normal during the early months of pregnancy, but if the incoming spirit is not able to settle in and stay, it is not able to attach to the body and claim it. Instead of attaching to the body and building a strong, safe home there, it learns that leaving is the way to feel safer. It learns to flee as soon as it feels scared.

Attention and energy go: away

This experience of repeatedly leaving the body conditions the person's attention and life energy to routinely flee the body at the first sign of trouble. This habit becomes the person's safety strategy and the root of the leaving pattern.

The effect of this Safety Strategy: failure to attach to the physical body

This habit of repeatedly leaving the body interrupts the process of embodiment. The incoming spirit is not able to attach to the physical body and ground to the earth. Without attachment to the body, it's not able to build a felt-sense of core in the body. Without grounding to the earth, it doesn't feel supported and safe here in the physical plane.

Without a felt-sense of core in the body, it is unable to create a strong energetic boundary around the body. The job of that energetic boundary is to act as a filter to keep other people's thoughts and feelings out of your space. This is important because many thoughts and feelings generated by other people are floating around in the world and can float into your personal space. If you have a strong energetic boundary, you can keep most of that stuff out. But if you don't have a strong energetic boundary, their junk gets into your space. And pretty soon, your space is full of all sorts of thoughts and feelings that aren't your own, and you don't know what you think and feel.

Without a felt-sense of core in the body, you also have a hard time forming a strong, cohesive, felt-sense of *self* in your body, a sense of self that can hold together even when hit by a big wave of energy. Without that,

Relating to the Leaving Pattern

your self remains so fragile that, if someone else throws a big wave of feelings at you, your self may shatter into many pieces. This internal shattering is terrifying for you.

When your self has been shattered into fragments, you need to reassemble it. To do that, you need a reference point in the body to use as the starting place. But if you can't feel the core of your body, you don't have a place from which to begin. That makes it even harder to gather all your fragments and reassemble your self.

This experience of being shattered is very different from the fears and anxieties felt by people who are more embodied. When your sense of self is not attached to your physical body, and then your self is shattered into fragments, you literally can't find a center from which to operate. You can't find yourself. You can't find your body and you can't find the earth. You're just a point of awareness. One person described it as "floating in a black void." But then they said that even "floating" sounds too sensuous. There are no sensations. You're just a point of awareness, suspended in nothing.

Being shattered is terrifying.

That's very different from just feeling anxious. When you're feeling anxious, your experience is something like *I am here in my body, on the earth, and I am having this sensation called anxiety.* But when your self has been shattered, your experience is more like *There isn't a me or an earth or anything right now. There's just a black void, where I'm lost and helpless.*

Without a felt-sense of core to start from, it can take a leaving-patterned person days to reassemble themselves. That means days of feeling lost, helpless, and scared. It's a horrible feeling, and they really don't like it. And that's why they are so focused on avoiding situations where someone might throw a wave of big energy at them.

That's also why leaving-patterned people feel safer in separateness than in connection. For them, connection to other human beings includes the risk that something will shatter them. In fact, this whole physical realm does not seem warm and welcoming, but instead feels kind of cold and hostile.

The Gifts of The Leaving Pattern

The process of developing any of these personality patterns involves successfully using the safety strategy that underlies that pattern many, many times. But in order to make that safety strategy work for you, you have to have the talents and skills needed to make it work. If you can't make it work, you'll abandon it and try a different safety strategy. If you can make it work, you'll continue using it, and each time you use it, you'll be practicing and improving those skills. After years of practice, you become an expert at those skills, and they become the Gifts of the pattern.

So, when a person repeatedly practices leaving their body and going back to the spirit world, what skills do they develop? One is the skill of energetic and psychic perception. They become Masters of the Airwaves.

Leaving-patterned people also develop a very facile attention. They are able to move their attention easily, not only from one subject to another, but even from one viewing place to another. They don't see their attention as confined to their body, or even confined to their head. For most people, if you ask, "*Where is your attention located?*" they'll say, "*Well, it's in my head. I can look down at my hand, but my attention is not in my hand, it's in my head, behind my eyes.*" But for a leaving-patterned person, it can go anywhere. It can leave their body and even leave this physical dimension. They can visit other dimensions, and there are many dimensions to visit. For them, this physical world is just one place to visit—and not necessarily the most interesting one.

Because they can go to other dimensions and get new, wonderful ideas and bring them back here, they are very creative. If you bring to mind all the people who have created new stories, music, poetry, mathematics, or found new, amazing solutions to old problems — very often they did that by going to other dimensions to get them. Not all creative people do the leaving pattern, but those creating seminal works usually do.

And, having this multi-dimensional view, they are able to see both the big picture and all of its parts. They're very curious about how things work, and they like to pull things apart to see how all the pieces fit together. And their facile attention allows them to view a physical object from multiple directions at once: from the front, back, sides, above, and below. This leads them to deconstruct things, especially in the visual arts. You can see this way of viewing things illustrated in cubist paintings.

Relating to the Leaving Pattern

Leaving-patterned people also like to play. When they feel safe, they can be fun and joyful, even childlike and open, with the flavor of a fairy or sprite.

Fears

What do leaving-patterned people fear? They fear living here in the physical world, where they are so vulnerable, and they fear other human beings in general. For them, people and the world are not warm and inviting, but indifferent or even cold and hostile. They often feel like they are way too sensitive and that things in this physical world are just too much for them.

And because they've been shattered in the past when hit by a big wave of anger, they have a fear that if anyone's energy gets big, they'll get shattered again. And that experience of feeling their self fragmenting is just terrifying — it feels like going crazy. There is literally "no one there," not even themselves. So leaving-patterned people are very focused on avoiding any big energy and the people who run big energy.

They also try to protect themselves by not bringing much of their attention into their physical body. If their body has a lot of old trauma stuck in it, and they are staying out of their body to not feel that trauma, bringing their attention back into their body will cause them to feel that trauma again. Naturally, they want to avoid that, so they tend to keep much of their attention and life energy outside their physical body.

To avoid being shattered, they avoid claiming the body and attaching to it.

This creates a self-reinforcing cycle: without settling into the body and attaching to it, they are not able to develop a strong felt-sense of their core and a resilient, cohesive self within that core. Without a resilient, cohesive self in the body, they cannot develop a strong energetic boundary to shield them from other people's energy, which leaves them vulnerable to any big energy. In the end, their habit of fleeing to feel safer leaves them unable to develop the skills that would actually protect them.

So remember that leaving-patterned people are usually more scared in any situation than you would be. Don't be surprised or take it personally if they're a little anxious and tentative about connecting with you. You may find that you have to do a lot to help them feel safe enough to connect with you, but knowing all this about them will help you understand why.

Emotions

Generally, leaving-patterned people tend to avoid feelings, especially ones that are personal and negative, such as anger, need, or grief, and they especially avoid such feelings when around other people. On the other hand, when they're alone, they often review what has happened and feel it much more deeply than they did while it was happening. When in the presence of others, their attention goes to their fear of being hurt, but when they're alone, they feel safe enough to let themselves feel more. They may also preview an experience before it happens and feel it much more deeply during the preview than during the actual experience.

When they're feeling safe, they can be very playful and happy. Typically, this happens only when they're alone or with others who also do the leaving pattern.

Each of the five personality patterns has a default emotion. This is the emotion that a person who does this particular pattern feels whenever too much energy hits their system. The kind of energy hitting their system doesn't matter — it could even be something positive, like pride or joy — but if it is enough to put them into overwhelm, they will start to feel their default emotion.

The default emotion for leaving-patterned people is fear, and even a small increase in the level of energy around them can trigger it. The extra energy hitting their system is shunted upward in the body to the head, where the mind interprets it as fear.

The default emotion is fear.

The mind then looks for the cause of the fear, but because it is constrained by its patterned beliefs, it looks only outside itself, sifting through all its perceptions of the outside world for any signs of danger. Usually it is able to find some evidence of danger, which reinforces the patterned feeling of fear and the belief that the world is dangerous.

If you know what your own default emotions are, you may be able to avoid being swept away by them when you go into overwhelm. If you can say to yourself, *"Oh yeah, there's my usual feeling again,"* and then ask yourself, *"So am I feeling this because of the actual situation around me, or am I in overwhelm and this is just my default emotion kicking in?"* you have a much better chance of re-orienting yourself and not getting lost in the emotion.

Beliefs

The beliefs of leaving-patterned people reflect their fears that the physical world is unsafe and the people in it are unloving. Some of their typical beliefs are:

"I am my mind, not my body."
"I don't physically exist."
"I'm like a leaf, blown in the wind."
"My actions don't matter. I can't change anything."
"No one cares."
"I am alone here."

Examples

- Robin Williams
- Albert Einstein
- Nikola Tesla
- Pablo Picasso
- Luna Lovegood in the *Harry Potter* films
- Lisa Kudrow's character Phoebe in the TV show, *Friends*

Communicating with Someone Caught in the Leaving Pattern

Energetic sensitivity

Leaving-patterned people are typically more energetically sensitive than others. This can make them very perceptive, although as with anyone, their perceptions are often distorted by projections of their own unconscious material. The upside of their perceptiveness is that they can be incredibly sensitive and attuned to others. The downside is that they may trust their own impressions so much that they don't bother to check them against reality, and so may feel certain about a "perception" that is actually a projection. If you are angry — even if it has nothing to do with them — they will feel scared. On the other hand, if you're loving them silently from the next room, they are likely to feel that, too.

When dealing with someone who does this personality pattern, you must keep in mind both their extraordinary sensitivity to energy and their inability to tolerate very much of it. Because their own energetic boundaries are so weak, any energy you are radiating can easily penetrate them. This means that if you're coming to them with an agenda, they may feel you and your agenda coming a block away. Or they may frequently sense how you feel before you do. However, their interpretation of what they sense in you may or may not be accurate.

Safety, vulnerability, and helplessness

Since people who do this personality pattern feel so vulnerable, their main priority in all interactions is safety. Everything else is secondary to their need for safety. And because they actually were totally helpless when they got stuck in this early state, they typically continue to think of themselves as helpless. They don't think of themselves as having the ability to cause change in those around them, so it does not occur to them to make demands or put pressure on others to change. Instead, they tend to just accept the current situation as a given.

Others often misinterpret this lack of complaint as a tacit acceptance of their behavior, and may take the lack of opposition as permission to continue doing things which are invasive or abusive. So, if you want to

Relating to the Leaving Pattern

know how safe someone who does the leaving pattern feels around you, pay attention to how long they stay in contact with you, not whether they complain. They're more likely to manage their inner state by simply leaving (either physically or energetically) than by complaining or asking that you change your behavior.

Difficulty navigating in time and space

Because their attention is not anchored in their physical body, it's harder for them to navigate here in the world of time and space. They don't really live in the physical realm, so this whole time-and-space thing is foreign for them. You may notice that they're frequently not in the right place at the right time for a meeting or appointment. They're wandering around somewhere else, because they're not really paying attention to time and space in the same way that others might. In contrast, rigid-patterned people are typically very good at time and space and keep track of it almost religiously. But for leaving-patterned people, time and space are not that important; they're just coordinates in one of the dimensions, and a pretty scary one at that.

Communicating on the psychic channel instead of in words

Leaving-patterned people don't really focus on the words when communicating. They use the psychic channel, so the words are secondary. A leaving-patterned friend of mine calls their way of communicating "speaking dolphin."

So here's what speaking dolphin is like: suppose we have two leaving-patterned people who are having a conversation on the psychic channel. And remember that on the psychic channel, they can send a picture or a feeling and the other person will get it. So suppose that one person just says, *"Hey, remember that time?"* (and sends a picture). *"Oh, it was so"* (and sends a feeling). And the other person, who got all that, replies, *"Oh, yeah, I was"* (and they send a feeling back).

Both of those people know what they're talking about. Using both the words and the psychic channel, they got the whole conversation. But if you're not good at listening on the psychic channel and you're only getting the words, all you heard was, *"Remember that time, it was so"* and

How to Have Better Relationships

"Oh, yeah, I was," and you have no idea what they're talking about. You may feel frustrated and left out — like they're speaking a foreign language and you can't understand it. Many fights between lovers arise out of these differences in communication channels, coupled with our own belief that everyone uses the same way of communicating that we use, so if they misunderstood us, it must have been intentional.

And that's the point here. To communicate successfully with anyone, you need to send your message on the channels they use, if you can. And if you can't, you need to get as close as possible. Almost none of us are able to use all the channels; we just don't have all those talents. But do what you can. With leaving-patterned people, if you're able to put your communication on the airwaves in pictures and feelings, do that. It's okay to also use words, but try to put as much as you can on the psychic channel, because they're not really paying attention to the words. And keep in mind that when they communicate with you, they're sending most of their message on the psychic channel, so that's the place for you to listen for it, if you can.

"It's like you haven't heard a single thing I've thought."

(www.CartoonStock.com)

Relating to the Leaving Pattern

If you're not so good on the psychic channel, at least listen for the melody and the feeling tone in their words. Think of their communication as a song and listen for the melody, because it will tell you something about what they're feeling. This is an important thing to remember when interacting with anyone who's caught in the leaving pattern.

Now, you may be wondering if there's a way to get leaving-patterned people to put more attention on their words so that they communicate with you in a way that's easier for you to understand. You can certainly ask them to do that, but you will have to put your request into simple, clear words. Let them know that you're not able to get what they're sending on the psychic channel and that you need this help from them. This might be a big surprise for them, because they may never have even considered the idea that others don't get what they're sending on the psychic channel. After all, they get that channel all the time, so it's easy for them to think that everyone gets it. So don't make them wrong for not putting it into words. Just tell them that you need this and ask if they will help you this way. And then reinforce it by thanking them each time they do it for you.

To communicate successfully with anyone, you need to send your message on the channels they use, if you can.

For much a more detailed discussion of this pattern, please see the book, The 5 Personality Patterns.

How to Relate to Them Successfully

So, given how sensitive and scared leaving-patterned people tend to be, what can you do to help them feel safer?

First, dial down your own energy

Your energy might naturally be quite big and enthusiastic. You might just be feeling full of energy and joy, or creativity and excitement. Maybe you just came up with this big, wonderful plan, or your sports team just won a game — you could have all sorts of good reasons to have big energy. But big energy scares leaving-patterned people, because it has shattered them in the past.

So before you approach them, you need a simple way to dial down your energy. Now, I come from the days when every device that played music had a big volume knob on it, and to turn down the volume, you just turned that knob to the left. So to dial down the amount of energy in my body, I like to just stick out my hand, imagine I'm grabbing a big volume knob, and then slowly turn it to the left. As I do that, I imagine feeling everything in my body settling down.

Your method of dialing down your own energy can be anything that works for you. Maybe you're more familiar with pushing a button on a remote control device or sliding something with your thumb. Whatever motion your body is used to doing to turn down the volume, physically do that motion. Actually use your body and do the motion. Doing the motion physically will stimulate your muscle memory of that action and help your body do it energetically. And as you do that, imagine feeling your body settling down.

Next, pull your energy back inside your own space

Remember, your bubble is the space right around you, your personal space. It expends about an arm's length out from your body in all directions. Ideally, you should keep your personal energy inside your own personal space and not let it expand into anyone else's space. To pull your energy back inside your personal space, you have to gather your own energy — which could be spread out through the whole room — and bring it back inside your own bubble.

I find the easiest way to pull my energy back is to physically go through the motions of pulling it back: I reach out with my hands, imagine I'm grabbing my energy field, and pull it back in. Then I reach out in a different direction, grab some more, and pull it back in. I continue grabbing it from different directions around me and pulling it back in until I feel like I've made a difference. Try doing that for yourself. As you pull it in again and again, what changes do you notice in your body and your inner state? I encourage you to repeatedly practice this skill by both intending and physically pulling your energy in like this and see how your experience of

Relating to the Leaving Pattern

yourself changes. Also ask your friends who do the leaving pattern to give you feedback on what changes they notice.

Shift your attention to a soft, field focus, rather than a sharp, point focus.

Often, we focus on just one thing in our whole field of vision — perhaps a tree, or a lamp, or a picture on the wall — but we can also let our attention soften and spread out to include everything around us. To experience these two states for yourself, try this experiment.

First, find something near you and narrow you attention to focus only on it. Hold this narrow focus for a bit. As you do this, you may feel a slight contraction in your body or head or energy field. This is known as 'point focus'.

And now let that narrow focus relax. Let your awareness relax and broaden as you open your field of attention to the whole space around you. Let your awareness gradually expand to include not just what's in front of you, but also what's behind you and on both sides of you. How does this feel different? If you tune in to your inner state now, you'll probably notice that something inside you has softened, opened, and expanded. This is known as 'field focus'.

Now let's explore the differences between these two states. Take some time to shift back to point focus and try to feel into that state as fully as you can. To do that, let your vision again narrow to just one object. As your vision contracts, does your attention also contract? Is there also a slight contraction in your body or energy field?

Then shift back to field focus and try to feel into that state as fully as you can. To do that, again open your field of attention to the whole space around you. Let your awareness gradually expand to include not just what's in front of you, but also what's behind you and on both sides of you. As your awareness expands, what changes do you notice in your body, or emotions, or anywhere? In myself, I notice that when I shift into field focus, my voice pitch lowers a little bit and something inside me slows down. As you shift into field focus, what happens for you?

To get familiar with these two states, take some time to experiment with gently shifting back and forth between them. By shifting back and forth, you'll have a chance to compare the two states and discover how they're different from each other. You may not feel much difference immediately, but keep gently moving back and forth until you can sense a change. The inner shift may be very subtle, so that may take some time.

Being able to consciously feel this difference is important because our bodies have evolved over millions of years to sense this shift unconsciously and respond to it instinctively. To understand our instinctive reactions, let's take a look at how predator and prey animals interact with each other.

In the moment before a predator animal pounces on its prey, its attention narrows to a point focus on that one animal. Let's say the predator is a lion, and it's stalking a whole herd of gazelle. As it lies hidden in the grass, one gazelle wanders over toward it, and the lion thinks, "Okay, I'll take that one." In the moment the lion's attention narrows to a point focus on that one gazelle, it's energy field contracts, and that contraction ripples through the larger energy field surrounding the whole herd. Since gazelles are prey animals, their survival depends on feeling that contraction. Their bodies are tuned to that larger energy field, and the instant they feel that contraction in the field, they all run from it. They probably don't see the lion hiding in the grass, but they all feel the contraction in the larger energy field, and they run from that.[1]

They are prey animals, and one of the ways that prey animals detect predators is by holding a field focus on the whole space surrounding them. This allows them to feel any changes in the field, and when they feel a contraction, they run. If you've ever seen a herd of peacefully grazing animals suddenly bolt, you've seen this survival instinct in action. The grazing animals probably didn't all see the predator at the same time, but they all felt a contraction in the energy field at the same time, and they ran from that.

The reason I bring all this up here is that we humans were prey animals for millions of years, and our bodies still unconsciously watch for this and use it to try to avoid danger. When our attention contracts to a point focus, our energy field contracts, too, and that can scare leaving-patterned people. In the past, they've felt other people's energy fields contract just before launching an attack, and their bodies remember that and want to get away from it. If they feel your field contract, they will want to get away from you, too. They will likely think that you're about to attack them, even when you're not. Your attention may have narrowed for a completely different reason. Perhaps you didn't understand their answer to a question you asked, and now you feel confused and you're just trying to get more clarity on what they meant. Your intentions may be innocent, but if your

Relating to the Leaving Pattern

attention narrows and your energy gets a little hard and contracted, they can feel that and it scares them. Instinctively, they will want to get away.

So, to avoid scaring leaving-patterned people, you need to learn to maintain a soft, field focus of attention while interacting with them. Mastering this skill is not easy, and developing it may take some time, but you will find that it allows you to skillfully navigate many situations in life with many different people, no matter what personality patterns they do. Mastering the skill of differentiating between field focus and point focus and learning to control your own attention in this way will repay your efforts many times over.

If they feel your field contract, they may think you're about to attack them.

Put your agenda aside

Here, the problem is simply that you have an agenda. Perhaps your agenda is that you would like something to happen or not happen. But when you put your attention on your agenda — whatever it is — your attention narrows, and a leaving-patterned person's body will feel that contraction in your energy field and react to it. They may well feel startled and scared and want to get away. And this can happen even though you didn't even mention your agenda. They didn't need to hear you say anything because they could feel the contraction in your field.

So, what can you do to put aside your agenda? Let me suggest something that seems to work for me. (You may notice that, because I'm more kinesthetic than visual, many of the tools that I offer involve physical movements and sensations. If those tools work for you, great. If not, please experiment with similar visual or auditory ideas to find tools that work for you.)

I was a stage actor when I was younger, so I imagine that I'm once again on stage and my agenda is out in front of me. Then I physically reach out and move it off of center stage. I put it off to the side, perhaps behind a curtain. This leaves a clear, open space in front of me. Now, I still know I have an agenda, but it's off to the side, behind the curtain. It's not bothering me so much. I'm not so focused on it. Only a little bit of my attention is on it, and most of my attention is more open and field focused.

119

Try doing that for yourself. Try going through the physical motions, just as you did with turning down the volume and pulling in your energy. Go through the physical motions, and see if that helps you move your agenda off center stage. You can move it off to the right or off to the left; it doesn't matter. Just somehow move it off of center stage. I like doing it with my body because that helps my body get it. But if you can do this using only your imagination, that's fine, too. Whatever works for you is just fine. But somehow you have to put your agenda aside so that your attention relaxes and you don't scare the leaving-patterned person.

Shift your attention up into your head

Most of us in the western world live up in our heads most of the time, so your attention may already be habitually up there, and this may not be an issue for you. But if you tend to hold your attention more in your heart or belly center, just gently bring more of your attention up into your head. Just intend and imagine you're doing that.

Intention is the key here. If you explore how you go about moving your hand, you'll notice that you don't have to think about *how* to do it. You don't focus on which nerves to fire and which muscles to contract to make your hand move in the way you want it to. You just intend for your hand to move, and it moves. And you can use the same method to move your attention up into your head and your mind (or anywhere else). Just imagine it and intend it, and see what happens. You may need to experiment and practice for a while, but gradually, you can learn to do this.

One important point: when I say "move your attention up into your mind," I mean artist's mind, not lawyer's mind. This shift is not for arguing a case in court (more point focus). This is for being more creative and spontaneous and fun (more field focus).

Also, remember that leaving-patterned people can be a little uncomfortable with personal feelings, especially negative or intense ones, so frame whatever you have to say as abstract, impersonal ideas rather than as personal feelings. They get a little anxious around personal feelings and often don't want to go there, so avoid that if you can, at least at the beginning.

If you want to present a plan or possibility to them, try to present it as a fun experience. Maybe as an adventure for the two of you, or as a game you can play together. Paint a picture of something that'll be fun.

Leaving-patterned people like fun. Don't try to get them to move into deep emotional intimacy, at least not initially. It doesn't feel safe to them, so they're not so comfortable going there. Remember, most of their early interactions with human beings were most likely not warm and fuzzy.

Keep your heart center warm, but light

Keep a gentle, warm awareness in your heart center. But make sure it's light, not an intense feeling like jealousy, rage, shame, or grief. Just a light, kind sensation in your heart. You want to be a warm presence, but not someone who's about to pull them into a full body hug. You can offer that, but let them come to you.

Similarly, don't pull on them emotionally. Don't try to get them to open up to you about their needs, hurt, anger, shame, or any difficult emotions too soon. Start with just a light interaction. A non-demanding, gentle, warm presence. And avoid any kind of intense feelings, if you can. Intensity is a bigger energy, so it can scare them.

Ask what you can do to help them

It's important to remember that leaving-patterned people got wounded while still in the womb or soon after birth, at a time when they were so young that they were actually completely helpless. They couldn't do anything for themselves and couldn't make anyone else do anything. They couldn't even speak about their distress, because they couldn't yet talk. So in their mind/body, the idea that they can act to improve their circumstances may not even exist. The notion that they can say, *"I need you to do this for me"* or *"Hey, I don't like this; I want you to do that instead,"* is outside their realm of experience. Often, it doesn't even occur to them. They still think of themselves as helpless and unable to cause any change in their situation, so they don't try to improve it or ask anybody to change. They just leave.

So if you ask them what you can do to help them, that's a new idea for them. They may think, *"Oh, really, you could help me? I could ask you to help me?"* Frequently, you will need to open that door for them. And as you talk with them, again, avoid confronting them. If you have to talk about something that's a little confrontive — for instance, if they did something and you didn't like it — instead of talking about it in first and second person terms, using 'you and I,' talk about it in third person terms. Tell them that some other, random person did such-and-such, and someone else didn't like it. And then ask, *"What do you think about that? How could they deal with it?"* Make it a thought experiment about other, abstract people, rather than a confrontation between the two of you.

Making a request of them

Again, keep your energy calm and your touch light. This can be especially difficult in this situation, since you do have an agenda and that's why you have a request. It will help a lot if you can shift yourself into a playful feeling and present your request as a fun possibility. As you speak, go to the psychic channel if you can, and put a picture of your fun idea there, as well as in the words you're using. If you can't put your request on the psychic airwaves, at least make sure that your energy matches your words and conveys your intention that this can be a fun possibility. Then invite them into this fun experience that you've figured out. Ask if they want to do that, but don't turn it into a demand by saying, *"Hey, I want you to do this. I think you should, and I think you owe it to me."* The demand in that will scare them away.

Their response to your request

If a leaving-patterned person is not able to reference their body to assess whether they want to agree to your request, they will instead use their mind to assess it. If their mind can figure it out, they will answer you from there. However, if the request can be answered only through referencing their body sensations (*"Are you tired?" "Are you hungry?" "Are you feeling sexy?"*) they may go into confusion. And if that confusion is sufficiently distressing, they may dissociate. So be aware of that and watch for it. If they do get confused, take a step back and offer to maybe let it go for now.

Giving them a compliment

As with all the patterns, frame your compliment to fit their values, not yours. So, what do leaving-patterned people value? They value fun, play,

Relating to the Leaving Pattern

games, big, abstract ideas, and anything new. So first shift your awareness up into your head center, and then make your compliment either fun or abstract and impersonal, but about them, rather than about you and your feelings. Compliment what they think is important, such as beauty, originality, creativity, fun, or playfulness. Compliment the beauty or originality of their creation, or how creative and fun they are. If you compliment them on something that they don't value, they won't really get it. It won't really make sense to them.

As always, keep your energy light and your body calm. No big energy. Don't overwhelm them with your enthusiasm.

During a Conflict

People who do this personality pattern typically want to avoid conflict at almost any cost. They have no history of winning or of conflict leading to anything positive, so they want to avoid it. When anger or conflict arises, they will leave the situation, either physically or energetically (dissociate). Their only thought is, *"Gotta get away."*

If they are unable to get away fast enough, the intensity of the conflict may cause them to shatter into fragments, and leave them unable to function. Falling apart like this is terrifying. Now they feel even more scared and helpless than before they fragmented. Now there isn't even an internal center, an "I" who feels terrified — there is only terror.

While shattered, they may be unable to follow the thread of the conversation and may go off on a tangent, as if trying to move the focus of the conversation away from the conflict. From the outside, this may appear intentional, like they're trying to avoid the problem, but if they are now fragmented, it's probably only an unconscious effect of their internal confusion and loss of an internal center.

When shattered, they may not be able to function or even speak.

They usually do not feel or express their own anger, but when they do, it will appear first on the psychic airwaves as a feeling of anger that floods the room. Although they avoid conflict in the physical world, they can be quite vicious and hateful on the psychic airwaves. They can even attack others by sending angry, hateful energy toward them. They can also control the psychic space by filling it with their anger. This is a little bit like someone filling the room with their anger verbally by yelling hateful things and shouting over anyone else. However, those who are not psychically sensitive may not notice anything.

Now there is one thing I suggest you do when expressing your anger, no matter who you're expressing it to. Don't send your anger straight into their space. Don't send it at their core or even at their edge. That becomes an energetic attack. It's too much. It's not good energy manners, and it's likely to put them into overwhelm and/or provoke a patterned reaction from them. Instead, turn your body at least 90 degrees away from them and send your anger out somewhere away from them. If you're inside, send it at the wall. If you're outside and there's a big space, send it out there. They will still hear your anger and your complaint, but they won't have to deal with being hit by a big blast of your energy.

So turn 90 degrees away, or if you're really angry or think your anger will overwhelm them, turn more than 90 degrees away. Then send your anger out in that direction and let them witness it, but witness it from a safe place, at a safe distance. That will make it much easier for them to take in your complaint and respond to it constructively.

In Romance

When the two of you are wanting to get physical together, remember to keep your touch light. For instance, don't grab them hard. Some people, who do other patterns, love it when you grab them hard. They can feel your desire in the strength of your grip, and they like that. But with leaving-patterned people, it will likely scare them. You'll feel their body flinch.

Before getting sexy, help them focus on their body by helping them find its edges. Start by gently stroking or touching them in a non-sexual way on their arms, legs, and back. No place that might be sexual. Help them get back into their body before moving toward arousal.

Before getting physical, they may want to do something themselves to get back into their body. They might want to do some kind of exercise, like going for a run or a swim. Swimming is especially good because they can feel the sensations of the water flowing over their skin, and feeling those sensations helps them find the edges of their body. And it's a non-threatening touch. They know that the water is not going to attack them or demand something of them.

Relating to the Leaving Pattern

And remember, if they're really caught in the leaving pattern, the sex can actually be more energetic for them than physical. It may be mostly physical for you, but for them, the energetic experience of it may be much more important. I have known leaving-patterned women who could orgasm without their lover ever touching them. Just by focusing on feeling the energy from their lover's hand penetrating their genitals, they could orgasm.

Summary

The core trauma suffered by leaving-patterned people sidetracked their process of embodiment, so they have never felt safe and loved enough to claim their body and their right to exist here. They have not been able to attach to the earth, develop a felt-sense of their core, or create a strong energetic boundary around their body to protect it. As a result, they still regard the physical world as unloving and unsafe, and they think of themselves as helpless and unable to cause any change in their situation.

So, if a leaving-patterned person feels uncomfortable, they probably won't say anything about it in words. They'll probably just leave. They might leave physically, or they might space out and leave energetically. They're not used to thinking that they can cause anything to change by saying something like, *"I feel uncomfortable"* or *"I'm scared"* or *"I want you to stop that."* Speaking up like that feels too confrontive to them. They fear it could lead to conflict, and they don't want conflict. They're not used to winning any fight, ever, so they don't want any fights. It's safer to just quietly escape.

So, if you want to know how safe they feel with you, watch how long they stay. If they stay, you're doing a good job, and they feel safe. If they keep going away, they don't feel totally safe. That could be caused by something you're doing, or it could be caused by something else entirely. But their behavior will be a more reliable clue to how safe they're feeling than what they say. Remember, they're not used to thinking that they're able to do anything to change the situation.

Also, if you yell at them or throw big energy at them — even happy energy, like joy or excitement — it may hit them so hard that they fragment and become unable to function. They may not be able to find a center to operate from, and that's terrifying for them, absolutely terrifying. And it may take them days to retrieve their pieces and reassemble themselves. That's an awful time for them, and it can last for days. So they will typically want to avoid any kind of big energy, and if you run big energy, they will want to avoid you. All that leaving they do is their attempt to avoid that experience of being shattered.

> **Tips for Relating to the Leaving Pattern**
> - do the Centering Breath daily
> - dial down your energy
> - pull your energy back inside your bubble
> - explore field focus versus point focus and switch to field focus
> - put aside your agenda
> - shift your attention up into your head
> - keep your heart center warm, but light
> - ask what you can do to help them

Questions

Comforting a leaving-patterned child

"My 10-year-old daughter runs this pattern. She will run off anytime she's upset. It's hard to comfort her or talk to her. She loses her temper and loses control, it's very hard to understand her and be the affectionate mom I'm wanting to be. Do you have any advice?"

Yes, you've probably tried to comfort her by moving toward her, which could be scary for her. Instead, focus on cultivating a strong felt-sense of your own core and grounding. After you've developed a deep grounding for yourself, gently slide that grounding under the whole room and the whole situation. Keep it way down below her. Consciously or unconsciously, she will feel that grounding under her, and it will help her feel safer and calm down. But don't let it touch her personal space, keep it way down under her.

Do this energetically, rather than trying to reach for her physically. My guess is that, if you were scared and 10 years old, you might want an adult who loves you to physically pull you into their arms and hold you tight. But that may not be true for your daughter. So try grounding and holding her energetically, instead of physically. Remember that she may be scared of too much physical contact.

The fact that she doesn't want you to hold her physically is not a failing on your part. It doesn't mean you did anything wrong, so don't beat yourself up over that. We all somehow choose our own personality patterns. And who knows why we choose them — perhaps to help us accomplish something later in life.

Preemies

"Might premature babies be more likely to use this strategy?"

Yes, there's a real possibility that preemies are more likely to do the leaving pattern. But I haven't seen any actual research on this, so I can't say for sure.

Eye contact

"As someone who goes into the leaving pattern, I would avoid making eye contact and had to learn how to do it; it still doesn't come naturally to me. In one-on-one conversations, sometimes it feels too intense for me. Any advice on how to manage this and what's the normal way to do it?"

Different cultures have different norms for this. I'm told that in Japanese culture, for a child (a person of lower status) to look directly into the eyes of their parent (a person of higher status) is considered an insult. Conversely, in North American and European culture, mother and child frequently look into each other's eyes. So part of it is cultural.

And I would suggest that you explore what feels comfortable for you, and even talk to the other person in each case about what feels comfortable to you. If you watch people's eyes, you'll notice that some people can look at you while they're listening to you, but while they are composing their answer and speaking, they need to look somewhere else to find their answer. They need to look up or down or to the side, depending on whether they process using mostly the visual, kinesthetic, or auditory channels. So a lot of this depends on the individual.

Fight response

"Can someone that does the leaving pattern get into the fight response?"

Well, it's uncharacteristic in the sense that they aren't likely to do that while they are caught in the leaving pattern. However, some people who do the leaving pattern also do the aggressive pattern as their backup. So during a conflict, they will try to get away, over and over, until they hit a certain threshold. Then they will flip into the aggressive pattern, and now it's fight time. Now they're like, *"Okay, you wanted this, now you get it."* But notice that they are no longer in the leaving pattern — they have shifted into the aggressive pattern.

Also keep in mind the fact that a person who is present, that is, not caught in a pattern, will likely respond in a way that is appropriate to the situation, and if fighting is appropriate, they will fight.

Fight, flight, freeze, and fawn responses

"How are the patterns related to fight, flight, freeze, and fawn responses?"

Those are automatic responses that people go into during distressing situations. And you can fairly easily connect them to the safety strategies and the personality patterns. Fight would obviously be the aggressive pattern. Flight is obviously the leaving pattern. Freezing is one way of seeing the enduring pattern. And since fawning means trying to be nice and trying to get them to like you, that would be the merging pattern. Notice also that the "fight, flight, freeze, and fawn" list does not include the automatic response of the rigid pattern, because when a child is "being good", most adults don't think the child might be in distress.

Relating to the Leaving Pattern

Recalling childhood

"Would one growing up with leaving pattern have a feeling that they can't remember their childhood? Because they left their body, because in a sense, they weren't there. Wondering if this could be why I can't remember many details of my childhood."

It could be, but I don't want to say it has to be. When a person is not present in their body during an experience, it is likely more difficult to remember. I would encourage you to explore more and look for more clues.

Accommodating them

"How do I find the balance between dialing down my energy so as not to scare them and being who I am unapologetically? This feels a bit like changing who I am or dimming my light to please someone else."

Well, let me reframe the question this way. Imagine that you've just found a baby rabbit in the woods, and the baby rabbit is scared. If you bring that rabbit home and you want it to feel safe with you and get comfortable snuggling up with you, do you think that yelling at that rabbit will make it want to get snuggly? It doesn't matter if yelling is "who you are," if you want another being to feel safe enough to move closer to you, you have to be willing to shift yourself to help them feel safer. That's just a fact of life. I imagine that you do this already with human babies. If there's a baby sleeping in the house, you try to be quiet. You don't yell or slam doors. So it's not just about unapologetically being who you are. It's also about learning how to not scare other people.

Managing big energy

"Is meeting outside, so my enthusiastic energy is dispersed, a strategy for protecting a sensitive person?"

It could be; I encourage you to try it out. There are lots of possibilities here, and anything that works, works. So I encourage you to find new ways

Patterns vs personality traits

> *"For the romance subject you went through, it sounds like this is more of a character trait — being more energetic and needing a light touch — of the leaving pattern instead of a stress response. Does the person need to be caught in the leaving pattern for them to experience this? Or is this a generalization?"*

What I'm saying is that a person who is caught in the leaving pattern will have these kinds of preferences. So yes, it does wind up looking like a personality trait. It arises out of the fact that they are easily overwhelmed and the safety strategy they use to avoid that. And people who do not do the leaving pattern may also be sensitive and skittish, but for other reasons. This is why, when you're discerning patterns, you'll see them more clearly if you pay attention to the person's safety strategies, rather than their personality traits.

Pattern names

> *"Why don't you call leaving-patterned people leavers and enduring-patterned people endurers?"*

This is a very important point. I suggest that you resist the temptation to turn the verb into a noun because, when you do that, you're turning the person into a thing. And also, when you do that, people will think that you're saying this is who they really are. But it's not who they are. Leaving is only a safety strategy. Enduring is only a safety strategy. Who people really are is their essence, and that does not change.

The Leaving Pattern in relationships

> *"How do leaving pattern people stay present and be successful in relationships?"*

They work at it like everybody else. None of these patterns are terrific at relationships; they all have their difficulties. Being present is always better than being caught in any of the patterns. So the goal of inner work is to get out of pattern as much as you can. Being present in the here and now will help you create much healthier and happier relationships.

Attachment theory

"Can you please go over the difference between attachment theory and the five personality patterns?"

First of all, attachment theory comes out of the world of psychology, which deals mainly with the time after birth and with what is physically observable. So it does not include the idea that an incoming spirit would need to attach to the physical body and the physical world. That process is called embodiment, and it's an extremely important first step, but psychology tends to miss it.

Also, keep in mind the fact that, while attachment theory maps the kinds of emotional attachment that a person may form, it's not a map of personality. You may notice that withdrawn attachment seems to apply more to some of the patterns and anxious attachment more to others, but they don't exactly match up because the two systems are actually mapping different territories.

Conflict between patterns within a person

"What if someone does two patterns that are very different, such as the leaving and merging patterns at the same time?"

Yes, lots of people do both the leaving and merging patterns. And they may mix them together, or they may clearly do one first and then switch to the other if the first one isn't working. In the last chapter, after we've gone through each of them, we're going to discuss how the patterns combine and interact. Right now, that's too big of a question for us to go into.

Leaving vs enduring

"Can you distinguish between a leaving-patterned person who doesn't respond in words and an enduring-patterned person who doesn't express?"

Yes. The leaving pattern is actually very expressive, but it doesn't have to be in words. If you're only listening on the words channel, you might not notice that there's a great deal of communication happening on the psychic channel. In contrast, a person caught in the enduring pattern is much less expressive and communicative on any channel.

Getting out of the leaving pattern

> *"What practices can I do when I'm caught in the leaving pattern and I'm around a group of new people?"*

Practicing and developing the basic energy skills discussed in chapter 2 will help you avoid going into pattern so easily and help you get out of pattern more quickly when you do. The more you develop a strong felt-sense of Core and Grounding down into the earth, the safer you will feel. And the more you practice Edge and Me/Not Me to keep other people's energies out of your space, the less their stuff will bother you. Developing those skills will make you feel safer everywhere, in all situations.

This book is on how to relate to others and their patterns, so we can't go deeply into how to get yourself out of pattern. But my earlier book, *The 5 Personality Patterns*, has much more information on that. At the end of chapter 7, there's a whole section on getting yourself out of and healing the leaving pattern. And chapter 13 is about getting yourself out of pattern in general.

Relating to the Leaving Pattern

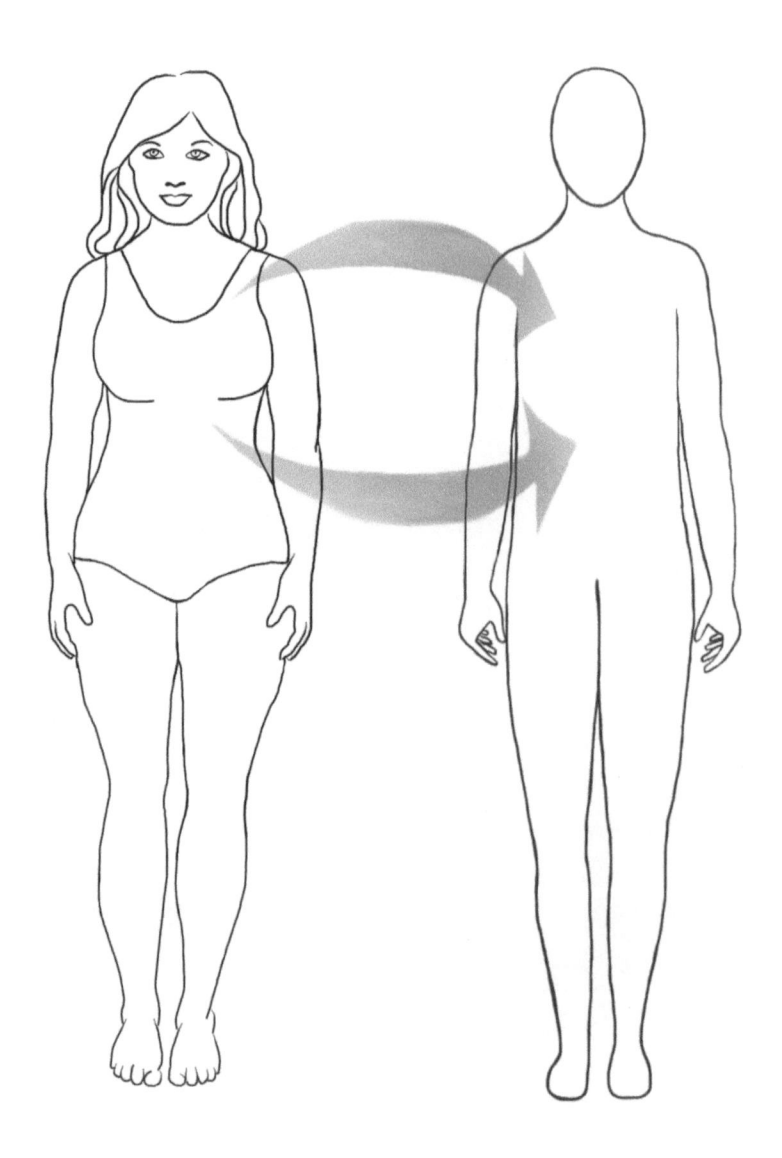

The Merging Pattern – body and energy flow

- 7 -

Relating to the Merging Pattern

Like all the survival patterns, the merging pattern is a way to buffer the self from feelings of overwhelm. It is a habit of attention, fueled by trauma held in the body. The original trauma was a difficulty with taking in, holding, and metabolizing food and energy as an infant.

Centering Yourself

Before we get into the chapter, let's once again do the Centering Breath. And this time, I'm going to add tuning in to your Core a little bit. Developing these skills is an important part of becoming a healthy adult, and it's critical for everyone who is caught in the merging pattern.

Imagine a column inside your body, from the crown of your head down to the bottom of your torso. And imagine that you can breathe in through the bottom of that column and fill it up. Now, breathe in through your nose and fill the whole column with breath, from the bottom up to the top. And then, breathing out through pursed lips, send all that breath down and out the bottom of the column. Do it again several more times: in and all the way up, then out and all the way down. Again, in and up, and out and down. And up once more, all the way up to the top, and then back down and all the way out.

> And now put your awareness on your Core, that column in the center of your body. Gently breathe into it or see it in your mind's eye. And just notice what you find there. This is the part of your body where you are the most you. This is the place to look to find the answers to your questions about *What do I feel? What do I want? Do I like this one or that one? Am I happy or sad or angry or scared?*
>
> Now just notice, how do you feel inside? Did something shift for you? Do you find yourself somehow more in your body and more in alignment with yourself? I encourage you to do these practices repeatedly, throughout the day, to bring you back to your center.

I also want to remind you that, although we're studying them one pattern at a time, that doesn't mean that a person does only one pattern. In fact, a person typically does two patterns.

What would your life be like now if . . . ?

What if the most important thing in your life, the thing you need to survive, was a present moment, heart-to-heart connection with another person? What if you were afraid that losing that heart-to-heart connection, even for a moment, would disorganize you and make you unable to function? Think about that for a moment. How would you handle life, if having a heart-to-heart connection in every moment was that important to you? And if you lived in a world where most people don't do heart-to-heart connections very well, what then? Would you feel anxious?

Furthermore, how would you experience life if you could feel other people's inner feelings and desires, but you couldn't feel your own? What if you weren't sure what you were feeling, but you were very sure about what everyone else was feeling and thinking and who they wanted you to be? Most likely, you would mistake their feelings for your own, and you would think that whoever they wanted you to be was who you wanted to be. And that is exactly what happens to merging-patterned people.

If you were feeling other people's inner experience more than your own, you would probably have trouble differentiating yourself from them. You would think their problems were your problems. If they felt happy, you would feel happy. If they felt unhappy, you would feel unhappy. If they

Relating to the Merging Pattern

wanted you to do something for them, you would think you wanted to do it. In energy work, this is called a Me/Not Me problem.

This is the situation that people who are caught in the merging pattern find themselves in every day. Remember, this is the experience they have all day, every day, so they think it is normal. And they make the classic human mistake of thinking that everyone else is having the same experience they are, when, in fact, they're just having the experience that is created by the merging pattern. We all make this mistake. No matter what patterns we're caught in, we think that everyone else's experience is like ours.

The Origins of the Merging Pattern

Nearly everyone uses this safety strategy in their first few years, when they're a nursing baby. At that age, will and strength have not yet come online, so if you're distressed in some way, you really can't fix it. All you can do is cry. Having to manage without will and strength makes the first two patterns different from the later patterns, which form after will and strength come online. As an infant, you also don't have much sense of a self, an "I" who can take action to get what you need. So the leaving and merging patterns are ways to feel safer before you have access to will and strength and an "I" that can take action to get what you need.

The Problem: can't hold enough, so feels empty

The main task of this developmental stage is to take in, hold, and metabolize the energy that you're receiving from the outside. Most of that energy is coming into your body through the love and nourishment you get from your mother and other caretakers. Ideally, when a baby feels hungry, it nurses and takes in the milk it needs until it feels full, and then it pushes away. It gets enough, feels satisfied, and stops.

But a child who will go on to develop the merging pattern is not able to complete that process. They encounter some sort of problem which disrupts their ability to take in, hold, and digest that nourishment. They cannot get to the experience of feeling full. Over and over, they can't get enough, so they feel empty.

The Healthy Taking-in Sequence

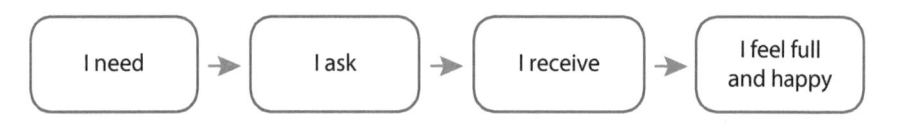

I need → I ask → I receive → I feel full and happy

The Not-Getting-Enough Sequence

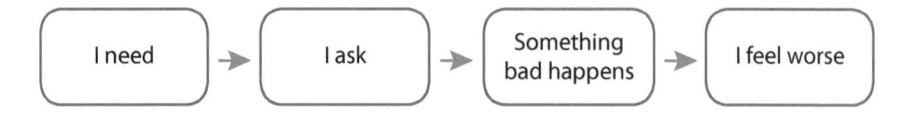

I need → I ask → Something bad happens → I feel worse

The Solution: turn to others

As they get older and try to understand why they feel so empty inside, they blame themselves. They decide, *"I feel this way because I'm not enough; I'm deficient."* And their solution is to try to stay the baby in the baby-mother relationship and continue pulling energy from others until they can finally get enough. They are trying to finish the developmental task of taking in, holding, and metabolizing the incoming love and energy. They are trying to get to the experience of feeling full and satisfied enough that their body spontaneously pushes away.

Attention and energy go: toward others

This experience of needing to continually turn to others for nourishment trains the person's attention and life energy to habitually seek connection by moving toward other people. This habit becomes the person's safety strategy and the root of the merging pattern.

The effect of this Safety Strategy: looking to others for everything

They learn to connect with other people to get what they need, and this becomes their safety strategy. So the attention of merging-patterned

Relating to the Merging Pattern

people habitually goes toward other people, trying to get them to solve their problems.

Because the core of the body is where the felt-sense of emptiness is strongest, people who are caught in the merging pattern learn to avoid feeling their core. If they are female, they may also be taught by their culture that they're not supposed to feel their own core, because doing so highlights what they feel and want, and knowing that makes them selfish and self-centered. Instead, they're taught to ignore what they feel in their core and focus on pleasing others. This method of ignoring yourself works because your core is the place where you are the most you. If you don't feel this part of you, it's hard to develop a felt-sense of self and know who you are. If you can't reference your core, you can't figure out what you want and need.

Not being able to reference the core of their body also makes it harder for merging-patterned people to form a strong energetic boundary around their body. And, without a strong energetic boundary, their body can't keep their own life energy in and other people's energy out. Without this container, they can't fill themselves up with their own life energy and feel full.

All of that makes it hard for them to grow beyond being the baby in the baby-mother relationship. In that relationship, the baby is helpless and the mother takes care of it. Because they're still stuck in that helplessness, when they feel overwhelmed, they collapse the way a child collapses. They dissolve into a puddle of tears. It's not a conscious decision, and it's not voluntary. It's natural for a three-year-old to fall apart that way. But if you're 33, others have less patience for that behavior.

So, under pressure, merging-patterned people collapse into helplessness and then turn to others to get what they need. That's their safety strategy. Remember, turning to other people to get what you need is age appropriate for a nursing baby. It is the best thing for you to do.

One other effect of being focused on getting help from others is that their attention becomes biased toward the positive. That means that they see what's positive in a situation rather than what's negative, which skews the way they see both the current moment and the whole world. Now, that skew helps them connect with other people, because they're always seeing the best in others, but it also makes them less able to see that something is not good for them. For instance, if alcohol dulls their heartache and makes them feel better, they may think that alcohol is their friend. Or they may not see that someone is manipulating them, so they fall in love with that person and marry them. When they can't see what's bad in a situation, they don't know that they're in danger. They're not totally blind, but their attention is biased against seeing the negative.

Another effect of this positive slant of attention is that they forgive easily and only rarely feel anger. I have known merging-patterned people who went into therapy with the complaint of *"I can't feel any anger, even when it would be wise and healthy for me to feel anger. I just can't find it."*

The Compensated Merging Pattern

The merging pattern is the only one of the five personality patterns that has both a simple and a compensated form. This seems to be caused by the fact that this pattern typically forms during the time when a baby actually is helpless, but continues into the time when will and strength are beginning to appear in the toddler. Psychology calls this the practicing phase, the time from about 18 to 24 months when the toddler can explore with confidence, because they still feel that they are one with the mother and therefore big and strong. The toddler's discovery at about 24 months that they are separate from the mother, and therefore small and vulnerable, reawakens their sense of helplessness.

This inner tension creates the rapprochement phase, the time when the toddler is constantly alternating between venturing out to explore and needing to return to the mother's lap for safety and reassurance. The toddler's budding psychological separation also creates a new need for autonomy, expressed as the Terrible Twos and their love of saying *"No!"* just to feel their new will and strength.

However, a person caught in the merging pattern has not completed the tasks of this stage. Developmentally, they are still stuck in the time before will and strength came online, so they don't yet have access to real will or strength. But they are old enough that they are able to compensate for that lack by pretending to have will, strength, and even core. It's not a real core — it's only a facsimile of a core — but it allows them to shift from being the small, helpless baby into being the big, strong Good Mother, the one who is the Giver and the Helper.

When a person is in the simple form of the merging pattern, they are in the role of the baby in the baby/mother dynamic. When they shift into

Relating to the Merging Pattern

the compensated merging pattern, they shift into the role of the mother, but they are still caught in the baby/mother dynamic.

However, being the Good Mother feels a lot better than being a baby. You don't feel so small, needy, and helpless any more. Instead, you feel big, strong and able to take care of the small, needy, helpless ones. But because you don't yet have a real core, you can't accurately measure how much strength you really have. And because you're identified with being the Giver, you need to keep giving to feel okay. You can't tell how much is too much, so you over give, and then you crash and burn. When that happens, the compensation dissolves, and you fall back into the simple merging pattern and back into that helpless, needy place.

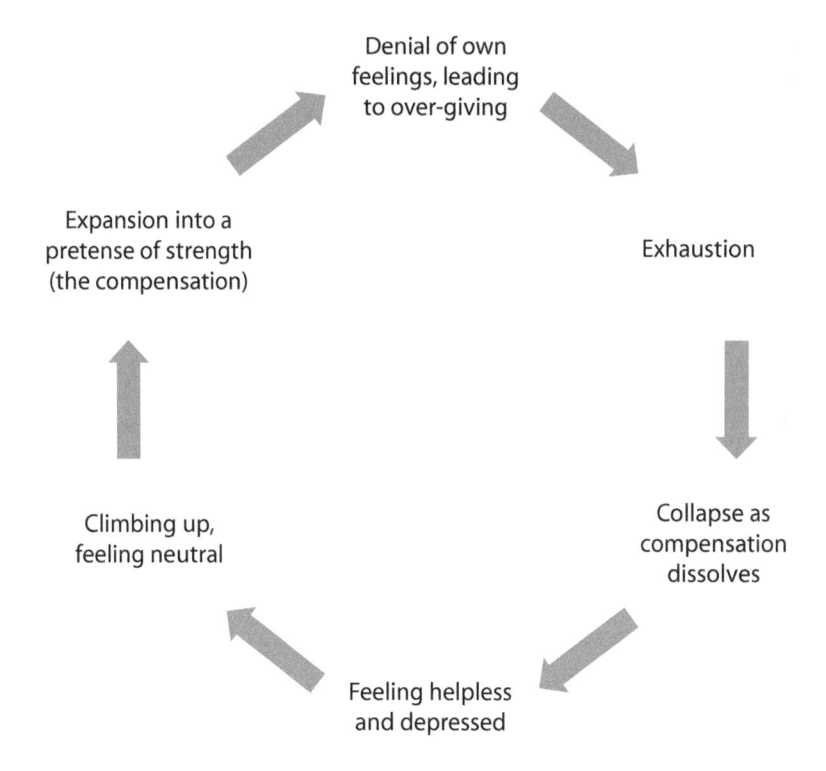

Cycle diagram:
- Denial of own feelings, leading to over-giving
- Exhaustion
- Collapse as compensation dissolves
- Feeling helpless and depressed
- Climbing up, feeling neutral
- Expansion into a pretense of strength (the compensation)

The Compensated Merging Pattern's Expansion-Collapse Cycle

This process creates a tendency for people who do the merging pattern to cycle between the simple merging pattern and the compensated merging pattern. Most of them have a preference for one role or the other: they spend most of their time in the compensated side, or they spend most of their time in the simple merging pattern side. But no matter where they start, they occasionally go through the whole cycle. If they're starting from the simple merging pattern, they build the compensation on a false core, expand into the compensated merging pattern and become the Giver, over extend themselves to the point of exhaustion, and then collapse back down into a puddle of tears. If they're starting from the compensated merging pattern, they over give and collapse first, and then begin rebuilding their compensation.

People who identify strongly with the compensated merging pattern do often have the appearance of will and strength. But that appearance lasts only until the pressure and demands on them become too intense, and then their core dissolves and they collapse. In contrast, people who are developmentally older and have developed real will, strength and core, like those who do the aggressive pattern, do not collapse under pressure.

The Skill of Referencing

There are three kinds of referencing: referencing yourself, referencing others, and referencing the rules. Most of us are skillful at one or two of these ways of referencing, but to be an emotionally mature adult, you need to develop all three.

To reference yourself, you put your attention on the core of your own body and ask yourself, *"What sensations am I feeling here? What do I want?"* And by doing that, you get information from your own body.

To reference another person, you put your attention on *their* core. By referencing their core, you can directly perceive what they're feeling and wanting. And by reading them in this way, you get information about them. This is an equally important skill, and very useful for navigating interpersonal situations.

To reference the rules, you put your attention on what society says you're supposed to do in a given situation. For instance, there are rules about how to get along with people, also called manners. Those rules include things like: don't hit people; don't interrupt them; don't lie, cheat, or steal. When you're driving your car, there are rules like: obey the speed limit and stop at a red light. Each culture has many rules, and most religions have additional ones. Those rules are part of our accumulated wisdom about how to get along with each other.

All three of these ways of referencing are important, but most of us don't do all three. In fact, many of us can do only one of them well. Most of the personality patterns use only one of these ways of referencing, so they don't make you practice the other two. For instance, developing the merging pattern requires referencing others, but not self or the rules. Developing the aggressive pattern requires referencing self, but not others or the rules. Developing the rigid pattern requires referencing the rules, but not self or others. So many of us are good at only one or two ways of referencing, and to be a healthy adult, we need to be good at all three.

The Gifts of the Merging Pattern

Remember, the process of developing any of these personality patterns requires successfully using the safety strategy that underlies that pattern many, many times. But in order to make that safety strategy work for you, you have to have the talents and skills needed to pull it off. If you can't make it work, you'll abandon it and try a different safety strategy. If you can make it work, you'll continue using it, and each time you use it, you'll be improving those skills. After years of practice, you become an expert at those skills, and they become the Gifts of the pattern.

Because of their ability to connect with other people's feelings so strongly, people who do the merging pattern become Masters of Connection. After doing a considerable amount of inner work and developing a real core, they may be able to energetically fill their core with love and then radiate that love out into the surrounding space so strongly that they change the feeling tone in the whole space. One merging-patterned friend told me she was manning a booth at a fair where there were hundreds of booths, and often people would walk by without even noticing her booth. So she stood in her booth, tuned in to her core, and filled the space around her with love. And in no time, there was a crowd standing in front of her booth.

Similarly, I've heard a story of a merging-patterned person using this skill to avert a developing conflict during Thanksgiving dinner, an American holiday meal with relatives that often includes people who don't usually get together and may strongly disagree. As some of them were starting to rev up for a fight, the merging-patterned person went inside himself, filled up his core, and started radiating love, and pretty soon they all forgot about the fight and started enjoying each other again. The ability to fill a space with love is a tremendous skill.

If you think of left-brain and right-brain distinctions, with the left brain being more logical and concerned with facts, reason, and numbers, and the right brain being more feeling oriented and concerned with music, space, and relationships, the merging pattern is the most right-brained of the patterns. It is also the most energetically feminine of the patterns. In contrast, the aggressive pattern is the most energetically masculine.

Another gift of this pattern is a very real generosity. Merging-patterned people are focused on others and genuinely want other people to be comfortable and happy. Remember, they're taking in everyone's feelings.

People who do this pattern are also Masters of Pleasure, in that they deeply enjoy sensuality and intimacy, whether in the form of food, sex, or love. And because they can directly sense the other person's inner state, they can take real pleasure in giving pleasure, whether that's sexually in a relationship or emotionally in the form of *"I made your favorite meal,"* or *"I got you exactly the gift that you wanted."* Just making other people happy is a joy to them.

Overall, merging-patterned people tend to have the best qualities of childhood, in the sense of being open, innocent, kind, spontaneous, bubbly, happy, and playful.

Fears

Merging-patterned people fear feeling empty inside. That feeling started in infancy when they were not able to complete the process of taking in love and nourishment, holding it, and feeling full enough to be ready to push away. Now, as adults, they still find themselves feeling empty and unable to get enough to feel full. Underneath everything, that empty feeling is still there, and any kind of deprivation reminds them of it.

Their need to get away from the empty feeling inside, combined with the fact that their positive bias of attention makes it hard for them to recognize an enemy, leaves them very vulnerable to problems with addiction. They may think, *"When I drink alcohol, I feel better, so alcohol is good for me."* Or *"I can't get you to love me, but the cookies give me some of the*

Relating to the Merging Pattern

sweetness that I want from you, so I'll have another cookie." By the way, if you're able to feel down far enough into the felt-experience of love, you'll find that it literally tastes sweet. On some level, we all know that, and we acknowledge it when we say *"Love is sweet."* So when you think that you want a sweet food, you may actually be wanting the sweetness of love.

Merging-patterned people also fear disappointing or displeasing others, because doing so might cause the other person to drop the heart-to-heart connection. That's a big loss for a merging-patterned person because they tend to organize their inner sense of self around their heart-to-heart connections, so suddenly losing that felt connection, even for a moment, can actually disorient them inside. For the same reason, they're also very afraid of being rejected or abandoned.

Emotions

The combination of weak energetic boundaries and little felt-sense of their own core creates a situation in which they have many feelings, but little sense of self. Their weak energetic boundaries allow other people's thoughts and feelings to get into their personal space and mix with their own thoughts and feelings, making it hard for them to distinguish between self and other, my feelings and your feelings. So they often have difficulty sorting out whose emotions they are and what they mean.

There is a strong flow of emotions. Love, happiness, joy, and sadness are often abundant. Play and delight are easily accessible. Even forgiveness for real injuries is not far away. Grudges and resentments are not nursed in secret and maintained for years, but just arise and flow through. Anger, however, may be completely missing.

Everything in the system is fluid and changeable, just as it is in a child. This also means that merging-patterned people are prone to mood swings, sometimes shifting rapidly through a big range of moods. However, since the empty feeling and their fear of abandonment underlie everything, anxiety is always nearby.

For merging-patterned people, the default emotions are shame and self-doubt. Whenever their system gets overwhelmed, they will start to doubt themselves, feel deficient, and fall into shame. However, this wave of feelings does not necessarily mean that they are deficient, but only that their system got overwhelmed.

Beliefs

The beliefs of merging-patterned people are mostly a reflection of their difficulty with taking in and metabolizing love and nourishment, combined with their attempts to maintain the heart-to-heart connection to others at all costs. Some of their typical beliefs are:

> *"There is never enough."*
> *"I am not enough."*
> *"I am deficient."*
> *"I can't do it alone."*
> *"My needs are not okay."*
> *"If I need, I will be abandoned."*
> *"If I am strong, I will be abandoned."*
> *"If I disappoint you, I will be abandoned."*
> *"You should love me totally and unconditionally, the way you would love a baby."*
> *"Love will solve everything."*

Examples

- The archetypal Good Mother
- the damsel in distress
- the heroines of romance novels who wait for rescue
- Drew Barrymore's character in the film *50 First Dates*
- Marilyn Monroe
- Bill Clinton does the compensated merging pattern (along with the rigid pattern)

Communicating with Someone Caught in the Merging Pattern

So how do you communicate with a merging-patterned person? What you need to keep in mind is that they are communicating with you through their heart center, not from their head or belly center. They're focused on feelings — on connection and self-expression. They're not focused on ideas, power, or correctness. And they tend to reference only others, not the rules or themselves, which means that they'll be much more aware of what's going on inside you than of what's going on inside them.

They are seeking safety through connection

Remember, their core wound was that they weren't able to take in and hold enough love and nourishment to feel full and ready to push away from their mother, so they're still trying to get what they need through others. They're still caught in the baby-mother dynamic — as either the baby who needs your help, or as the mother who needs to help you. Either way, they see connecting as the way to get their needs met.

That's why they're so focused on creating and maintaining emotional connections. For them, safety is in connection. When they have a strong, stable heart-to-heart connection with someone, they feel safe. That is their safety strategy.

They are referencing you, not themselves

You will also have to keep in mind the fact that their habit of referencing others hijacks their inner attempts to reference their own feelings and agendas. When you ask them what they want, they are likely to reference your core for the answers, not their own core, so their answers will mirror yours. If you're not aware of this habit, you are likely to mistake their mirroring of you for agreement with you.

In order to get to their actual thoughts and feelings, you may often need to help them find their own core and feel into it for their own answers. We'll discuss how to do this in the next section.

*For much a more detailed discussion of this pattern,
please see the book, The 5 Personality Patterns.*

How to Relate to Them Successfully

Remember that each personality pattern grows out of its own particular safety strategy, and we create our patterns in childhood by repeating those safety strategies until they get conditioned into our body and become automatic. We are all seeking safety in our own ways, and we all need to feel safe before we can focus on you and hear what you have to say.

The key is to give them a heart-to-heart connection.

And what makes merging-patterned people feel safe is a heart-to-heart connection with you, so the key to interacting with them successfully is to give them that connection.

Shift into your heart center

Shift your awareness into your heart center in the middle of your chest, and then connect with them from there. The heart-to-heart connection is not just a metaphor. It is an energetic cord that goes from one heart to another. Energy and information go back and forth through that chord, so there is actually connection and communication through it.

Creating a heart-to-heart connection means sending an energetic cord from your heart to their heart, almost like you're plugging the power cord of a kitchen appliance into a wall socket. You can do this simply by imagining it. A merging-patterned person will feel this immediately and like it. The hard part is in maintaining it, because as soon as you get unhappy or distressed, you will probably unconsciously pull out that cord. A merging-patterned person will feel that, too, and that's often upsetting for them because, if they were using that connection to organize themselves, losing it disorganizes them.

It won't disorganize them so much that they're unable to function, the way that shattering can disorganize a leaving-patterned person, because the merging-patterned person won't lose contact with their physical body. But they may lose contact with their sense of self, which can be very distressing. And for a person who does both the merging and leaving patterns, it can be even worse.

Practicing this skill

So let's take a moment to practice shifting your awareness to your heart center. For some of you, this may be easy, because you do it all the time, but many people don't. I didn't grow up that way, so I have only an outsider's view of this, but here's the best guidance I can give you. Think of the location of your awareness as the place you're looking from. For instance, if you're in your head, you're looking out from your head through your eyes. But if you shift down to your heart, you're looking out through your heart, which sees in a different way than your eyes see. If you shift down to your belly, you're looking out from your belly and seeing the world from there and in that way. Each location has its own way of perceiving the world and so sees the world differently.

At this point, you're probably wondering how you shift your attention from one location to another. Again, you just intend it and imagine it. You already do this when you want to move your physical body. For instance, when you want to raise your hand, you don't have to stop and figure out which muscles to contract to make your arm go up. You just *intend* for your hand to go up, and it goes. You can move your awareness in the same way, just by intending it, though you may need to practice it many times to learn to do it well, just as you practiced moving your arm over and over as a child until it became second nature.

First, just notice where your awareness seems to be right now and imagine bringing it to your heart center. Your heart center is not your physical heart, the muscle that pumps your blood. That's a wonderful thing, but it has a completely different function. The heart center is at about the same level, but in the center of your chest. The heart center is not a physical organ, but an energetic organ in your energy body, just like your head center is an energetic organ in your head, and your belly center is an energetic organ just below your belly button.

So just take a moment. Imagine that you're moving your awareness to the middle of your chest and looking out from there. It may help to also imagine that you're breathing into your heart center. What's it like to be here, even a little bit? Do you feel more connected to the world in general or to anyone in particular? Do you like feeling more connected?

Now, think of something you love — it could be a person, a pet, a place, a song, or even a favorite food. Let yourself focus on that and soften into that loving feeling. Do you notice a change in the sensations in the middle of your chest, even a small change? Most likely, what you're feeling in the middle of your chest is the sensation of a loving, heart-to-heart connection.

Take some time to savor the feeling. Breathe into it to feel it more deeply. Take all the time you like to get to know it and enjoy it. The idea here is to get familiar with it so that you can tell the difference between having that feeling and not having it, because that is the difference between having a heart-to-heart connection with something and not having one.

For you, that difference may be small and it may take some practice to even find it. But for a person who is naturally heart-centered and runs the merging pattern, that difference is big, and it's important. Remember, if they're using it to organize themselves inside, losing it may disorganize them so much that they fall apart. You would not judge this in a young child, so don't judge it here. They are doing the best they can, given the skills that they have acquired so far.

So, whenever you're relating to a merging-patterned person, do your best to maintain your heart-to-heart connection with them all the time, even when you're upset, even when you're frustrated, annoyed, bored, scared, or angry. That's the hard part.

Put your attention on the melody, not the words

People who do the merging pattern talk a lot, but not about actions or ideas. They talk about feelings, and because they care much more about feelings than words, their words may get jumbled up. Their grammar may be messed up. They may say the words in the wrong order. Instead of saying the word they meant, they may say another word that sounds similar. You may care about all those details, but they don't, so let the words go and listen for the feelings behind the words. That's the part that's important to them.

Listen for the feelings behind the words.

Think of the communication as a song, with both words and melody. The feelings are in the melody, not in the words. And keep this in mind when you're speaking, as well as when you're listening. While you're speaking, notice the melody you're sending: is the pace fast or slow? Is the pitch high or low? What feeling tone are you sending in your melody? Does it sound angry, sad, scared, ashamed, or happy? They will hear your melody more loudly than your words, so pay attention to it.

When they're talking, listen to them in the same way — what melody are they sending? Is it fast or slow? High or low? Happy or sad or scared or angry? That is the part they care about and focus on, so you will receive their message more clearly if you put your attention there, also.

Make your communication personal and emotional, heart-to-heart

Furthermore, make your communication with them personal and emotional. Consciously send it from your heart to their heart. Tell them about your personal feelings, and ask them about their feelings. They care about your feelings, and they want you to care about their feelings. They care much less about ideas, rules, and reasons, so don't expect that or emphasize those things. Instead, keep your communication personal and emotional.

Reassure them that you like them

Like most people, merging-patterned people need to feel safe before they can really focus on anything else. And the way to help them feel safer is to connect with them and tell them that you like them. This is important because, to them, being liked feels like a survival need, and until they can feel you liking them, they may find it hard to pay attention to anything else.

I'm not suggesting that you lie to them. I'm suggesting that you shift your awareness into your heart center, and while looking from your heart, find something about them that you actually do like. Remember, the heart does not judge or criticize — it just loves what it loves. So use your heart-centered awareness to notice something that you do actually like about them — maybe a bit of affection you have for them, or some detail about their behavior that pleases you. Or, if you're glad you're with them at the moment, simply say that. But be sure to express to them whatever good feelings you do have toward them, no matter how small.

Hold space for them and help them reference themselves

You'll also need to remember that people who do the merging pattern will unconsciously abandon themselves as they attempt to please you. They're not good at referencing themselves in the first place. Instead, they will reference you to discover what you feel and want, and who you want them to be. And then they will try to become whoever you want them to be. This makes it very hard for them to figure out what they want and even harder for them to say what they want, because they fear that saying what they want might lead to conflict and to you not liking them.

In order to help them reference themselves, you need to be able to hold space for them. This is a very important skill, a skill that everyone needs to develop. It will help you navigate many, many situations in life, and it's essential for having better relationships. When you know how to hold space, you know the difference between making the interaction about them, about you, or about both of you. For more details on how to hold space, please look back at the section in chapter 3 called "Holding Space for Someone".

As you learn this skill, you can use it to help merging-patterned people reference themselves. The main thing to remember is that they need your support in moving their attention back to themselves and what's going on with them. So ask them, *"How do you feel about this?"* and *"What do you want?"* And then wait and hold space for them while they try to find their answer. It may take some time. If they answer too quickly, it may be that they simply read *you* and then said what *you* want them to want. You can help them by repeatedly bringing their attention back to them, thereby showing them that you're interested in *their* answer. Remember, they aren't sure anyone even cares what they feel and want, so they feel that it's safer to focus on what you feel and want.

By holding your attention on them and asking, *"Well, what do you think? What do you want? How do you feel about this?"* you're showing them that you do care about them. Over time, they may come to trust that you actually are interested in what's going on inside them. And, with your support, they will be practicing the skill of referencing themselves, finding out what they feel, and then putting that into words. It may take time. Give them time. Keep in mind, they're not used to doing this, so they won't be good at it until they've practiced it a lot.

In terms of language, they'll tend to avoid saying 'I' or 'me' and instead will talk about 'you' and 'us.' For instance, if you ask, *"What movie do you want to see?"* They might say, *"Well, I think we would both like _____."* Did you notice that they didn't say *I* would like this movie? They said *we* would like it. They unconsciously shifted from talking about *me* to talking about

Relating to the Merging Pattern

us, which shows that, unconsciously, they're mainly referencing you and how to make you happy.

So when they go to 'you' and 'us' and 'we', try to gently bring them back to referencing themselves. Don't be nasty or aggressive about it. Be kind and supportive, the way you would be when teaching a new skill to a child. But try to gently bring them back to referencing themselves.

Here's a tip — it is easier for them to reference themselves when it's framed as helping you, so say something like, *"Well, before we decide, I would like to hear about which movies you want to see."* By saying it this way, you are framing their act of self-referencing as a service to you. That makes it safer than doing it for themselves, which may have been punished as 'selfish' in their past.

When they need help

Ideally, whenever an adult needs your help, they would just come to you and say, *"Hey, I have this problem, and I need your help to solve it. Can you help me with this?"* But merging-patterned people generally don't do that. Instead, they just talk about their problem and wait for you to fix it. They will tell you all about how bad it is and how helpless they feel about it. They will likely say something like, *"This always happens, and I don't know what it is, and there's no way I can fix it. It's just — it's an endless problem. And I don't know how to fix it. But it's really bad, and I feel really bad about it, and it's just a terrible problem."* They will just talk about the problem endlessly, as if telling you about it will somehow magically fix it.

Keep in mind that this pattern forms before will and strength come online.

To understand this, recall that this pattern forms during the nursing stage, before will and strength come online, when all a distressed infant can do is cry out and wait for other people to come and fix whatever is wrong. On some unconscious level, a merging-patterned person is still stuck in that state, so it may not occur to them that they can act or even directly ask for your help. They do not have a sense that *they* are responsible for solving the problem, or that *they* can act to solve it. Instead, they will just say something along the lines of *"Oh, I can't. It's too hard."* And then they will wait for you to solve it.

It's important for you to know about this when they go into a long, rambling saga about their problem. If you start to feel annoyed, remember that in some ways they're still caught in the nursing stage, unaware that they may be able to solve the problem themselves, or at least directly ask for your help.

So how you can help them? You can help them find their way through the process of solving their problem. When they have gone into talking about their problem, you can acknowledge that they have a problem and ask, *"Are you asking me to help you with this?"* By saying it out loud, you're reminding them that they actually can ask for your help.

By asking them about their problem, you can also help them define the problem, gather their resources, and find their way to a solution. Along the way, you can gently remind them of the strengths and resources they do have, and express confidence in their ability to solve this problem, especially if you've seen them solve a similar problem before.

If you've raised children or worked with children, you're probably familiar with these steps:

1. Assess their emotional age and abilities in this moment, remembering that a person can shift in seconds from being emotionally 15 to being emotionally 3.
2. Compare their current age and abilities to what is needed to solve this problem. Can they do it on their own, by themselves? Can they do it as long as you watch and encourage them? Do they need you to hold their hand and talk them through it, step by step? Or is it totally beyond them, and you will need to do it for them?
3. If it's possible for them, give them enough direction and help so that they can actually do it, but let them struggle a little bit so that their abilities grow, and so that when they succeed, they feel victorious.
4. Praise and celebrate their successes at each step if they're emotionally younger, or at the end if they're emotionally older and doing it on their own.

Making a request of them

When you want to make a request of them, shift your awareness into your heart center and make your request simple and personal. Because of your own patterns, you may have the impression that you have to prove

Relating to the Merging Pattern

something to them — maybe that this is what they should do, or that the rules require it, or that there's a logical reason to do it. They don't care about any of that. They only care about your feelings and needs, so just connect heart-to-heart and ask them for it.

It often helps to follow up your request with a simple question like, *"Would you do that for me?"* That will make it simple and personal, from your heart to their heart. This sort of feelings-based request will touch their heart and make them expand into wanting to do it for you.

Now, I want to point out that, while this is a lovely way to get a person who does the merging pattern to do something for you, it's also a way to manipulate them. Please be careful how you use it so that you don't do that. There are a lot of con men in the world who use this maneuver to manipulate people who do the merging pattern. That's not good. Don't be one of those people.

And if you do the merging pattern, be aware that a person who understands this maneuver can use it to manipulate you. It's the perfect hook, and before you know it, you're doing what they want. And you didn't even notice that you had a choice.

There are many different ways to get people who are caught in different patterns to do or not do something. And for the merging pattern, it's really simple — you just make a heart-to-heart connection and ask. But please don't use this to manipulate or hurt them.

Their response to your request

When you ask them, *"Would you do this for me?"* they will want to say *"yes"* because they want to please you. The danger is that they will not reference their own core to find out, *"Do I want to do this? Do I have the ability to do this?"* They will instead check your core. And of course, since you want them to do it, your core says, *"Yes, I want you to do this."* So they will say *"yes"* without knowing whether they can do it or even if they want to do it. Also, they will say *"yes"* without giving any thought to *"How would I do this?"* It's as if you asked them, *"Do you want to make me happy?"* and they answered, *"Yes, of course, I want to make you happy,"* and the details don't matter.

They want to please you.

155

How to Have Better Relationships

Merging-patterned people often agree to do something without first checking their own core to find out whether they want to do it and are able to do it. And then later, when the time comes to deliver on their promise, they panic. For instance, suppose you ask them, *"Can you drive me to the airport next Monday morning instead of going to work?"* And they think, *"Oh, sure. I'd love to do that for you,"* so they say, *"Yes."* But then, when the day comes, they have an awful, panicked feeling inside because they realize, *"Oh, no! I have to go to work! They'll be mad at me if I don't go to work. And besides this is rush hour. The traffic will be awful. It'll take hours!"* A lot of fights arise out of this skipped step in the asking and answering process, and they sound something like, *"But you said you would!" "Yes, but I didn't think about it. You wanted me to, so I just said yes."*

So what can you do to solve this problem? You can help them stop and think it through. You can ask, *"Do you actually want to do this? Can you do it?"* It's also important for you to ask yourself, *"Can they really do this?"* because it may be that they can't. And if they can't, the two of you will have a problem later on. That's not good. And maybe you shouldn't be asking them to do something they cannot do, or something they really don't want to do. Remember, you're dealing with a person who's very good at saying "yes", but not good at all at saying "no".

With all the above being true, keep in mind that they probably have a sincere and generous desire to please you and give you what you want. But wanting to please you is not the same as having the capacity to do what you're asking.

Giving them a compliment

As with all the patterns, frame your compliment to fit their values, not yours. So what do merging-patterned people value? They value heart-to-heart connection. So first shift your awareness into your heart center, and then make your compliment personal and about your feelings. Tell them how good whatever they did made you feel.

If they did something for you, think of it as *"Oh, this is them loving me. This is them wanting me to be happy."* Focus on that. If they baked you a cake, it's not about how good the cake tastes. It's that they are showing you their love by baking a cake for you. The cake might taste great, but it also might not. That's not the point. When you compliment them on the cake,

Relating to the Merging Pattern

remember that you're not complimenting their skill as a cook. You're complimenting their generosity and their desire to make you happy. Focus on that. Tell them how good it makes you feel. Don't get sidetracked into critiquing their cake. They are trying to make you happy — just appreciate that.

During a conflict

Remember how, when facing a possible disagreement, a leaving-patterned person would move away from you. Here, we have the opposite safety strategy: a merging-patterned person will move toward you. They will try to connect with you in some way. They may move closer physically or reach out to you. They may agree with you or flatter you. They may try to please you or appease you. In some way, they will try to connect with you emotionally and get you on their side.

They will try to connect with you.

They may also try to manipulate you to get their way. Typically, that will involve offering you a gift that will later turn out to be a trade. They will give you what you want, believing that if they give you what you want, you will then reciprocate and give them what they want, and that transaction will resolve whatever disagreement you're having.

They're presenting it as a gift, but it's really a trade. And they think you know this because, in their world, this is what everyone does. They think you know that accepting this gift implies accepting the trade. However, if you're not a merging-patterned person, you'll likely think it's really a gift. So you may say to yourself, *"Oh wow, they're giving me exactly what I want! And at no price! This is great!"*

But that's not what's happening. Later on, they will send you the bill. They will say, *"Wait a minute, I gave you that, so you owe me this."* If you didn't know it was a trade, you may feel surprised and ripped off. At the same time, they will likely feel frustrated because they believe that all relationships operate on the principle of reciprocity and that everyone knows that. They would immediately see such a gift as part of a trade, so they think you would see that, too.

This sort of personality-pattern-based misunderstanding turns out to be the source of many fights. In this case, the misunderstanding arises from the fact that they're proposing a compromise in the form of a trade, and they think you know that, but you think you're just getting a free gift. If you have not been aware of this, it's time to learn about it.

As we said earlier for the leaving pattern, when expressing your anger, don't send it straight into their space. Don't send it at their core or even at their edge. That becomes an energetic attack, and it's likely to put them into overwhelm and provoke a patterned reaction from them. Instead, turn you body at least 90 degrees away from them and send your anger out somewhere away from them. If you're inside, send it at the wall. If you're outside and there's a big space, send it out there. They will still see and hear your anger and your complaint, but they won't have to deal with being hit by a blast of your energy. That will make it much easier for them to take in your complaint and respond to it constructively.

In Romance

In a romance, all that we've talked about so far becomes more intense, on both the plus side and the minus side. Because the heart-to-heart connection between you is stronger, there's even more at stake. The connection feels like more of a survival need, and its loss feels like more of a survival threat. A merging-patterned person's fear of losing the relationship may be so intense that it manifests in frequent jealousies and demands.

For instance, one of Taylor Swift's music videos shows her cutting up the shirts of a boyfriend who betrayed her and then smashing his new sports car with a golf club. This is a little beyond the ordinary, but it gives you a sense of how deep the wound can be when the love connection is lost. If the woman has abandoned herself in order to be who her lover wants and is then abandoned by him, she has nothing left but her fury. The popular saying is "Hell hath no fury like a woman scorned."

If you drop the heart-to-heart connection, they will feel it.

So measure the person you're in love with for how strong a felt-sense of self they have and how much they are able to tolerate not having the support of a heart-to-heart connection. And if you tend to drop the heart-to-heart connection when you get unhappy, factor that in before you judge their behavior. Or if you're intending to leave them, factor that into what you expect will happen.

Relating to the Merging Pattern

Now, with all that being said, remember as well that, as long as they feel loved and safe, merging-patterned people can be very skillful and generous lovers. In fact, they have a reputation for being wonderful lovers, because they have two marvelous qualities. One is they can often directly perceive your inner experience, so they can feel what you're feeling and know what you're wanting. That means they can give you what you want without you even asking for it. Their ability to do this is one reason that they may expect you to give them what they want without them having to ask for it. They think you can perceive their inner experience the same way, even when you cannot.

And their other wonderful talent is that they can genuinely take pleasure in your pleasure. Making you feel happy makes them feel happy, and giving you pleasure gives them pleasure. And that creates a self-reinforcing loop within them, which can lead to you both feeling deeply loved and sexually satisfied, even though they were mostly pleasing you.

The fact that they can be both the generous lover and the jealous lover sometimes makes their romantic relationships very dramatic. A person who's deeply caught in the simple merging pattern typically doesn't have much felt-sense of self in their core, so if you pull the plug on your heart-to-heart connection with them, they may fall apart inside. And their fear of falling apart like that can make them clingy and demanding. So in a romance with a merging-patterned person, you may get both jealous rage and great sex — sex like you've never had before. It can be a really rocky relationship.

One more thing — for a merging-patterned person, sex is generally more about feeling loved and connected than about having orgasms. It's about causing a strong current of love to flow between the two of you. That's the feeling they're going for, more than the buildup of sexual tension in the body and its sudden release in an orgasm.

It's the sudden discharge that creates the orgasm, but in order to build enough charge for a big orgasm, a person needs to have a strong energetic container. And to create a strong container, they have to have strong energetic boundaries. It's like filling a jar with water: the jar has to be strong enough to hold the water. If the jar is so weak that filling it with water makes it burst, you'll never get a full jar. In the same way, not having a strong energetic container makes it hard to build a big charge of energy in your body and then discharge it as an orgasm. So a person who has weak energetic boundaries may not be able to build enough charge to have an orgasm. I have known women who were deeply caught in the merging pattern who never had orgasms at all, but they felt the current of love during sex and took great pleasure in that.

Summary

The main thing to keep in mind with merging-patterned people is that they tend to believe that connecting with others is the way to solve all problems. Whether it's their problem or your problem, they expect to find the solution through connection. If it's their problem, they will want you to solve it for them. If it's your problem, they will want to solve it for you.

They see the world this way because they're habitually referencing you rather than themselves. Because they haven't developed a strong felt-sense of their own core, they don't have the skill of referencing their own body to find out what they feel and want. But they have developed the skill of referencing another person's body, so they can easily perceive what you feel and want.

This also makes it hard for them to separate outside from inside, and leads them to think that whatever you feel and want is what they feel and want. It also causes them to habitually abandon themselves and ignore their own wants and needs.

In order to interact with them skillfully, you'll have to keep this in mind. You can help them bring their attention back to themselves by asking, *"How do you feel about this?"* and *"What do you want?"* And you'll have to stay aware of whether they are abandoning themselves and giving away too much as they try to please you. By doing this, you're protecting both of you, as well as the relationship.

Tips for Relating to the Merging Pattern

- do the Centering Breath and Core practices daily
- listen for the melody and feelings in what they say
- ask them how they feel and what they want
- shift your attention into your heart center
- speak from your heart, simply and personally
- tell them what you genuinely like about them, even small things
- hold space for them to help them reference themselves
- help them develop the skills they missed, step by step

Questions

Collapsing

"If someone feels overwhelmed and collapses into tears and self-deprecation, is that the simple merging pattern?"

Probably it is, but I suggest that you think of it as only one indication and keep noticing everything else about them before trying to decide. And keep in mind that they do two patterns, so the picture will be more complicated.

Avoiding hurt

"How do you help a merging-patterned person not get hurt by their loss of heart connection and the daggers from others?"

We're all sensitive to certain things in life. And others aren't always sensitive to those same things. Often, they don't even notice those things. So they may inadvertently do something that hurts us. If you're trying to help a merging-patterned person become more resilient, you'll need to help them develop a felt-sense of Core, a strong connection to the earth, and a firm Edge.

Merging vs opening your heart

> *"So as a heart-centered person, is the goal to be less heart centered with people who are not so heart centered? It's hard to figure out when I'm merging, versus when I'm simply opening my heart."*

I wouldn't say be less heart centered, but I would say add more awareness of your belly center as a support for your heart center. The goal is to cultivate all three centers — head, heart, and belly — and integrate them within your core. I would suggest that as a goal for all people, whether you tend to start from being more heart centered, or more head centered, or more belly centered. All three of those centers of intelligence have real value, but they do different things, using different skills and talents. So we all need to develop all three of these centers and then integrate them.

Being an empath

> *"Is leaving or merging the most empathic of the patterns?"*

Typically, it's the combination of the leaving and merging patterns that leads to being an empath, because the person has both strong psychic skills and attention on what others are feeling.

Fear of centering and core

> *"From a trauma-informed perspective, what strategies would you recommend to someone who has a very difficult time with centering, or even the idea of centering, and who also runs the compensated merging pattern strongly?"*

It sounds like you're asking this question as a therapist who works with merging-patterned clients, so let me answer it this way. A big part of developing the merging pattern is learning to ignore your own core. The person has been trained to ignore their own core and their own feelings, and instead to reference the other person's core.

So a person who does the merging pattern definitely needs to practice the Centering Breath and develop a felt-sense of their own core. However, doing so will likely bring back into their awareness many old, buried hurts and traumas. So when that happens, you will need to proceed in very small

Relating to the Merging Pattern

steps, in bite-size chunks, if you will. And as each old hurt surfaces, you will need to clear that particular trauma out of their body, using whatever trauma-clearing tools you have, before going on to the next one.

The idea is to take such small bites that the process feels safe and manageable for the client, and they can gradually develop a sense of confidence in it. Above all, you want to avoid re-traumatizing them, so start with very small bites. And remember, a person who does the compensated merging pattern has a habit of over-estimating their abilities, so it's your job to regulate the pace of the process and keep the bites small enough that they don't over-do it and re-traumatize themselves.

Feeling off when heart-centered

"When I shift my attention from my head to my heart, I feel unsettled. I tried to shift to my heart when I was angry, to see how I'd feel, and I noticed that I felt okay. Not quite solid or centered, but okay. What can explain this?"

It may well be that you are quite used to having your awareness in your head and not very used to having it in your heart. Of the three centers, people typically have one that's their favorite, that they use most of the time, and then one that's maybe a close second or a distant second, but it's definitely their second. And then the third option is frequently undeveloped, since they hardly ever go there.

It may be that the heart center is the third choice for you, and that you felt unsettled there because you're not used to it. But when you were angry and shifted to your heart center, you felt okay. Perhaps your heart center isn't interested in anger. But I want to encourage you to keep investigating and see what you discover. You may find something that you hadn't noticed before.

Reciprocity

"Isn't reciprocity something good in relationships? Culture is built on reciprocity. If I give someone empathy, is it wrong to want empathy and thoughtfulness in return?"

It's not wrong to want it, but it's wrong to assume that everyone believes in it as strongly as you do. For some people, that is a very deeply ingrained value, and they would always give you something back. But for other people in other cultures, that is not a deeply ingrained value. They may talk about reciprocity, but then slam the door on you. So be aware that just because you value and want something, that doesn't necessarily mean that everyone values it equally or that they will provide it.

If you want to set up a trade, I would suggest that you make the trade explicit and negotiate it by saying something like, *"Well, if I do this for you, will you do that for me?"* That's a more explicit trade. You're making it clear by putting it into words. You're not just automatically expecting it and then feeling disappointed and saying, *"Well, if you loved me, you would."* Those are classic words for people who are caught in the merging pattern.

Functioning with two patterns

> *"When the patterns are energetically different, such as leaving and compensated merging, how can that person function?"*

Initially they will switch from one pattern to the other, and their energy field will switch at the same time. As they do more inner work, their patterns will get more integrated. But usually, people are not doing two patterns at once, especially if they haven't done much inner work. First, they do their primary pattern, and then, as their distress increases, they switch from their primary pattern to their backup pattern.

Explaining "I'm not enough" to the rigid pattern's inner critic

> *"Can you explain the merging pattern's, "I'm not enough" to the rigid pattern's inner critic?*

The inner critic is generally not interested in learning, so explaining anything to it rarely works. But each of us is more than our inner critic, and there are other parts that do want to learn. It's always better to ask a question than to make a statement, so try finding a paragraph or two in this or my first book that you think really does catch what you're trying to convey and then say to your friend, *"This sounds like it's about me. What do you think?"* and then read the paragraph to them and see what they say. You're getting them involved in the thing you want them to learn about, but you're not saying anything about them. You're just inviting them to

Relating to the Merging Pattern

express their thoughts about the paragraph and you. If they ask *"What does it say about me?"* invite them to look through the book and see what they find, but remember to avoid declaring anything about them. People don't like being told who they are, but they do like discovering it for themselves.

Susceptibility to religious cults

"Are people with the merging pattern more susceptible to religious cults than other patterns? And if not, which patterns may be?"

Well, people who do the merging pattern definitely want to belong, right? They want to belong to a group, a family, a partner, to something. They want to be part of something bigger and feel like they belong and they're emotionally connected. So I would guess that merging-patterned people would be more susceptible to identifying with any kind of group, including a cult, than the average person.

Getting out of the merging pattern

"How does a person get out of the merging pattern?"

Self Care is the way out of the merging pattern. Whether it's the simple merging or compensated merging pattern, developing a strong felt-sense of core, learning to self-reference, and practicing self care is the way out.

This book is on how to relate to others and their patterns, so we can't go deeply into how to get yourself out of pattern. But my earlier book, *The 5 Personality Patterns,* has much more information on that. At the end of chapter 8, there's a whole section on getting yourself out of and healing the merging pattern. And chapter 13 is about getting yourself out of pattern in general.

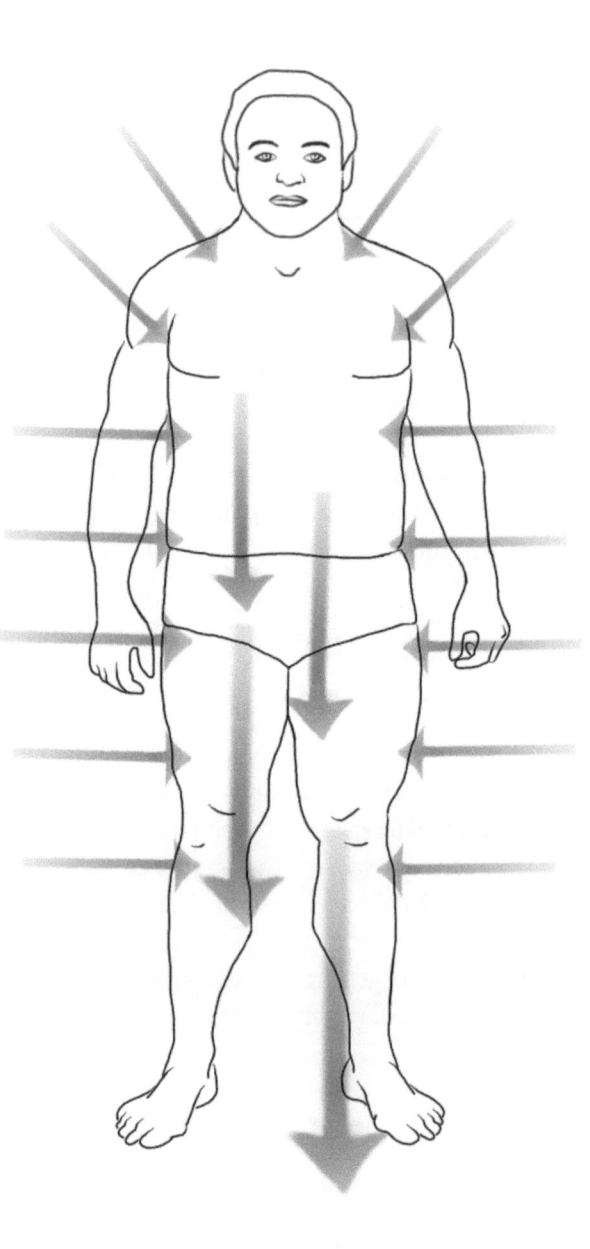

The Enduring Pattern – body and energy flow

- 8 -

Relating to the Enduring Pattern

Like all the survival patterns, the enduring pattern is a way to buffer the self from feelings of overwhelm. It is a habit of attention, fueled by trauma held in the body. The original trauma involved repeatedly being defeated and punished for attempting to separate or be different from whoever was raising you. At some point, you realized that you couldn't win, so you learned to just hunker down and endure it instead.

We're focusing on one pattern at a time because that's the clearest way to study them, but keep in mind that people do more than one pattern.

> **Centering Yourself**
>
> Before we get into the chapter, let's practice the Centering Breath and Core again. Each time you do these practices, you're developing the core skills you need to get out of whatever patterns you do and become an emotionally healthy adult.
>
> Imagine a column inside your body, from the crown of your head down to the bottom of your torso. And imagine that you can breathe in through the bottom of that column and fill it up. Now, breathe in through your nose and fill the whole column with breath, from the bottom up to the top. Then, breathing out through pursed lips, send all that breath down and out the bottom of the column. Do it again several more

times: in and all the way up, then out and all the way down. Again, in and up, and out and down. And up once more, all the way up to the top, and then back down and all the way out.

And now put your awareness on your Core, that column in the center of your body. Maybe gently breathe into it and feel into it, or imagine that you can see it. And just notice what you find there. This is the part of your body where you are the most you. This is the place to look to get the answers to your questions about *What do I feel? What do I want? Do I like this one better or that one?*

Just notice, how do you feel inside? Did something shift for you? Do you find yourself coming more into your body and into alignment with yourself? I encourage you to do these practices repeatedly, throughout the day, to bring you back to yourself.

What would your life be like now if . . . ?

What if, when you were a child, you were punished every time you spoke up, initiated an action, or said "*no*?" What if, every time you tried to do something for yourself, you were defeated? And not just defeated, but punished and humiliated for trying? What would you have done to try to avoid those humiliations? What automatic responses would you have formed to try to protect yourself? And how would those have shaped your ways of behaving now?

You might believe that you can't do anything, so it's better to not try. After all, you really were helpless in all those early situations when you were defeated, over and over. And you would probably hate all those defeats and rebel inside, but you wouldn't show it on the outside, because if you show it, they're going to punish you again.

You might be very sensitive to any kind of evaluation from the outside, any kind of getting a grade or a score or being seen as succeeding or failing. So you might want to withdraw from others and stay in an imaginary world inside yourself where no one sees you or judges you.

You might be in a lot of pain. And you might hate yourself for being this way. You would probably feel scared and alone, and maybe ashamed of yourself. But you would avoid expressing your emotions, because that would just attract their attention again. You might find it difficult to even know what you want, because knowing leads to expressing and acting and further defeat. So you might have learned to hide and keep yourself small, instead. And now every time you come into a new situation you find yourself wondering, *"Where is the danger here, and how can I hide from it?"*

It's like you're hiding in a foxhole, and you have to keep your head down, because if you put your head up, it'll get shot off. One of my clients described this very eloquently. His mom was very good at psychically tracking him. So he learned that he had to hide himself so completely that even he didn't know where he was hidden. Because if he knew, his mom would know, and she would find him and attack him. That's the kind of thing that enduring-patterned people are dealing with all the time.

The Origins of the Enduring Pattern

A toddler most often begins developing this pattern at around 2 years old as a way to protect themselves when their caregiver cannot tolerate the new separateness and autonomy that they start to assert at that age. Each of the patterns has its own developmental stage, but there's an unusually big developmental change that happens around age 2 because will and strength begin to come online then. And as a separate self begins to form, the child begins to think in terms of *me* and *mine*. So now there's not just a *want* to do something, there's also an *I* who wants to do it.

The child is beginning to develop autonomy, that is, the feeling that they are a separate person with their own will and power and their own ability to do what they want to do. By the time the child is two years old, this new assertiveness is clearly present. It creates the period known as 'the Terrible Twos,' the time when a child discovers the word *"No"* and finds that they love saying *"No,"* that they glory in saying *"No."* And that's because saying *"No"* gives them this feeling of separateness and power. This is part of the child beginning to separate psychologically from their caregiver.

Now, if the child's caregivers are okay with this, they will find ways to allow them to say *"No,"* while still keeping them safe. They will give the child choices. They might think, *"You want to choose for yourself now, so I'll offer you choices where I'm okay with both options, like 'Would you like milk or orange juice?'"* The child gets to feel, *"I chose, and I got what I wanted!"*

And there was no fight because the parent was okay with both choices and with letting the child exercise their autonomy.

The Problem: punishment for separateness and autonomy

But if the parent is not okay with the child beginning to separate and develop their own autonomy, they will try to stop it. They will try to thwart the child's will by forcing the child to do as they're told. To do that, the parent will over-control the child. This may include refusing to let the child decide anything for themselves by dictating what the child does, eats, and wears long after this is age-appropriate. It may include invading the child's space and privacy, even in the bathroom. It may even include invading the child's body with forced feedings, forced enemas, and the like.

To suppress the child's will, the parent will punish the child for expressing it, such as by voicing their own feelings or taking their own actions. Typically, the parent will mock, humiliate, threaten, or beat the child. They may emotionally manipulate the child with statements like *"You'll break your mother's heart"* or *"No child of mine …"* They may confuse the child with statements like *"I know you want …"*

The Solution: hunker down and endure

Now, the child will fight against this, over and over. They'll fight it to the point of exhaustion, again and again. But if the child finally concludes, "I cannot win. I've tried everything. There's just no way I can win," then the child will change their strategy. They will abandon trying to win. Instead, they will switch to trying to avoid losing. They will try to minimize how much they lose and how often they lose.

How do you do that? You stop playing the game. You stop expressing yourself. You stop taking a position. You stop initiating your own action. If you are involved in any sort of contest or evaluation, you don't let it finish, because it's at the finish that you win or lose. You don't emotionally invest in anything, so you don't care whether you win or lose. You learn to hunker down and endure so you can survive not being able to do what you want or get what you want.

Attention and energy go: in and down

To do that, you pull your attention in and send it down into the lower part of your body and even down into the earth below you, so you can hide there. You learn to hunker down and let the storm blow over so you don't get hurt. And remember, wherever you put your attention, your life energy goes, also. So if you habitually pull your attention in and send it down, you are also pulling your life energy in and sending it down into your legs and down into the earth below you. This habit becomes the person's safety strategy and the root of the enduring pattern.

The effect of this Safety Strategy: stuck in hiding & resisting others

To protect itself, this child learns to hide itself and avoid self-expression and self-action. To stop self-expression and self-action, the child learns to pull in the life energy that would normally be filling their personal space and send it down into the earth.

To hide and avoid self expression, enduring-patterned people learn to slow down the flow of life energy through their body, because it's the flow of energy in your system that causes you to have feelings and want to express them. So they pull their energy in, send it down, and slow down its movement. But with so little flow, they get stuck down there. Well hidden, but stuck.

So enduring-patterned people wind up stuck. They're able to resist other people's agendas, but they're not able to initiate their own agenda and take their own action. They have a deep strength, but it is the strength of the immovable object, not the strength of the irresistible force. They become the immovable object. And I mean literally immovable. Don't think that you can make an enduring-patterned person do something, because you probably can't. This is where the term "the strong, silent type" comes from.

But that also means they cannot make themselves do something, because they cannot bring their own life energy up and fill their body with it. That is what allows a person to take action and accomplish things. Enduring-patterned people have a hard time doing that, so they feel deficient and weak, and they conclude "I'm not enough."

And they learn to automatically resist all agendas, because it's hard for them to tell whose agenda it is. They think, *"Is this my agenda? Is it your agenda? I don't know. I'll just resist everything."* So hiding and resisting become the safety strategy for people caught in this pattern.

What long-term effects does this have? Well, the child forms a deep sense of grounding into the earth, but it's more of a death-grip than a flexible connection. And, although they're able to form a felt-sense of core in the body, they're not able to form much of an energetic boundary around themselves, so they can't protect their core.

Not having a strong energetic boundary makes it difficult to separate *me* from *you*. So it gets difficult to distinguish my feeling from your feeling, my intention from your intention, my agenda from your agenda. That difference remains vague, and the person is unsure what is me and what is not me.

The Gifts of the Enduring Pattern

Remember, the process of developing any of these personality patterns involves successfully using the safety strategy that underlies that pattern many, many times. But in order to make that safety strategy work for you, you have to have the talents and skills needed to pull it off. If you can't make it work, you'll abandon it and try a different safety strategy. If you can make it work, you'll continue using it, and each time you use it, you'll be practicing and improving those skills. After years of practice you become an expert at those skills, and they become the Gifts of the pattern.

One of the gifts of the enduring pattern is an Awareness of Space. By that I mean not only an awareness of their personal space and intrusions into it, but also a larger awareness of space. Enduring-patterned people are aware of space as itself, not just as the background of other things. Most of us who don't do the enduring pattern will look out at the yard or the room we're in, and our vision and attention will automatically go to the objects in the space. We will see the tree, the horizon, the table, the lamp, the picture, etc. Our attention will go only to the objects there. We will see the objects, but we will not see the space between the objects. We will automatically ignore the space.

They are aware of space as itself, not just as the background of other things.

Relating to the Enduring Pattern

Enduring-patterned people are aware of the space itself. And they care about the space itself, because the space is their friend, the part of reality that makes them feel safe.

That also means that they're able to hold space for other people. Since they're so aware of personal space, they will not invade your space. People who do not do the enduring pattern tend to invade other people's space, in one way or another. But people who do the enduring pattern will not invade your space, and they don't want you invading theirs.

Because they send their energy down into the ground, they develop a very strong connection to the earth. Since that's one of the main ways that people get their energy and strength, they have an enormous strength. And it's a deeply grounded strength. This makes enduring-patterned people strong, stable, and steady. Because they are so deeply grounded, you can't tip them over.

And they know how to ground not just themselves, but a whole group or situation: an office, a family, a home, even an elevator full of people. They're aware of the need for grounding, and they do it for themselves. But they're also aware that most people are not grounded and don't know about it, so they have to do it for everybody. Often they feel some resentment about that, and they think *"Damn, you guys, I have to do this for you all the time."*

If you know what to look for, you can see this fact demonstrated in many offices and businesses. Usually there is someone whose desk is kind of in the middle of the whole big workspace. Maybe it's an administrative assistant or a low level supervisor. In the army, it's often a sergeant. Typically that person does the enduring pattern and, because they are deeply grounded, they ground the whole space and everyone else. So everything goes well when they are present, but if they're out sick for a day, things get a little chaotic. Others notice their contribution and depend on it, even though they often don't know what it is.

Another gift of this pattern is the ability to not over-react. If you can slow down your energy flow, you can also stop yourself from over-reacting, no matter what's happening around you. This gives enduring-patterned people a real ability to be patient, to be tolerant and diplomatic, and to not automatically over-react to whatever craziness is going on around them.

They're able to simply be, without having to do. And they can take pleasure in just being quiet and alone. Remember, space is their friend, even though other people may not be.

People who do this pattern can be steady, loyal mates and workers, if you give them enough space. It's a marvelous set of skills.

Fears

What do they fear? Well, as children, they were invaded, over-controlled, and humiliated, and they want to keep that from happening again. So they want to stay away from others and avoid attracting attention as much as possible. When they are around others, part of their attention is scanning for possible trouble, checking on *Who is here? Are they tracking me? Are they invading my space? Are they sending in little feelers to find out what's going on with me? Are they messing with me in some way? Do they have an agenda? Is there something that they want me to do?* They want to avoid anything like that.

Emotions

Because their life energy is moving so slowly, they generally feel stuck and numb. If you ask how they're feeling, they'll usually say "*I'm fine*," both because they're not sure and just to get you to leave them alone.

They don't like big emotional swings and drama. They don't fall desperately in love or erupt in anger, and they will avoid conflict, if they can.[1] Beneath the surface, there's a sense of vague, chronic dissatisfaction, of heaviness, burden, and pressure. In more extreme cases, they may feel downright miserable.

The default emotions for those in this personality pattern are resentment, guilt, and shame. Their resentment is a passive manifestation of the deeply buried anger they feel at all those invasions and humiliations. It is the tip of an iceberg of fury. Their guilt arises from a suspicion that they have somehow brought all of this on themselves, and their shame comes from the thought that, since this is what they're getting, maybe it's what they deserve.

Any failure, then, can provoke a shame attack — a feeling of intense self-loathing that can spiral down into depression. On the other hand, any success can provoke an anxiety attack, since they fear that it will bring attention and punishment. So they are caught in a dilemma, in which both success and failure bring up difficult feelings. Their solution is to neither

Relating to the Enduring Pattern

succeed nor fail, but to remain suspended in between. To do this, they have to find ways to not act, take a position, or express themselves. And the only way to do all that, of course, is to suppress all movement of energy and emotions within their body.

Beliefs

The beliefs of enduring-patterned people arise mainly out of being controlled and defeated in early life. Some of their typical beliefs are:

"I can't win."
"Life is hard."
"I have to carry it all."
"You can't make me."

Since their basic strategy is one of outer compliance and inner resistance, the illusion of the enduring pattern is *"I'm trying to please you."* This means that, while they may be outwardly complying with your wishes and may sincerely believe that they're trying to please you, on the inside, they may also be unconsciously resisting your agenda.

Examples

- Eeyore in *Winnie the Pooh*
- Charlie Brown in the *Peanuts* comic strip
- Hagrid in the *Harry Potter* series
- Samwise Gamgee in the *Lord of the Rings*
- Michael Caine's character in the film *Secondhand Lions*
- George Costanza in *Seinfeld*, played by Jason Alexander

Communicating with Someone Caught in the Enduring Pattern

They have been invaded, punished, and humiliated for expressing themselves and acting to get what they want. And because of that, they've learned to mistrust other people. If you want them to trust you and reveal themselves to you, you will first have to win their trust. How do you win their trust? You do not invade their space. They do not find safety in other people. They find safety in space, that is, in space without people in it. *Space is the most valuable thing you can give them.*

This may be something that's not easy for you to give. You may want much more frequent contact and communication than they do. That's a difference that the two of you will have to negotiate. But the first step is for you to understand that, for them, space without your energy in it is much more valuable to them than it would be to you.

Space is the most valuable thing you can give them.

Respecting their space

To win their trust, you must respect their space by not invading their bubble. In a moment we're going to practice a series of actions you can take to make sure you're not invading their bubble.

As we go through this, there is one important detail to remember. While it's crucial for you to not invade their bubble, they are not protecting it. They are not guarding the edge of their bubble. They are not even claiming that space. This behavior is very different than the behavior of the rigid and aggressive patterns, both of which strongly claim their personal space. With the rigid pattern, you'll find there's a very strong energetic boundary at the edge of their personal space. And with the aggressive pattern, there's a real filling up of their own space with their own life energy to try to be as big and strong as possible. So with a person who does either or both of those patterns, you'll probably be much more clearly aware of the edge of their bubble, because they're claiming that space, filling it with their own life energy, and holding a boundary around it.

In contrast, a person caught in the enduring pattern needs you to respect their space by noticing its edge and not violating that edge, but they are not helping you to do that. There is no sign at the edge of their bubble saying "NO TRESPASSING." They are not claiming that space, filling it with their own life energy, and maintaining a strong energetic boundary around it. In essence, they need you to respect their space, even though they are not respecting their space.

They learned to do this because, as a child, claiming and defending their own space was exactly what led to trouble. It was interpreted as defiance by someone bigger and stronger, who then attacked them. So the safest thing to do was to hide, and the way to hide was to pull in their energy, hunker down, and become invisible. Taking a stand by claiming their own space would have been like waving a red flag at their attacker and yelling, *"Hey, Stupid, I'm over here!"*

For much a more detailed discussion of this pattern, please see the book, The 5 Personality Patterns.

How to Relate to Them Successfully

So what can you do to respect their space? Let's go through that series of actions we spoke about above.

Move your attention down into your Belly Center

Remember how we practiced moving your attention and energy from your head center down into your heart center? Here, we're going to do the same thing, except we'll move your energy further down into your belly center. Remember, you have three centers: your head center, heart center, and belly center. They are three different centers of intelligence, each with its own kind of intelligence.

The intelligence of your Head Center is focused on concepts, which usually occur in pairs, like right and wrong, good and bad, up and down, and yes and no. It also deals with reason, logic, and mathematics.

The intelligence of your Heart Center doesn't care about concepts and logic. It cares about connection and love. Who do you love? What do you love? What do you want to move toward? What do you want to move away from?

The intelligence of your Belly Center deals with space and with moving through space. All the martial arts are belly centered. Most physical sports and activities are belly centered, including swimming, running, football, soccer, dancing, and even walking. The belly center is often called the moving center because, if an activity involves moving through space, your attention needs to be located there in order to be good at it. The belly center is also called the instinctual center, because it seems to be the place where instinct lives in the body.

It's located about two inches (five cm.) below your belly button and about that same distance inside you. To feel your belly center, imagine that you have a warm, glowing ball there and try breathing into it. Maybe you can visualize the ball, or feel some warmth there, or even hear a soft buzzing coming from below your belly button. As you put your attention there, your life energy will begin to go there, also.

As your attention begins to find it, you may have various reactions. It may be that you habitually reside there, so you may think, *What's different? I always do this.* Or it may be that your attention usually stays up in your head center or your heart center, so you may be wondering, *How do I move down into my belly center?* As we said before, you just imagine and intend it, just as you do when you want to raise your hand. You don't have to figure out what muscles to contract to make your hand go up. Your body already knows how to do it, so you just intend to raise your hand and it goes up. In the same way, let yourself imagine that your attention is centered in your belly. You may need to practice for a while to perceive anything, but keep playing with the possibility that you can somehow see it, feel it, or hear it.

As you begin to be able to sense your belly center a little bit, imagine that the place from which you are experiencing the world also moves down into your belly. Your physical eyes and ears won't move down there, of course, but let yourself imagine what it would be like if your awareness resided down there and looked out at the world from there. Take some time — maybe hours or days — to explore experiencing the world from your belly center.

Pull your energy back inside your own space

We've done this already, in the chapter on Relating to the Leaving Pattern, so you may have practiced this and already have some sense of it. To

Relating to the Enduring Pattern

pull your energy back inside your own space, imagine that your energy is like a big, fluffy cloud and you can grab it with your arms and hands and pull it back inside your own bubble. Then reach out in a different direction, grab some more, pull that back in. Grab it from all around you and pull it all back in. Keep doing that until you feel you've gotten most of it back inside your own space.

Ideally, your life energy should stay mostly inside your own bubble and not fill up the whole room. When you let your energy fill the whole room, it intrudes on other people. Having good energy manners includes keeping your energy inside your own space.

Notice where the Edge of their bubble should be and respect it

You don't have to be psychic to do this. Just imagine a space around their body, perhaps in the shape of a big egg, that extends out about a yard (a meter) beyond their body in all directions. The edge of that egg is the edge of a person's bubble. Now, since space is their refuge, enduring-patterned people typically want a larger bubble than that, so increase that distance to 3 - 4 yards/meters beyond their body in all directions and hold that image in your mind as you interact with them and don't let your energy invade it. Some enduring-patterned people may want 10 yards/meters in all directions, so don't be surprised if they do.

Notice where their edge should be and respect it.

Your job is to notice where their edge should be and respect it, even though they're not holding an energetic boundary there. Make it your job to be aware of and hold that boundary for them. They lost the battle for that boundary years ago, so they stopped even trying to maintain it. Now they expect that everyone will cross it and invade their space, and most people do. But if you can respect their space and not invade it, they will notice that fact, and gradually, they will begin to trust you.

Speak to their Edge (not to their core)

When you say something to them, send it to their edge or just outside their edge. Don't send it to their core. When we get to the aggressive pattern, you will find that it's important to speak directly to their core, but here, when relating to enduring-patterned people, you need to do the opposite. If you send your energy directly at their core or even into their space, enduring-patterned people will feel invaded, and they won't like it.

Now, it's difficult to manage your energy so well that it stops halfway between you and someone else. Remember, wherever you look, your attention and your life energy goes there. So, when interacting with an enduring-patterned person, instead of looking directly at them, look a little to the side of them. Look at their edge or a little outside their edge, and even turn your body so that you're not facing their core, but instead facing their edge. Then speak to that place.

Here's another way to think of this: imagine that you've just made some wonderful brownies and you want to give some to your neighbor. But you do not have permission to just open your neighbor's front door, walk into their kitchen, and put your treats down on the counter. That's not okay; you would be invading their space.

Instead, bring your gift to their front door and leave it there. Imagine there's a little table right next to the door so you can leave your gift there. Maybe ring the doorbell to get their attention and call out "*Hey, I left you something.*" But don't go in. And don't send your attention or energy in. Keep it outside their bubble. This applies to any interaction, whether it's a gift, a question, or something else.

Then Walk Away – and take your attention with you

This last step in the process is really important. After you deliver whatever it is, just turn and walk away. And as you go, take your attention and your energy with you. Don't check on them. Don't leave part of your attention back there, feeling for where they are and if they came out and picked it up. They will feel you tracking them, and it will feel to them like you're hunting them. They won't like it.

When they were little kids, it is likely that one or both of their parents would track them energetically, and that tracking would often be followed by an attack. It's similar to the way that the military use a targeting radar to find and lock on to an airplane in the sky so they can fire a missile at it. Enduring-patterned people are very wary of anybody energetically tracking them. Feeling your attention on them feels to them like you're hunting them, just like their parents did. It will make them want to hide. That's why you have to take your attention away and give them the space to process their own thoughts and feelings and find their own decision.

So to respect their space, you need to do these five things:

- drop your awareness down into your belly center
- pull your energy back inside your own bubble
- notice where their edge should be and do not cross it
- interact with their edge, not their core. Leave your gift or request outside their edge
- then turn and walk away, and take all of your attention with you

This last step is important because enduring-patterned people can't consider your question or request if you're standing there watching them. They need space and time to take in whatever you have offered, differentiate what is you from what is them, and figure out what they think and feel about it. If you need a decision, they can't find it while you're standing there watching them. They need privacy to do that.

So leave your question and walk away. Take your attention with you and put it on something else. Read a book, watch TV, cook a meal, or whatever you like. But take your attention off of them and put it somewhere else.

Respect their timing

Along with respecting their space, you also need to respect their timing. Their pace is slower than most people's and probably slower than yours. Belly-center pace is slower than head-center pace, so being pushed, rushed, and hurried was likely part of their childhood wound. If you rush them now, you're simply re-wounding them. So as you interact with them, you will probably need to slow your pace down to match their pace.

You're probably noticing a theme here: match them and give them what they need in the way they need it. That's true for all the patterns — do it the way that works for them. Interact with them in their style and their native language.

Wait with them while they find their statement

When they're speaking, respecting their timing also means waiting while they find their entire statement. If you watch closely, you'll probably observe a speech pattern which is different from the pattern you see in most people. The speech pattern is this: they go inside, they find part of what they want it to say, they say that part, and then there's a pause. It may be a very long pause. It may be much longer than you would pause. It may start to drive you a little crazy. They're doing two things during this pause.

First, they're going back inside (at their slow pace) to find the rest of their statement. To do that, they have to go inside, find the feelings, find the words for those feelings, compose the words, bring their attention back out, and then say it. At their pace, that probably takes more time than it would take you.

But they're also doing a second thing. They are testing you. They're testing to see if you really want to hear what they have to say. They're testing you because when they were a child, people interrupted them, didn't listen to them, and regarded what they said as unimportant. So they're a little skeptical now about whether you really want to hear from them, and they're making you prove it.[2]

They're testing you to see if you really want to hear what they have to say.

You will probably feel pulled to interrupt them during this long pause. You'll want to finish their sentence, make a suggestion, or add something to "help them out." They do not experience this as help. They experience it as an interruption and as proof that you don't really want to hear what they have to say. And if you interrupt them, they may lose the thread inside and have to start again to find it, which will just take longer.

And most importantly, if you interrupt them, you have failed the test. They will trust you less and pull in further. Remember, you're trying to build their trust in you by showing them that they're safe with you. To do that, you have to wait with them while they find their statement and bring it out, bit by bit, no matter how long it takes. While you wait, I suggest that you practice grounding yourself. You can do that while also attending to them, and it will help you wait longer. It will give you something to do that's both good for you and good for them.

Avoid surprising them

Another way to respect their timing is by not surprising them. They don't like being surprised. If you have a question, that's fine, but don't just blurt it out. First say, *"I have a question for you. Is this a good time?"* You're doing them the favor of alerting them, asking their permission, and giving them a moment to prepare. This is important to them, and they will be grateful. If they say *"yes,"* go ahead and ask your question.

If they say *"no,"* ask them when would be a good time, and then say, *"Okay, I'll come back and ask you then."* By asking their permission, you're respecting their autonomy and their timing, and acknowledging that they don't have to answer your question right now. They don't even have to listen to it right now. You're showing that you know you cannot force them to do anything. If you can acknowledge that, it's less likely that they will need to prove it to you.

If you need an answer to your question soon, say that and ask them when would be a good time to come back. Maybe the two of you can negotiate a time, or if you know when you need an answer, say that.

When you come back, don't come back pissed off. Remember that they need time to find their actual answer, so come back calm, stay a little outside their bubble, and say, *"Hi, I've just come back to hear your answer to my question."*

And then wait. Your presence at their edge will bother them. They don't like having somebody standing there, waiting. It's a little annoying to them. So they will respond to you to get you to go away and leave them alone. Remember, they feel safest when alone, and their motto is *"I'm fine. Go away."*

When presenting something new, walk side by side with them

Here's another great clue: when you're presenting something new to a person who does the enduring pattern, walk side by side with them. Don't be sitting down or facing them. Here's why: when they're up and walking, their hips are moving, which keeps some energy moving in their system. That moving energy makes it easier for them to take in and process whatever you're saying.

Secondly, if the two of you are walking side by side, you're not facing them. When you're facing them, it feels to them like you're energetically intruding into their space. And maybe you are, especially if you're looking right at them and right at their core. That may be normal for you, but for them, it's an invasion. So that feeling of being invaded is filling up the foreground of their experience, and they're feeling something like, *"Damn, get out of me!"*

Whereas, if the two of you are walking side by side, they have open space in front of them. That feels safer to them. This is a very important clue about how to interact with an enduring-patterned person, so try to set up the interaction that way. Maybe you can say, *"There's something I want to ask you, but I'd like to get a walk in, too. Will you walk with me, and we'll talk it over?"* And then while you're walking, say, *"You know I have this question for you. Is it okay if I ask you?"*

Notice that I'm suggesting you get their permission at each step, before you go to the next step. If you ask their permission, they will likely feel honored and respected. They will like it, and they will trust you a little more. Remember that their childhood probably included a lot of times when their autonomy was just ignored, times when the big person just ran over them, so they are very aware now of who is respecting their autonomy and who isn't.

In fact, they're keeping a record of how much you respect their autonomy. It's often a point system, and each time you respect their autonomy, you get a point, and they trust you a little more. Then they're more willing to open up and reveal themselves to you. But each time you trample on their autonomy, you lose points, and then they trust you less and reveal less. So, if you want them to reveal themselves to you, you have to be skillful about how you approach them.

When they need help

Enduring-patterned people find it difficult to ask for help, and they find it difficult to receive help. So they probably will not directly ask for your help. Instead, they will complain about their problem and their situation.

You may remember that a merging-patterned person also tends to complain, but their complaining has a different purpose than an enduring-patterned person's complaining. A merging-patterned person will complain to get you to solve the problem for them. They don't want to learn how to solve it themselves, and they don't want to do it themselves. They want you to do it for them.

Relating to the Enduring Pattern

In contrast, an enduring-patterned person does not want you to do it for them. They very much want to do it themselves, because they are still trying to develop their own autonomy and strength. But they can't say that because taking a position like that might attract attention and expose them to an attack. So, if they have a problem, they cannot ask directly for your help. Their safest option is to just complain about it.

It's also possible that they grew up in a family with a lot of other enduring-patterned people, and in their family, complaining was their normal way of sharing feelings and connecting with each other.[2] So you may need to assess what kind of complaining this is and what they want.

Since you're probably used to the way most people complain, you'll have to pay special attention to do that. For example, suppose they say, *"Oh, God, I don't know what to do about this car insurance thing. I don't know whether I should keep this policy or get another one."*

Now, people who don't do the enduring pattern are often asking for your advice when they say something like that, so you may automatically interpret it that way and then begin to offer your advice. If they listen to your advice and reply, *"Thanks. That's great. I'll try that,"* then congratulations, you read their complaint correctly and gave them what they were asking for. Problem solved.

However, doing that probably won't work with an enduring-patterned person because they want to find the answer themselves. So watch what happens. If you go through a few exchanges in which you make a suggestion and they shoot it down, then you suggest something else and they shoot that down, then you suggest something else and they again shoot it down, that means they actually don't want your advice. They want to figure it out themselves. The conversation may sound something like this:

They want to find the answer themselves.

> *"Oh, I don't know what to do. I just don't know. It's just terrible."*
> *"Well, how about if you do ABC?"*
> *"No, no, I tried that. That won't work."*
> *"Well, how about if you do DEF?"*
> *"No, no, that won't work. I thought of that."*
> *"Well, how about if you do XYZ?"*
> *"No, that won't work."*

Does this sound familiar? They're not doing it to frustrate you, so don't take it personally and get angry. They're trying to tell you what they need, but without ever actually stating that they have a need. To get the message, watch their behavior more than their words.

You can do two things to help them. One is that you can express confidence in them. You can say something like, *"Well, You're a smart person. I've seen you solve problems like this before. I'll bet you can figure out this one."* Your expression of confidence is helpful to them. But don't get excited about it. Don't overwhelm them with your energy. Let it be simple and matter-of-fact.

The other thing you can do for them is simply to be there with them as they wrestle with the problem. You might say something like, *"Well, what do you think you can do? Do you have any ideas?"* You can be a sounding board for them by listening to them but not adding anything of your own. They may want you there as they sort through the options, but they don't want you to choose; they want to choose. Remember, they want to do it themselves.

You may have seen this same need in a young child as experiencing their own power and autonomy comes into the foreground. If you've been a parent, you've heard the cry of, *"Mom, I want to do it myself!"* That's what this is. They don't want you to do it; they want to do it themselves. They might need you to express confidence in them, encourage them, or just witness them, but they want to do it themselves, because they need to feel their own power and autonomy.

Making a request of them

When making a request of them, you'll need to do all that we've already named. First, slow down your inner pace to match their inner pace. Then, present your request, one piece at a time, at their pace. Wait for them to process each piece before you go on to the next piece. This pace can be a lot slower than you would like, and a lot slower than you would use with someone who does other patterns.

Secondly, don't invade their space by putting your request inside their bubble. Place your request at the edge of their bubble or even a little outside. If you put your energy inside their bubble, your energetic invasion will distract and overwhelm them so much that they can't pay attention to your request, because they need to deal with the invasion problem first. So turn a little to the side and put your request off to the side of their personal space, away from their core. Then turn and leave, taking your attention with you. And come back later at the agreed time and ask them for their answer.

Also, don't ask them to take initiative. This is really hard for them, perhaps a lot harder than it would be for you. They are wary of taking any sort of initiative because doing so tended to lead to getting humiliated and defeated when they were young. So don't phrase it that way. Instead, tell them you're going to initiate whatever it is and invite them to join you (keeping in mind that you will actually have to do it). For example, don't say that you want them to go to the gym and exercise. Instead, tell them that you're going to go to the gym and invite them to go with you. The difference is that it's easier for them to join your project than to start their own project all by themselves. By doing this, you're sidestepping their fear of taking initiative and giving them an easier path.

And they don't like being left behind — but they're willing to join you, because they'll feel safer joining your action than initiating their own. This way, they don't have to be out there by themselves. And if something goes wrong, they can always blame you. They can say, *"Well, I didn't want to do that. It was your idea."*

Their response to your request

Pay attention to how they respond to your request. Their silence is not agreement. An enduring-patterned person's silence just means that they don't yet have an answer for you. Here, silence is not consent.

Their first answer will probably be an automatic *"No."* That first automatic *"No"* is just a placeholder; it's just a way of getting some time and space to go away and think about it. And if they start complaining about your request, that's also not a real *"No."* That probably just means *"I don't know, I haven't had a chance to figure it out yet."* Complaining can also be a placeholder for people who do the enduring pattern.

Their silence is not agreement.

When they do say *"Yes,"* their first *"Yes"* is probably not a real *"Yes."* It's probably only an agreement to actually consider your request and figure out what they think and feel and then give you a real answer. The real answer won't come until you get to the second *"Yes,"* if there is one. But you won't get a real *"Yes"* until at least the second one, or even the third or fourth one.

Seeing how fraught and convoluted this whole process is for an enduring-patterned person, you may be getting a sense of how difficult it is for them to form a preference and then move to self-expression and self-action. But if you put yourself in their shoes, their avoidance actually makes sense, because as a child, self-expression and self-action were exactly what brought attention, attack, and defeat.

Giving them a compliment

First, as always, make sure you're not in their space. If you're in their space, they won't be able to hear you, no matter what you're saying. Then softly place your compliment outside the edge of their space.

Tell them what you admire about them and why you admire that. But keep your enthusiasm smaller than theirs (and theirs is probably pretty small). If your enthusiasm and emotional investment gets bigger than theirs, your compliment will start to feel to them like an obligation. It starts to become a requirement that they always do it that well. To them, your compliment is becoming a new standard, and the old standard is being raised. So they don't get to enjoy your praise about how well they did and think, *"Well, good for me!"* Instead, they think, *"Oh, no, now I have to do it that well every time!"* So keep your level of enthusiasm and emotional expression smaller than theirs.

During a conflict

Because enduring-patterned people are able to hunker down and let the storm blow over, they can tolerate your anger and not react to it better than people caught in any other pattern. They don't want to get into a fight with you. But they can listen to your upset and anger, as long as it's authentic. They value authenticity, and they watch for authenticity. They don't want to be manipulated; that's happened to them too much already. But, even if you're really angry, it's okay to feel it and say it.

They can witness your anger, but do not put them in the line of fire. As described earlier, turn at least 90 degrees away from them and send your

Relating to the Enduring Pattern

anger in that direction, not at them. That will make it much easier for them to take in your complaint and respond to it constructively. If you hit them with the blast of your anger energy, they can't hear whatever you're trying to communicate. They're overwhelmed, and they're busy trying to deal with their overwhelm.

Also, be aware that their initial responses to your anger will be passive ones, like silence and inaction. They'll probably just hunker down and may get quite stubborn. They may even say out loud, *"You can't make me."* And that's true, you absolutely cannot. You can't make them do anything. You cannot raise their level of distress high enough to make them surrender. They're better at this than you are. They've been doing it their whole life.

> *Their initial responses to your anger will be passive ones.*

If you push them farther than just passive silence, they will probably shift into passive-aggressive responses, like forgetting to meet you at the agreed time and place, forgetting to do the thing they agreed to do, or making a mistake when doing it. It might include having an accident, especially if that accident inconveniences you.

There is one other passive-aggressive thing they'll do which you need to know about. And that is, they will bait you with a series of small provocations. They will bait you into getting angry, which serves two purposes for them. One purpose is revenge; they are getting back at you. They are punishing you for whatever wrongs they feel that you (or people in general) have done to them. And the other purpose is that, if you take the bait and get angry, your anger gives them an excuse to get away from you. They wanted to get away anyway, and now they have an excuse. Remember, they don't like conflict and they don't want to fight; they'd rather get away.

So be aware: they will punish you with a series of small provocations, but they will disguise each provocation so that their fingerprints aren't on it and you can't really blame them for it. Your best defense is, don't take the bait. Remind yourself that it's not personal, this is just their way of trying to stay safe. They're probably not doing it to hurt you, even though it sure does aggravate you. This is just their habitual way of trying to protect themselves. And it's not about you, even though it sure does feel like it.

189

In Romance

When it comes to romantic relationships, the main thing to remember is this: you're dealing here with a person who was likely punished by someone they loved for simply asserting their own power and autonomy. So now, the experiences of loving, being punished, and losing their power are all cross-wired in them. That makes them afraid that falling in love with you, or accepting your love for them, will once again cost them their autonomy and their power. It's a very realistic fear, given their history. It is not about whether you would actually do that to them. It's caused by the fear that still lives in their body from things that happened to them long before they ever met you.

When facing this situation, enduring-patterned people believe that they have to choose between love and autonomy. One path they can take is to just refuse your love. In doing that, they are choosing to protect their own autonomy, even though it means giving up your love.

The other path they can take is to accept your love, but then dis-empower themselves by becoming passive and submissive. By doing that, they are defeating themselves before you can defeat them, which allows them to retain at least a little bit of power and control. They are still being defeated, but by doing it this way, they get to choose when and by whom they are defeated.

In romantic situations, it's also important to remember that they have learned to avoid initiating any action. So they probably won't ask you out; they will wait for you to ask them out. They won't suggest that the two of you go deeper with this relationship, they will wait for you to suggest it. If it's not going well, they won't say, *"I want to end this."* They'll wait for you to say it. They are much more comfortable going along with your initiative than initiating something themselves.

Their capacity to hunker down and endure allows them to tolerate a lot, which means that they can be very steady, loyal mates and partners. As long as you give them enough space, they can put up with a lot. They can stay with you for years and years, even through very difficult times.

It also means that they have a tendency to stay too long, to not notice that it was time for them to leave years ago, and that it would be good for them to take action now. All of this follows from the simple fact that, for enduring-patterned people, initiating any action is scary and difficult.

Relating to the Enduring Pattern

Summary

With enduring-patterned people, the main thing to remember is that long ago, they were punished for self-expression, self-action, or for simply showing up. To protect themselves, they learned to hunker down and hide whenever they're around other people. So, for them, the only real safety is in avoiding interaction as much as possible. That means not talking and not acting, or at least not initiating any action.

So you will have to earn their trust by respecting their space and their timing—by not invading or messing with them. It means not sending your energetic feelers into them when you're with them and not energetically tracking them when you're apart. If you need to feel constantly connected, this may be difficult for you, but it's what they need to feel safe enough to reveal themselves to you. Most people don't have the patience for this unless they also do this pattern. If all this seems strange, I encourage you to ask your enduring-patterned person about it and see what they say. It's quite likely that no one has ever asked them about this before, and they may be (quietly) very grateful that you're even thinking about what they want.

Tips for Relating to the Enduring Pattern

- practice the Centering Breath and Core daily
- drop your awareness down into your belly center
- pull your energy back inside your own bubble
- notice where their edge should be and do not invade their space
- interact with their edge, not their core
- respect their space: stay out of it, leave your gift at their edge and go away
- respect their timing: wait, don't interrupt, come back later for their answer
- sit or walk side by side, rather than facing them

Questions

Belly center

> "If your attention doesn't sit in your belly center, does that mean you don't do either the enduring or aggressive pattern? I personally related to so much about the enduring pattern, but feeling into my belly was so foreign to me."

It may indicate that you don't do either of those patterns, since doing either of them pretty much requires starting from your belly center. But it may also be that, even though the enduring pattern is one of your patterns, it's not the one you identify with most strongly.

When thinking of the three centers — head, heart, and belly — remember that each of us has one that we use the most and that's probably where we think of ourselves as being centered. Then we have a second one, which we use less than the first. We may be familiar with it, or we may not. And then we have the third one that we hardly ever visit and probably aren't familiar with. So see what happens in attempting to center yourself in your belly center. Don't assume yet that you do the enduring pattern — keep watching what you do as you try to feel safer.

Self-sabotage

> "Any suggestions on how to be effective with this pattern as a health coach? I find it really hard to see any changes in clients running this pattern."

That's right. Enduring-patterned people don't want to display successes, even when they occur, because claiming a success would draw attention and punishment as a child. These are the clients who defeat psychotherapists, and I would imagine the same is true for health coaches. Self-sabotage is an essential part of their safety strategy, but going through the details of how it keeps them safe requires a longer explanation than we can go into here. But it's a great question, and you'll need to understand it to successfully coach them, so I suggest that you look at the chapter on the enduring pattern in my earlier book, *The 5 Personality Patterns*.

Relating to the Enduring Pattern

Procrastination

"Which patterns would be most likely to procrastinate?"

This one. Procrastination and self-sabotage are some of the main defense mechanisms for an enduring-patterned person. Again, in *The 5 Personality Patterns* book you'll find whole sections on procrastination and self-sabotage.

Pausing as a test

"Is this way of testing you by pausing unique to the enduring pattern?"

As far as I know, yes. People who are caught in other patterns may pause to collect their thoughts, but I doubt that it would be a test of your ability to wait for them.

Feeling pressured to speak

"Do people who do the enduring pattern tend to have difficulties in situations where they're rushed or forced to speak?"

Yes, they typically do have difficulty with being rushed or forced to speak, since their pace is usually slower, and they're used to being cut off or run over. In my experience, feeling pressured would typically not cause them to speed up and might even cause them to slow down. But if it's a situation that really matters to them, they might try to speed up.

Getting them to do something

"I have an older relative who does the enduring pattern and I'm worried about their health. I've tried to not be invasive, but when I worry, I do feel like telling them. And sometimes I do tell them to take care of their health. But I also think it probably creates resistance. In such a case, where you can see someone doing something unhealthy or harmful, how do you tell them? Or do you just not tell them? I've also tried not doing anything, but it feels hard."

How do you get them to do something? It's a great question, and a really tricky one with a person who does this pattern. The short answer is you ask them to join you in the thing you want them to do. You announce that you're going to do it and ask them if they'd like to join you. And then you have to actually do it, of course. They most likely will not take any initiative to do it on their own, because as a child, taking action would draw attack and punishment. But they may well be willing to join you in it. Remember, they don't like to be left out.

Critic attacks

> "When I shared with my partner my feelings of hurt and loneliness after a conflict, he felt very criticized and got so angry. He couldn't handle it and rushed away. Which pattern could that be and how to better share my feelings?"

I'm not able to tell what patterns your partner does, just from a description like that. I do hear that he felt criticized, which suggests to me that maybe he has a strong inner critic and is pretty identified with it. But everybody has an inner critic, and most of us are identified with our inner critic.

I also hear that he rushed away, rather than moving toward you with empathy or starting a fight. Responding to distress by moving away suggests that maybe he does either the leaving pattern or the enduring pattern, but it's just one data point, so it's not enough to conclude anything. It might help if you and he read the sections in *The 5 Personality Patterns* on the inner critic. Maybe even read them together. There's a short section in chapter five. And then, in the chapter on the rigid pattern, there's more about it.

Warrior energy

> "What if a child comes in with a lot of warrior energy? Wouldn't they be less likely to settle for the enduring pattern? In other words, isn't it ultimately the child who decides?"

Yes, they would be less likely to develop the enduring pattern and more likely to choose the aggressive pattern's safety strategy, but there may be other reasons to adopt the enduring pattern. If your life purpose is to learn about managing warrior energy, you would need to set up life experiences that will help you learn how to do that. And maybe adopting the enduring pattern would help. Also keep in mind the fact that people do two or three patterns, not just one, so this person might also adopt the aggressive pattern.

Merging vs enduring patterns

> *"What's the difference between the 'I'm not enough' of this pattern, compared to the 'I'm not enough' of the merging pattern?"*

Their experience of themselves as weak, deficient, and helpless is similar, but they use different safety strategies to deal with it. A merging-patterned person will try to handle their feelings of weakness and helplessness by getting you to solve their problem. An enduring-patterned person actually does want to solve their problem themselves, but they don't think they can, so to protect themselves from one more defeat, they avoid even trying.

Both people will need some support to make progress, but they are at different developmental stages, so they need different kinds of support. The merging-patterned person will most likely need you to hold their hand, actually or metaphorically, and talk them through doing whatever action they need to take. The enduring-patterned person will ask you for help, but then refuse everything you offer because they actually want to find the answer themselves. What they need is for you to hold space for them while they do that. If you understand why they need to go through this process, it will be much easier for you to hold space for them as they haltingly do that. Again, there is much more on this in my book, *The 5 Personality Patterns*.

Merging-Enduring conflicts

> *"Yes, as a person who does the merging pattern and needs attention, the need of enduring-patterned people for space and alone time is a real problem for me."*

This is a problem that I see frequently in couple's therapy. The usual situation is that the woman does the merging pattern and the man does the enduring pattern. She loves the man and wants to connect with him, so she sends little feelers into his space to see what's up with him. He feels invaded and doesn't like it, so he pulls away and gets more silent. She misses him, so she moves closer and sends out more feelers. He dislikes it even more and moves farther away. And you can imagine how this would become a 10-year fight that neither of them could understand or resolve.

Neglect

> *"Instead of being squashed in their early years, what if a child was totally neglected and got no attention? Could this also cause the enduring pattern?"*

Yes, I think it could. It's not as classic, but keep in mind that we're mainly talking here about the typical situations that cause a person to adopt a pattern. There can be other reasons for a person to adopt a pattern, and neglect certainly could be one of those situations.

If the child feels totally alone and has no one to rely on, they could go into this pattern in order to endure the neglect. Or they could go into the aggressive pattern and try to do it all themselves, or into the rigid pattern and try to figure out the right way to solve the problem. They could go into the merging pattern and search for someone to connect with, or go into the leaving pattern and live mostly in an imaginary better life. There are lots of different possible solutions, depending on the child's talents and the whole situation.

High maintenance

> *"This pattern seems to be high maintenance. So many maneuvers one has to do to accommodate them. It's overwhelming and exhausting. Can you speak to this?"*

You know, if you really get into it, all of the patterns are high maintenance in one way or another. With the aggressive pattern, you have to defend yourself against their big energy. With the rigid pattern, you have to manage their inner critic, because if it gets activated, it takes over. And it's the same with the merging and leaving patterns. With each pattern, you've got to know what's okay and not okay when interacting with a person who's caught in that pattern. I'm not saying that relating to everyone skillfully is simple or easy. I'm just saying that it's possible and you can learn how to do it.

Martyr behavior

"Would enduring-patterned people be more likely to act like a martyr than those who do other patterns?"

No, because playing the martyr would mean attracting attention to themselves, which a person currently caught in the enduring pattern would want to avoid. Playing the martyr is much more usual for someone caught in the simple merging pattern. But remember that people typically do two patterns, so if this person does both the simple merging and enduring patterns, the martyr behavior may show up while they're caught in the merging pattern.

Asking for help

"Why do people with the enduring pattern have a hard time asking for help? Is it because they don't want people coming into their space?"

Look at it from their point of view. If someone had repeatedly punished you for saying what you were feeling or for taking any action on your own behalf, would you feel safe going to them for help? Probably not. So a person who's been wounded that way in childhood tends to be wary. And asking someone for help is like opening your front door to them. They might just barge right into your house, even though you didn't want that. So asking someone for help can be dangerous, and they fear it will lead to invasion.

Leaving and enduring patterns together

"My husband is very much this pattern. However, I always find myself telling him how in the clouds he is. He's a shaman and works in the astral realm a lot. He lives between the worlds and has difficulty acting on the earth plane. Yet the enduring pattern is considered to be grounded. How can he be so in the clouds and yet be considered so grounded at the same time?"

My guess is that he does the leaving pattern along with the enduring pattern, and he spends a lot of time in the leaving pattern, working, as you say, between the worlds and in other realms and dimensions. I would guess that the fact that he also does the enduring pattern helps him find his way back to the physical plane and to his body again, so that's a real benefit. But while doing the enduring pattern does make a person grounded, it does not help them act on the earth plane – in fact, it stops them.

Complaining

> *"My mother does this complaining a lot. How can I gently call her forward to get out of this pattern?"*

Well, there may be ways you can help her understand what she's doing. You could accidentally leave a copy of this book on the table at her house and see if she picks it up and reads it. Or you could find another way to help her understand this behavior, but don't ask her if *she* does it. You could ask her about a friend of yours. You could say, *"You know, I have this friend who does this complaining thing a lot. What do you think that's about? Why would a person complain like that?"* And then see what she says. But don't ask her to reveal herself. Ask her to tell you what she thinks about someone else.

Complaining

> *"In the enduring way of complaining, it seems like they stay mostly in the victim role. What will help them take responsibility? My husband does this pattern, and I get exhausted from hearing the daily complaining. My main pattern is leaving."*

When he's complaining, don't assume that he is asking you to do something about it. You can ask him, *"Are you asking me to do something about this? Or are you just telling me about your feelings?"* And if he says he's just telling you about his feelings, you can say, *"Okay, great; please, tell me all about your feelings."* That may help him shift into actually talking about his feelings rather than complaining. Or if he really does want your help with something, saying so will clarify that.

But don't take responsibility for his feelings, just because he's complaining. Ask him, *"What is it you're wanting, and how do you want me to respond?"* You might be surprised at how he answers. And at the least, you will be putting the ball back in his lap by asking him to tell you what he actually wants from you, instead of you thinking that you have to provide something when you don't even know what it is.

Tracking others

> *"Since enduring-patterned people are wary of people tracking them energetically, does this mean they're more likely to track others?"*

No, they will not do that. They will notice whether you're coming into their space, but they are not going to track you when you're far away. Their energetic manners are actually the best of any of these five patterns. The rest of us are much more likely to energetically track someone or invade their space. Enduring-patterned people typically do not do that. They will stay out of your space in the same way that they want you to stay out of theirs.

Anxiety about time

> *"Do people who utilize the enduring pattern have increased anxiety when waiting for others? Like when waiting to be picked up for dinner or for a delivery that is supposed to arrive today?"*

I'm not aware of that. I think an enduring-patterned person would have an attitude of *"well, whatever happens, happens"*. A more passive attitude. Getting anxious while waiting sounds to me more like the rigid pattern. But I want to encourage you to keep your eyes open and keep collecting data yourself.

Getting a hunkered down person working on the marriage

> *"How does one deal with an enduring-patterned person in regards to working on the marriage when they're hunkered down and don't want to change? 'You can't make me.' That's true. But change needs to happen on both sides for the marriage to work. What can I do?"*

You will have to acknowledge that you can't make him engage and instead find a way to invite him to engage. So you'll probably have to back off of whatever pressure you're exerting.

If there's a paragraph in this book or my earlier one that you think really is true about him, you could read him the paragraph and then ask, *"Is this how it feels to you inside?"* and see what he says. If he feels that it's an accurate description of himself, he'll be glad that you're seeing him more clearly. And he might even get curious about the book you're reading from.

Or if you find a paragraph that you feel really describes you, and can read it to him and then ask if that's how you look to him. But use questions. Don't make a statement. Don't assert anything. As soon as you take a position, you've offered him the opportunity to resist your position.

Developing a stronger energetic Edge

> "How can people with the enduring pattern make their energetic boundary more visible to others? Because others often are absolutely clueless."

That's true, most people haven't studied anything about this, and they are clueless. You can't change other people, but you can learn how to protect yourself more effectively. You'll need to learn to claim your own space, fill it with your own life energy, and strengthen your energetic boundary around it. And the way to do that is to practice, practice, practice. Practice is the key to all of the energetic skills.

I taught the whole series of energetic skills in a video class called *How To Create a Self*. You can find it on the book website, thefivepersonalitypatterns.com. It takes you through practicing and developing Core, Edge, Ground, claiming and filling your own space, and all the energetic skills.

Getting out of the enduring pattern

> "How does a person get out of the enduring pattern?"

One simple thing you can do to get yourself out of the enduring pattern, or to at least lighten it up for yourself, is to get your energy moving every day. Every morning, spend half an hour moving your legs and hips. You can dance, run, swim, bike, kickbox, or anything that really moves your lower body. That'll do a lot to get your energy moving. For instance, an enduring-patterned friend of mine decided to bicycle to work every day. He had to peddle for half an hour each way, which really helped him get his energy moving. That practice is very helpful for an enduring-patterned person.

This book is on how to relate to others and their patterns, so we can't go deeply into how to get yourself out of pattern. But my earlier book, *The 5*

Relating to the Enduring Pattern

Personality Patterns, has much more information on that. At the end of chapter 9, there's a whole section on getting yourself out of and healing the enduring pattern. And chapter 13 is about getting yourself out of pattern in general.

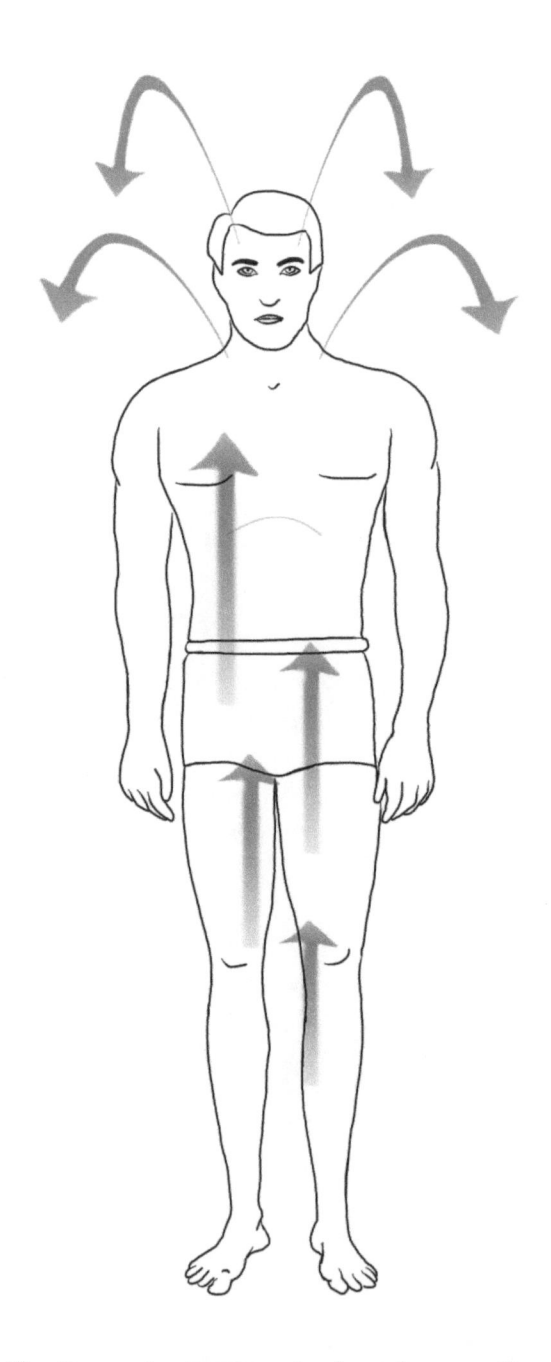

The Aggressive Pattern – body and energy flow

- 9 -

Relating to the Aggressive Pattern

Like all the survival patterns, the aggressive pattern is a way to buffer the self from feelings of overwhelm. It is a habit of attention, fueled by trauma held in the body. The original trauma involved distress that was so intense that the person feared they would die, coupled with a strong enough flow of life energy that they were able to use their own will and strength to fight their way through. In a very real sense, they have never come out of that early life-or-death struggle and continue to perceive life as a fight for survival. They believe they are alone, without love or support, so they try to be bigger and stronger than everyone else in every situation.

We're focusing on one pattern at a time because that's the clearest way to study them, but keep in mind that, in life, people do more than one pattern.

Centering Yourself

Before we get into the chapter, let's practice the Centering Breath and Core again. Each time you do these practices, you're developing the core skills you need to get out of whatever patterns you do and become an emotionally healthy adult.

Imagine a column inside your body, from the crown of your head down to the bottom of your torso. And imagine that you can breathe in through the bottom of that column and fill it up. Now, breathe in through your nose and fill the whole column with breath, from the bottom up to the top. Then, breathing out through pursed lips, send all that breath down and out the bottom of the column. Do it again several more times: in and all the way up, then out and all the way down. Again, in and up, and out and down. And up once more, all the way up to the top, and then back down and all the way out.

Now just put your awareness on your Core, that column in the center of your body. Maybe gently breathe into it and feel into it, or imagine that you can see it. And notice what you find there. This is the part of your body where you are the most you. This is the place to look to get the answers to your questions about *What do I feel? What do I want? Do I like this one better or that one?*

And just notice, how do you feel inside now? Did something shift for you? Do you find yourself coming more into your body and into alignment with yourself? I encourage you to do these practices repeatedly, throughout the day, to bring you back to yourself.

And I want to remind you again that, although we are studying them one pattern at a time, that doesn't mean that a person does only one pattern. In fact, a person typically does two different patterns and sometimes even three.

What would your life be like now if . . . ?

What if, when you were a child, there were times when you feared for your life and cried out, but there was no help? No one came, and it seemed to you that no one cared about your distress. So, to save yourself, you called up every resource inside you and fought your way through by willing yourself to survive. What would you have decided about life?

And what if the person who failed to come to your aid was the very person that you most loved and trusted and depended on? What if you concluded that they had manipulated or betrayed you? Would you have said to yourself, "*You will never do that to me again*"? Would you have closed your heart in order to protect yourself?

Relating to the Aggressive Pattern

If all that had happened to you as a child, what would you be doing now to make sure that doesn't happen again? You would probably be saying, *"I can't trust anyone else. I have to take care of myself. It's a jungle out there, and only the strong survive."* You'd think, *"I've got to make myself as big and strong as possible. Those people failed me, so I can't trust anyone now. The only person I can depend on is me."*

Also, in order to save yourself when you were terrified that you might die, you would have gone into the adrenalized, fight-or-flight state. And you'd probably still be stuck there now, trying to push down the fear by being angry and aggressive.

The Origins of the Aggressive Pattern

Typically, this personality pattern begins to form when the child is between about two and four years old, in the time after will and strength have come online.

The Problem: facing survival fear alone

The problem was that, in a time of fear for their survival, no one came to help them. They felt abandoned. They may have felt betrayed and feared that their love and trust in the other person had been used to trick them. And they concluded *"No one cares. There is no help. I am alone, and I must fight my way through alone. Only the strong survive."*

The Solution: get big and strong enough to survive anything

So, what could they do to try to feel safer? This is a child who naturally has a big flow of life energy, because if you don't have a big energy flow, you can't make this particular safety strategy work for you. In order to make any of the safety strategies work for you, you have to have the talents required to actually pull it off. Without that, it won't work for you and you won't feel safer.

Because people who do this pattern have a big flow of life energy and are old enough that will and strength have come online, they are able to will themselves to survive. To do that, they call up all their inner strength and shift their sense of themselves from being the small one to being the big one. Now they have switched roles. They're still caught in the same scenario, but instead of being the small, helpless, scared one, they now see themselves as the big, strong, dominating one. And then they fight their way through and survive on their own, without any help. And the lesson they take away from this is, *I have to be the big, strong one all the time.*

You may remember that when a person is shifting from the simple merging pattern to the compensated merging pattern, they also shift from being the small, needy baby to being the big mother who gives the baby what it needs, so you may be wondering *How is this different?* The difference is this: the merging pattern forms when the child is younger, before will and strength have developed. So they don't yet have access to real will and strength, and they can't yet form a real felt-sense of their own core. Without real will, strength, and core, their pretend core and fake strength dissolve under pressure, and they collapse back down into the simple merging pattern. But the aggressive pattern tends to form when the child is older and does have access to real will and strength and therefore can form a real felt-sense of core in the body. That gives them the foundation needed to develop the aggressive personality pattern.

Attention and energy go: up and out in front

The flow of attention and life energy for this pattern is up and out in front, toward others. Remember that with the leaving pattern, attention and energy goes away from others. With the merging pattern, it goes toward them to connect and get help. With the enduring pattern, attention and energy is pulled in and sent down in order to hunker down and hide. Here, the person brings up as much life energy as they can to puff themselves up and appear big, strong, and intimidating. Then they throw that energy at others to try to scare them into compliance and agreement. That habit becomes the person's safety strategy and the root of the aggressive pattern.

The effect of this Safety Strategy: needing to dominate

What are the effects of using this safety strategy? One effect is that aggressive-patterned people are still stuck (at least partially) in the

Relating to the Aggressive Pattern

fight-or-flight state, and it is distorting their feelings and actions. When a person goes into the fight-or-flight state, their emotional heart goes offline. That is survival adaptive. If you have to run away or climb a tree or fight an animal with big fangs and claws, you cannot afford to be distracted by fears and feelings. You have to focus on the fight. You have to act to save your life. So your heart goes offline.

Now, if you remain in the fight-or-flight state, your heart remains offline. So for aggressive-patterned people, their emotional heart is not easily accessible. And without it, they can't really feel what's going on for other people. That may be very different from your experience of the world, and that's an important thing to keep in mind as you relate to them.

If you remain in the fight-or-flight state, your heart stays offline.

But because they did form a strong felt-sense of their own core, they are able to feel themselves. You have to have a felt-sense of your own core to reference yourself, because that's what you feel into to find out *What do I feel? What do I want and what do I need?* So people who do the aggressive pattern can feel themselves, but they're not able to reference anyone else's core and know what they feel and need. They also don't reference external rules, such as manners. Rigid-patterned people prioritize that, but people caught in the aggressive pattern don't really care about rules.

Another effect of developing the aggressive pattern is that the person trusts only their own will and strength, nothing else. They believe they can't afford to trust anything else because it may betray them again. They've learned to pull their energy up and push it out at other people to intimidate them, and now they're conditioned to habitually inflate themselves and fight or at least threaten to fight. It's a self-protective mechanism. And because they're still stuck in the fight-or-flight state, they hardly ever feel safe. Instead, they believe they always have to be ready to fight.

The root of the problem is the fact that their old terror, the terror from the times when they really did feel that their life was in danger, never got healed, it just got frozen. And then it got disowned, so that now they don't consciously feel it at all. But it's still there in their unconscious, making them think they're in danger. It's still running their life. And to ward off that danger, aggression and dominance have become their habitual safety strategy.

The Gifts of the Aggressive Pattern

Remember, the process of developing any of these personality patterns involves successfully using the safety strategy that underlies that pattern many, many times. But in order to make that safety strategy work for you, you have to have the talents and skills needed to pull it off. If you can't make it work, you'll abandon it and try a different safety strategy. If you can make it work, you'll continue using it, and each time you use it, you'll be practicing and improving those skills. After years of practice, you become an expert at those skills, and they become the Gifts of the pattern.

One of the natural talents of aggressive-patterned people is a big flow of life energy. And because they practice using that big flow every time they use the pattern's safety strategy, they develop it and get better at it. So people who do the aggressive pattern become Masters of Energy. They're able to pull up a big flow of energy and use it to make things happen in the world.

Because they carry a high energy charge in their body, they need ways to discharge that energy. Most of the time, they use action to discharge it, which is why they engage in action so much of the time.

Aggressive-patterned people are highly charged, embodied, and intense. They're alive, engaged, and aware of their situation on the physical plane. They have a strong, focused attention and will, and if you've ever studied manifesting in the physical plane, you know that a strong intention and will are exactly what's needed to do that. So aggressive-patterned people are good at manifesting and often seem able to just will something into existence. It's an amazing thing to watch.

They are belly-centered, so these are people who are physical and active, athletic and sexual; they're good fighters, good hunters, and good trackers. They track other people energetically by putting a fiber of attention on them. Others may experience that fiber of attention as intrusive, and they're right; it is intrusive. But that's how people who do this pattern try to keep track of everything.

Relating to the Aggressive Pattern

You may recall that the merging pattern is the most feminine of the five personality patterns. This one, the aggressive pattern, is the most masculine. I don't mean that only men do this pattern. Women can do this pattern, too, but they do it by shifting from feminine into masculine energy. You have to be running more masculine energy than feminine energy in order to make this pattern work for you.

Because doing this pattern means developing a strong felt-sense of your own core, another gift of this pattern is that people that do this pattern can reference themselves and know who they are, at least in terms of the physical world. And because they are full of their own life energy, they also feel full of themselves, which makes them confident and natural leaders. They're able to make decisions, initiate action, and persuade others to join them in that action.

Aggressive-patterned people like to break boundaries. They like to go beyond the established limits, challenge themselves, take risks, and try new things. And they love competition. Think of the downhill skiers you've seen in the Winter Olympics who are going as fast as possible, sometimes 80 miles (130km) an hour. People who do this pattern are juicy, bold, passionate people, full of energy.

Many of our movies and books are about people who do this pattern, because their stories are about adventure and conflict. And when it's the good guys versus the bad guys, usually they both do this pattern. That's because they're in a fight with each other, and this is the pattern that's most connected to fighting and the warrior archetype. The people who do this pattern want to ride into battle, storm the castle, and either rule the world or save it.

You can see this clearly in some of our big recent stories, like *The Lord of the Rings*. Sauron, the main bad guy, is so caught in the aggressive pattern that he wants to dominate the world. Aragorn, the good guy who becomes king at the end, not only does this pattern, but also has enough self-awareness to know that there is something unhealthy about his relationship to power and therefore something to fear inside himself.

Similarly, in the Harry Potter stories, Voldemort, the main villain, is completely caught in this pattern. Because he is unable to trust anyone, he wants to dominate the world. Harry Potter, however, does not do this pattern, which is one of the reasons he's such an appealing hero. He's not just another strong guy with a gun, a sword, or a wand. Although he clearly has some of the gifts of the aggressive pattern, he is not caught in the pattern.

How to Have Better Relationships

He doesn't want to fight or dominate others, and he demonstrates that at the end of the story when he becomes the legitimate owner of the Elder Wand. With the Elder Wand, he could literally rule the world, but he doesn't want that, so he destroys it.

Fears

What do aggressive-patterned people fear? They fear that they're alone in a hostile world and have to fight for survival. They're afraid that trusting or needing anyone will, once again, set them up for betrayal. And they hold a deeper, usually unconscious, fear that inside they're actually bad, as if they have a monster inside. They're afraid the monster will get out, because they see that, even though they try to be a good person, sometimes a blast of energy comes out of them and hurts someone. After a while, they see that they're leaving behind a trail of destruction, and that makes them afraid of what's inside them and afraid that others will see it and abandon them.

Emotions

The emotions of the other patterns are more on the surface and appropriate to the situation. Here, things are a little different. An aggressive-patterned person distrusts their own feelings and therefore devalues and ignores them. In fact, they tend to ignore everyone's feelings and emotions, both their own and yours. Their attitude is, *I don't care how anyone feels, just do it.*

Their fear meter is broken.

Often, they don't consciously feel fear. That's because they have a broken fear meter inside them. To understand this, imagine that you have a meter inside you with a little needle that moves back and forth to show *How scared am I right now?* In their time of survival terror, they broke their meter so that they could ignore their fear and get through it. If you think of the meter as having wires going into it, they ripped out the wires. Now, because their fear meter is broken, they often can't feel fear inside themselves. Even though their body is scared, they don't know it because they're not consciously feeling it.

The fact that their fear meter is broken also means that they often don't notice when other people are scared. They're not as able as others to notice when they're scaring those around them. That's a real blind spot for them and a real problem for everyone else. But it's part of the situation with people who do this pattern.

On top of that, they fear any sort of weakness. They're afraid that feeling fear or need or any sort of vulnerability will make them weak. And, since they're still caught in the fight-or-flight state, they fear that any weakness threatens their survival. They have split off and buried all of that inside, which makes it easy to project it onto other people. They will say that you are small and weak and needy, but they are not. And they will believe that you need your relationship with them, but they don't need their relationship with you. Remember that their safety strategy is to try to always be bigger and stronger, so one-upping you is just another part of that strategy.

There's an easy way to tell when they are scared or overwhelmed. Their energy will suddenly get bigger and they will try to take over by overpowering everyone with their big energy. They will get angry or demanding and try to blast others into submission and compliance. That's a sure sign that they're scared, even though they don't feel it and will probably deny it. They may not know they're scared, but they're acting scared.

For aggressive-patterned people, the default emotion is anger. Whenever their system gets overwhelmed, they will start to feel and act angry. However, anger is a secondary emotion, not a primary one; it's a reaction to a deeper feeling. Underneath their anger, there is probably an unconscious fear, sadness, shame, grief, regret, or some other emotion that they have disowned out of a fear that it will make them weak. So this wave of anger does not necessarily mean that their deeper feeling is anger, but only that they felt something strongly enough that their system got overwhelmed.

Beliefs

The beliefs of aggressive-patterned people reflect both their history of feeling alone and their strong will to survive. Some of their typical beliefs are:

"I am all alone."
"There is no help."
"No one cares."
"It's a jungle out there."

How to Have Better Relationships

> "Only the strong survive."
> "Only the truth is trustworthy."
> "I have to do it all myself."
> "It's all a matter of will."
> "Rules are for other people"
> "Abuse is normal."

Examples

- special forces in the military (Navy Seals, Army Rangers, Green Berets, etc.)
- the head of security in the film *Avatar*
- Lucy in the *Peanuts* comic strip
- Tigger in *Winnie the Pooh* ("Bouncing is what Tiggers do best!")
- Jack Nicholson in nearly any role
- Tom Cruise
- Arnold Schwarzenegger
- Senator John McCain
- Sarah Palin ("don't retreat, reload")

Communicating with Someone Caught in the Aggressive Pattern

Remember, as children, aggressive-patterned people felt abandoned by the people they depended on, so they learned to get tough and fight their way through difficult situations. No one saved them; they saved themselves. And they concluded, *"No one cares. There is no help. I am all alone, and I must fight my way through alone. To survive, I have to be big and strong all the time."*

Relating to the Aggressive Pattern

They are still stuck in the fight-or-flight state

They are still stuck in the fight-or-flight state, believing that every moment is a fight for survival. So their heart is still offline, and they're just trying to stay safe in a dangerous world. But there is one thing that they will trust, and that is the truth. They will accept the truth. They will even surrender to the truth, though they won't say they're surrendering.

For example, suppose an aggressive-patterned guy has gone into a bar. He's had a bad day—he's pissed off and kind of looking for a fight. He's being mean to the people around him and baiting them into a fight. And suppose the bouncer confronts him and says, *"Hey, you can't do that here. You need to step outside."* If he sees only one bouncer, he might reply, *"Screw you, I'll take you right here."* But if he sees that two more bouncers have just stepped in behind the first one, he may think, *Uh-oh, wait a minute, it's now three to one, and if I start something, they're gonna kick my ass.* He will most likely accept the truth of the situation and say, *"Okay, I'll just grab my hat, and I will be leaving."* He will surrender to the reality of the situation, though he would not surrender to a person.

They have a terrific bullshit detector

The most valuable thing you can offer them is the truth. Don't try to soften it or sugar coat it. That will sound to them like a lie. Just tell them whatever is really true for you right now, no matter how bad it is. They can deal with that. But don't lie to them or try to manipulate them. You probably can't do it anyway. To them, lies feel like a survival threat, and they've developed a terrific bullshit detector. So the most valuable thing you can give them is the truth.

> *The most valuable thing you can give them is the truth.*

They are going to test you

They also value competence and reliability. They want to know, *Can you do this thing I need you to do for me?* So they will test you repeatedly to gauge your competence. Although it will certainly feel personal, don't take it personally. Instead, notice that they're also constantly testing themselves. A student of mine reported a typical example of this. She is not an aggressive-patterned person, but her husband is. He took her rock climbing, and she felt terrified. The danger makes her husband feel more alive, so he thinks rock climbing is great. He's testing himself and he loves it. She doesn't love it because she can feel how scared she is. But he's not feeling how scared he is; he's feeling more alive. That's a very typical situation.

If you run any kind of group or organization, keep in mind that the aggressive-patterned people in the group are going to test you. And when they do, remember, it's not about you. It's about their own survival. They're checking to make sure that they can trust you to lead them.

Their communication style

First, be aware that aggressive-patterned people always have an agenda. They're not making small talk with you. They don't just want to connect or share a feeling with you. For them, that's bullshit. Why even bother? For them, life is about getting stuff done, so when they communicate with you, they have an agenda. They want something, and they want it from you, or they wouldn't be talking to you.

And the way they get you to do what they want is to speak directly from their core to your core. They direct their energy right into the core of your body. For you, that feels very compelling and persuasive. It moves you into compliance with their agenda, and you find yourself somehow going along with it, even if you didn't want to.

Remember how, for the enduring pattern, I said repeatedly, *"Don't speak directly to their core; they don't like it; speak to the edge of their bubble?"* Here, the situation is totally different, and that's why it's so important that you pay attention to who you're dealing with and what pattern they're caught in so that you can adjust your behavior to what works for them. If the person is caught in the enduring pattern, do not send your energy right into their core; they will hate it. If they're caught in the leaving or merging patterns and you send a big blast of energy into their core, you may disorganize them so much that they can't function.

But if they're caught in the aggressive pattern, and you speak strongly right to their core, they will hear you. They will get that you are really there and you really mean it. They will believe you, and they will trust you more. They'll still test what you say to see if it's true and if you really believe it.

But speaking to them directly, core to core, is the key to getting them to pay attention to you and care about what you say.

Also, be aware that when they tell you what they want, they're simply being practical and pragmatic. They don't care about morality or ethics. They don't even care if it's fair. Their inner question is, *What do I need to do to get you to give me what I want?* That's the whole calculation. It's not about being fair or polite or nice or anything like that.

They are focused on power

One last thing — be aware that they're always tracking the power dynamics in the situation: who has more power? who has less? who is using their power right now and who's not? whose power is obvious and whose is hidden? They are very focused on power, because for them, power is the key to surviving. They want to know how much power you have and how much everyone has.

*For much a more detailed discussion of this pattern,
please see the book, The 5 Personality Patterns.*

How to Relate to Them Successfully

Match their style

To relate to them successfully, you need to match their style as much as you can. Matching their style is like speaking to them in their own language, or on their own wavelength. You won't be able to do it all, the way they do, because they've been practicing their whole life. But you can get closer. And each step closer is going to improve your relationship with them.

Develop a strong felt-sense of your own core

To match their style, you will need to develop a strong felt-sense of your own core. To do that, you will need to practice the Centering Breath frequently to help you feel your core. As your felt-sense of your core becomes stronger, you will need to practice holding your attention on it as much as possible. Your goal is to embody it so deeply that you do it all the time as you go through daily life. The good news is that developing a strong felt-sense of core (and all the energetic skills) is good for you. All these skills are part of developing emotional maturity and becoming an adult.

To help you embody this skill, let's practice it again now, so that you can see how it helps you feel your core. First, notice the column in the middle of your torso and breathe in the bottom and all the way up to the top of your head, breathing in through your nose. Then out and all the way down through pursed lips. And then again in the bottom and filling the column all the way up. Then out and all the way down. And a third time, in the bottom and all the way up. Then out and all the way down.

Now, notice how you're a little more aware of your core — maybe only a little, but some. Like all skills, this skill takes practice. To fully embody it, you will need to do it many, many times. That's because you have to get it into your body. Just knowing about it in your mind isn't enough. But since it takes less than 10 seconds to do each in-and-out cycle, it goes very quickly.

And the great thing about the Centering Breath is that it's the doorway into feeling your own core. The actual skill of Core is having awareness in that whole column, from the crown of your head down to the bottom of your torso, but it's a little hard to develop that awareness with just your imagination and intention. That's why I've been asking you to practice the Centering Breath. It helps you find and feel your core, so it opens the door for you. (You can also get audio recordings and a whole video course at www.the5personalitypatterns.com to support you in your practice.)

Speak directly from your core to their core

We discussed this above, but I want to repeat it so that you get how important it is. Speak directly from your core to their core. Aim your words and your energy straight into their core. That gets their attention and causes you to show up on their radar screen. If you don't speak directly to their core, aggressive-patterned people may not even hear you.

Speak straight from your core to their core.

Present yourself as an equal

Remember, their safety strategy is to one up everyone else in order to dominate and control them, so they're used to thinking of other people as somehow inferior. To counter that, you need to present yourself as an equal. You don't have to actually get bigger than they are, but you do need to shift the power dynamic and the physical situation enough to get them to listen to what you're saying.

First, stand up. Standing up will make you taller, and standing firmly on your own two feet will help you feel stronger and more grounded. It will also help you feel your own core.

Next, position yourself so that your head is higher than their head. This might mean you need to stand on something or go to the stairs and go up a few steps so that your head is higher than theirs. This allows you to look down at them. All of us feel bigger and stronger when we're looking down at the other person.

This also causes them to look up at you. Our bodies are still conditioned from our childhood years when we looked up at the big people who knew what was going on and told us what to do. So our bodies still tell us that, if we need to bend our head back to look up at someone, we need to regard them as at least an equal. Positioning yourself so that your head is above theirs will help you shift the aggressive-patterned person into seeing you as an equal.

So stand up on your own two feet, get your head higher than theirs if you can, feel your own core inside you, and speak directly from there.

State your agenda simply and plainly

Next, state your agenda. Remember, they believe you have an agenda, and you probably do or you wouldn't be engaging them, so state your agenda. But say it simply and plainly. Make your statement short, simple, direct, and emotionally congruent.

Don't pretend that you're not feeling whatever emotions you're feeling. If you're angry, let yourself express how angry you are. If you hate them, let yourself feel and say that. If you love them, let yourself feel and say that. If you feel sad, feel and say that. Whatever it is, you can feel it and say it. They will trust that.

Don't waste their time by trying to soften it or be polite. They don't care about politeness or manners, even if you do. Just say it to them. Make it simple and short; don't give them a long speech. They know you want something from them, and they're trying to figure out what it is. Don't let your fear of really asking for it sidetrack you into a long speech like, *"Well, I wonder if, perhaps at some point, if it's not too much trouble for you, you could do this little thing for me that I'm going to tell you about in a minute, but I haven't told you about yet . . ."* That won't work for them. While they're waiting for you to get to it, they're getting confused and frustrated. They can't track all of that, so just tell them what you want in simple, plain words.

Also, don't waste time trying to justify it. Don't tell them *why* they should do this. Or that the law says they should do it, or the rules say they should, or they have to do it to be fair, or that you gave them something before, so now they owe you. They don't care about any of that. Their decision about whether to give you what you want will not be based on any of that. It will be based on whether doing it will benefit them.

So just tell them how doing what you want is going to benefit them. You may have to think it through beforehand to figure that out. Then emphasize how it benefits them when you present it to them.

Remember, aggressive-patterned people do not habitually notice other people's needs. They're focused on protecting themselves, because they think they're in danger all the time. So they need to know how whatever you want them to do is actually going to benefit them, too.

Speak the truth, no matter how bad it sounds

Finally, tell them the truth, no matter how bad it sounds to you. They are listening for the truth, and they are able to hear the truth, no matter what it is. This is part of their strategy for surviving in the jungle. They watch for the reality of the situation and use it to orient themselves. In a world they regard as dangerous and manipulative, the truth is the only thing they can trust. So they watch for it and use it to guide them. It is their North Star and their safety.

So tell them the truth. Say it simply. Say it directly. Say it clearly. No being polite; no sugar coating it; no trying to soften it or save them from your

Relating to the Aggressive Pattern

emotions. Your truth might be *"I hate your guts right now and I wish you were dead. And I wish I'd never married you!"*

First of all, they've already picked up most of that energetically, so it's not a surprise. Secondly, when you say it, they're able to measure whether it's true for you. Suppose they get *"Yep, that's true for you,"* and then they think *"Wow, that really is true for you!"* That's important. They needed to hear you say it to be sure of it. Remember, the truth is the one thing they trust, and when they hear it, they will trust it.

So don't lie to them or try to manipulate them. When their assessment of your words is that you're lying or trying to manipulate them, it makes them scared, and they will need to fight to defend themselves. But if their perception is that you're telling the truth, it calms them down, even if that truth is painful to hear. And even if that truth is something that would be emotionally devastating for you.

I've known of situations where one person in a monogamous relationship had recently had a secret affair. The other person, who did the aggressive pattern, didn't know anything about the affair, but they could feel in their body that something was wrong. And it kept bothering and confusing them until they finally just got angry and said, *"I don't know what it is, but something is wrong here! Just tell me what it is!"* And then the person who'd had the affair burst into tears and confessed, *"Oh, I'm so sorry, It happened while I was away. I had an affair with so-and-so."* And on hearing that, the aggressive-patterned person did not get angrier. Instead, they felt their whole body relax, because they actually felt safer. Their inner experience was, *"Finally this makes sense! Now we can deal with it. Now we can decide what to do about it."* The truth helps them feel safer, so give them the truth.

They probably will not ask for help

When they need something, an aggressive-patterned person will avoid acknowledging that they have a need. They will not come to you and say, *"I need some help from you. Would you please do this for me?"* That would make them feel needy and vulnerable, so they won't do it. Instead, they will start criticizing and devaluing whoever or whatever is not giving them what they need. If it's a company or an institution, they'll say something like, *"They're so stupid. You can't trust them. They don't know what they're doing. I don't know why I ever depended on them."*

Their criticizing, devaluing, and insulting remarks may be signs that they need something, but they're not able to ask for what they need. If you want to help them, listen for the buried need behind all the put downs, and then do what you can to give them what they need. It may be that you can provide something that will help them a lot, even without them being able to ask for it. But be sure to take good care of yourself while you're doing this, and don't over extend yourself.

If you're able to hear what they need and give it to them, they may take notice and start to trust you more. Keep in mind, they don't believe that anyone cares or wants to meet their needs. That's part of why they won't ask. But if they see that you do notice what they need and try to give it to them, they will start to trust you more. They may even come to depend on you, but don't wait for them to say so out loud.

Because they're assuming no one cares, when they need help, they won't get vulnerable and ask for it. They also won't risk asking because you might say no, and then they would feel weak. Instead, they will probably just command you to give them what they need. They'll just say, *"You, do this for me."* Or maybe just, *"Do this."*

Asking for their help

When you are making a request of them, do all the things we discussed above:

- speak straight from your core to their core
- make it direct, short, and clear
- use simple language
- tell them exactly what you want and how it will benefit them

Don't try to be polite, and don't justify it. They don't care about manners, and they don't care about your justifications. Their question is, will doing what you want benefit them?

Their response to your request

If they believe that complying with your request will benefit them, they will do what you want. If they believe that it won't benefit them, they will not do it. Notice that it's got nothing to do with you. They're not referencing you. They are referencing only themselves. And their calculation is not moral; it's practical and pragmatic.

Now, helping you may give them some real benefits. They may get to feel big and strong (or at least, bigger and stronger than you). They may get to feel important in your life. They may get to feel like they're valuable to you, or capable of doing something that others can't do. Those are all real benefits for them and may be important in their decision about whether or not to help you.

Giving them a compliment

When you're giving them a compliment, as always, speak directly from your core to their core. And as with anyone, no matter what patterns they do, reference what they value. They will value your compliment more if it's about something that they already care about. Now, the things that aggressive-patterned people care about most are competence, reliability, and the truth. So if you compliment how competent they are at something, that you can always rely on them, or that something they told you turned out to be true, they'll probably feel good about that. They will value your compliment.

But be sure to make it something that's true for you. Don't try to "support" them by saying something that isn't true for you. Instead, find something about them that you do actually admire and compliment them on that. Remember, they're testing what you say for truthfulness, and if it doesn't ring true to them, they may think you're trying to deceive or manipulate them and get mad. So keep it true.

During a conflict

This is where things may get difficult for you. These are people who are used to winning fights, so they are not shy about fighting. In fact, aggressive-patterned people often embrace conflict, because they were the kids who won most of the fights. The kids who lost most of the fights developed other patterns. But these are the kids who won the fights in childhood, and they plan to keep winning them.

They often like the challenges of being in a fight: the big energy, the sense of danger, aliveness, and risk. They're thinking, *"Oh, boy, let's see if I can win this one. Let's see how I deal with this."* And since they're still caught in the fight-or-flight state, fighting feels normal to them.

Also, when they're in a fight, they get to be angry and yell a lot. This allows them to vent the energy that they're holding in their body from emotions that they're suppressing — emotions that they don't want to feel, like fear, guilt, shame, sadness, and grief. They don't want to feel those emotions because they believe feeling them will make them weak and vulnerable to attack. But if they have an excuse to get big and angry and blast someone, they can vent all that pent-up energy without having to feel those suppressed emotions. Venting that energy actually helps calm them down inside. So even though you may be in overwhelm, they will feel calmer after blasting you.

Fighting feels normal to them.

However, in the long term, doing this does not help them. They don't learn anything from their explosion and venting, because they don't feel what's going on for them underneath the anger. Without feeling those suppressed emotions, they cannot discover anything about their buried wants and needs. Instead of exploring their buried feelings, they just diverted them into anger and vented their energy.

You may recall from the last chapter that enduring-patterned people prefer to use passive aggression. Here, the opposite is true: aggressive-patterned people will almost always use active aggression. It will be straight out, not hidden or denied. But their active aggression may take several different forms. The most well known forms are force, violence, and threats, but they may also use charm, manipulation, and reason.

The form of active aggression that they prefer will depend on the other patterns they do and the gifts of those patterns. For instance, a person who does both the aggressive and leaving patterns can be very charming. Often, they can charm the pants off you — especially if getting your pants off was part of their agenda. Similarly, a person who does the compensated merging pattern with an aggressive-patterned compensation may be very good at flattering and manipulating you. And a person who does both the aggressive and rigid patterns may use logical argument, even relentless

Relating to the Aggressive Pattern

logical argument, against you. So don't think that all aggression has to be violent or threatening; it can also be charming, manipulative, or logical.

With aggressive-patterned people, there is less danger that your anger will put them into overwhelm, but there is more danger that their response will put you into overwhelm. As we've said before, when you are expressing your anger, don't send it straight into their space. That becomes an energetic attack, and it's likely to provoke a counterattack. Instead, turn your body at least 90 degrees away from them and send your anger out somewhere away from them. They will still see and hear your anger and your complaint, but they won't have to deal with being hit by a blast of your energy.

If they feel that you're attacking or challenging them, they will escalate. They will not just match you; they will get bigger than you. Again, this is part of their safety strategy of trying to feel safer by being the bigger, stronger person in the interaction. This means that if you're in any sort of relationship with a person who does the aggressive pattern, you are going to have to learn about boundaries, both how to set boundaries and how to enforce them.

Now, there are two kinds of boundaries, behavioral and energetic. Traditional psychology is very good at helping you develop behavioral boundaries, and there are good self-help psychology books on the subject, so I suggest that you read several of those books or go into therapy. Remember that you will have to actually practice setting and enforcing those boundaries in real life to develop them.

Then there is also your energetic boundary, also known as your Edge. This is one of the basic energy skills that everyone needs to learn. Without a strong energetic boundary around your bubble, other people's thoughts, feelings, and energies can easily get into your space and mix with your own thoughts, feelings, and energies. This will confuse you and make it hard for you to sort out what you think, feel, and want.

We covered how to develop a strong energetic Edge back in chapter 2, in the section on The Basic Energy Skills. And on the5personalitypatterns.com website, you can also get audio recordings about each of them and a video course called *How to Create a Self*, which teaches you all of the energy skills.

How to deal with their big explosions

Their anger typically takes the form of an energetic explosion or storm. It's big and loud, but it's not precisely aimed, so it just tends to flatten everything nearby. Sometimes it looks very much like a young child throwing a tantrum. During these times, it's easier to see that they're venting their terror, while not actually feeling it.

When they do that, one way you can protect yourself is to leave the situation. Leaving may be your best option, especially if the blast disorganizes you so much that you become unable to function. Blasting others this way can quickly cross the line into abuse, which has no place in a healthy relationship.

Turn sideways so their blast of energy goes around you.

If you want to stay through the storm, here are a couple of suggestions. First, don't just face them and take it. Don't take the spear in your chest or the force of the blast into your body. Instead, turn sideways and use your shoulder to make their blast of energy divide and go around you. Think of your shoulder as the bow of a ship or the blade of a plow cutting through the earth. Imagine that you have a sharp edge on the side of your body that divides the big wave of energy hitting you, forcing it to go around you, rather than through you.

If you do the enduring pattern, you may be good at the duck-and-cover technique. Imagine that you can drop down deep into the earth, where a blast on the surface won't harm you. Or that you can dive under the wave of energy, like diving under a wave at the beach. That can be very helpful in this situation, if you can do it.

If you do the leaving pattern, you will probably dissociate and jump out of your body to get away from the explosion. However, your body is still there, so your body still takes the blow, which is not good for you. Also, when you leave your body, the aggressive-patterned person will feel you leave. They will feel abandoned, which will make them more angry, and they may blast you again, just for that. So jumping out of your body may not be a great solution. Instead, you'll need to develop a strong felt-sense of your core and learn how to set and enforce your boundaries and your energetic edge. However, physically leaving the situation may still be your best way to both protect yourself and enforce your boundaries.

One last tip about navigating conflict with an aggressive-patterned person: their angry rant is also a call for attention, so listen for the seed of truth in it. In their rant, they're actually telling you about their feelings and needs, while doing their best to not feel them. If you can catch that information, you may be able to help them. If you can stay through the storm, hear the need behind it, and reflect that back to them, they may feel heard and seen in a way they never have before. And if so, they will trust you more. But remember, that is only a temporary fix. Ultimately, it is their job to learn to communicate skillfully about what they feel and need, not your job to constantly manage their inner state. If you cannot protect yourself during the storm, it may be wiser to just get away. Either way, take good care of yourself.

In Romance

Remember, this is a person who, as a child, probably loved and depended on the person who failed them when they were afraid that they would die. So now, they still have an unconscious fear that if they open their heart, that openness will make them vulnerable again. Their fear that they will be betrayed once again makes them scared to let themselves fall in love.

So, to protect themselves and minimize their fear, aggressive-patterned people often choose mates who do not or cannot challenge them and therefore feel less threatening to them. They choose people who are smaller, weaker, quieter, and willing to agree to whatever they want. Often, that leads them to choose a mate who is caught in the merging pattern — not necessarily a happy or healthy match, but a frequent one. Or they may choose a mate who is caught in the enduring pattern. The enduring-patterned mate does not get blown away by the aggressive-patterned person's big energy and can actually use the energy to get themselves moving, so that's actually a healthier match.

Also keep in mind the fact that an aggressive-patterned person is probably still caught in the fight-or-flight state, which means their heart is offline. So for them, sex is usually more about the energy discharge afforded by their orgasm than about emotional attachment or a heart-to-heart flow of love. Now, that doesn't mean it's not going to be good sex; it might be terrific for you. They may take great pride in being big and strong and able to move you enough to give you mind-blowing orgasms. But they're probably less interested in surrendering into mind-blowing orgasms themselves. They will want to have orgasms, but they probably won't trust you enough to surrender into letting you move them energetically and emotionally.

How to Have Better Relationships

Summary

The most important thing to remember about people who are caught in the aggressive pattern is that their bodies are still in the adrenalized, fight-or-flight state, with all that entails about fearing for their survival, believing that there is no help and no one cares, and needing to fight through it all alone. It's a very scared and lonely place to be, and it takes a lot of energy to keep all that fear and loneliness buried in their unconscious.

And, these are the children who had a big flow of life energy, which they found they could use to win fights and get their way, so they still think that fighting is the way to stay safe and get what they want. They fear that any weakness or need will be used against them, just as it was in the past, because "It's a jungle out there" and "Only the strong survive."

As you can imagine, being stuck in the adrenalized, fight-or-flight state doesn't leave much room for trust or emotional needs. Instead, it demands that anyone offering help must prove their competence before their help can be accepted. And it means that everyone must be tested before they can even be taken seriously.

So keep in mind, as they're getting big and intimidating, that for them, life is a fight for survival in a hostile world, a world without love or trust or safety. And they want you to prove your competence, pass their tests, and become someone they can trust. But it's hard for them to believe that you can.

Tips for Relating to the Aggressive Pattern

- do the Centering Breath and Core practices daily
- develop a felt-sense of your own core
- speak directly from your core to their core
- present yourself as an equal
- state your agenda simply and plainly
- tell them exactly what you want and how it will benefit them
- speak the truth – no matter how bad it sounds

Relating to the Aggressive Pattern

- turn sideways so their blast goes around you
- learn how to set and enforce boundaries

Questions

Throwing tantrums

"How do children throwing tantrums relate to the aggressive pattern?"

People caught in the aggressive pattern are a lot like a child having a tantrum. Just like a kid, they want something, they can't get it, and they're having a big burst of energy. They're kind of overwhelmed and not handling it very skillfully. When a kid is throwing a tantrum, they may just be venting their overwhelm, but they may also be doing it to try to get what they want. Aggressive-patterned people are like kids who have gotten much more skillful at throwing tantrums in order to get what they want, so there's a lot of similarity. But remember that people who aren't caught in the aggressive pattern can also throw tantrums.

CEOs and bosses

"I recently had my home renovated, I noticed that the contractors who founded their business tended to run the aggressive pattern."

Yes, the people who begin businesses often do the aggressive pattern, because they're willing to take a risk and want to be in charge. They don't want to work for somebody else and often don't trust others to do the job, so they want to run it themselves.

Many people who run businesses — the CEOs, bosses, and team leaders — run the aggressive pattern. They want to be in charge and they're probably better at keeping the whole team working and on track to accomplish the goal than most people. During my time working with the military, I noticed that most of the commanders, master sergeants, and fighter pilots did the aggressive pattern. They have the skills needed to hold it together and perform well under fire.

Not feeling fear

> *"How can they not know that they're scaring people, when they are threatening and intimidating them?"*

Well, when your fear meter is broken, you don't notice fear anymore. You don't notice it in yourself and you don't notice it in others. I can understand that, for you, that's an unimaginable experience. But it's a regular experience for people who are caught in the aggressive pattern. They don't feel their own fear, and they often aren't aware of fear in others. It's just like what happens in your car when your fuel gauge is broken: you just don't know how much gas is in the tank because you have no way of measuring it.

Also, remember that the habit of behaving in an intimidating way gets so conditioned into the person's body as a child that they automatically act that way as an adult, even when they're not intending to be intimidating. That same process happens in each of the personality patterns: an early safety strategy gets so deeply conditioned into the person's body that they automatically act that way as an adult. That's why changing our adult behavior requires more than just wanting to; we have to develop the energy skills needed to avoid going into pattern and, if we do go into pattern, the energy skills needed to get out of pattern.

Narcissism

> *"Have you seen narcissists do one pattern more than others? Is it the aggressive pattern?"*

This is a big, important question. My understanding is that narcissism is actually quite different from the aggressive pattern. In Steven Johnson's books on character structure, he conflates them and says that narcissism and the aggressive pattern are the same thing. I think that's wrong, because an aggressive-patterned person has a strong felt-sense of core, but a person stuck in narcissism does not. And more broadly, I would say that the personality patterns appear in people who have a good-enough ego structure, the sort of people that psychotherapists refer to as garden-variety neurotics. Whereas, people with narcissistic personality disorder do not have a good-enough ego structure. Their ego structure is incomplete.

If you think of a good-enough ego structure as a house, it would include a foundation, walls, a roof, and a door, because those are the basic parts

Relating to the Aggressive Pattern

needed for a complete house. In narcissism, the structure of the ego is not complete. It's like you're missing the foundation and a wall or two, which makes the whole structure so unstable that it starts to cave in unless it gets constant support. That's why a narcissistic person needs the support of constant attention and affirmation. They need you to look at them and admire them and praise them. And they need it constantly. Without it, they start to collapse inside. By contrast, a person who does the aggressive pattern doesn't need others' approval. They have their own approval, and that's the only approval they need. You can like them or not. What they want to know is whether you're useful to them.

So I would say that narcissism is not one of the five personality patterns, and that borderline personality disorder isn't, either. The narcissistic and borderline personality disorders are both the result of an incomplete ego structure, which is a much more fundamental problem than anything we're discussing here.

Compulsive eating

> *"Does the aggressive pattern have problems with compulsive eating for more energy? What pattern would probably have problems with compulsive eating?"*

People who do the aggressive pattern do love to eat and drink, and they might eat and drink too much, but it's unlikely to be compulsive. Remember, they want to have conscious control over everything, including themselves. And they have a strong will, so they can say no when they want to say no. If they're eating too much, it's more likely just their habit of over-doing everything, such as partying "too long, too loud, too late."

The people who often have problems with compulsive eating are those who are caught in the merging pattern. And this is especially true when what they really want is love, and they're confusing the sweetness of sugar with the sweetness of love. The big processed food companies know that our bodies are physiologically and psychologically programmed to seek the sweetness of sugar, so they put sugar in everything in order to get us to eat more of it. Merging-patterned people typically have trouble stopping themselves, both because they don't have a strong will, and because they can't reference themselves and measure, *Am I hungry? Am I full? Is it even food that I want, or is it something else?* Without a felt-sense of core and the ability to self-reference, they cannot find the answers to those questions.

Perception vs projection

> "I have a few aggressive-patterned people in my life, and they really think their intuition is on point because they can track energy. And I don't always agree. But they truly believe they are seeing the situation clearly and their perception is accurate."

This is a problem that happens for everybody who's perceptive about the energy or psychic world. It's the problem of perception versus projection. The problem is, the more of our own stuff we're projecting, the more distorted our perception is. It's one of the things that every school that teaches psychic or subtle perception spends a lot of time helping you deal with. You have to heal and clear out most of your own internal traumas so that your own buried wounds and needs are not unconsciously distorting your perceptions. And it is true that people who do the aggressive pattern are quick to assume that they're right. If they also do the rigid pattern, that's doubly true. That's part of the safety strategy of both patterns.

Relating to aggressive-patterned kids

> "These are great strategies for big people. But how do we talk to kids when they're running this pattern? This standing up can be intimidating."

Well, if you're with a kid, your head may already be higher than theirs, so you don't need to stand up. Let's modify what I'm suggesting to fit the situation. If your four-year-old is already strongly in the aggressive pattern and you feel intimidated, standing up may reassure both of you that you're still the parent. Or, if you feel grounded and confident in your authority, maybe sitting down on the floor so your head is more even with theirs may allow them to just be a kid, instead of needing to compete with you. But try out different things. Don't take my suggestions as requirements. Take them as suggestions, see if they help, and be guided by your experience. There is no one-size-fits-all strategy for all situations.

Relating to the Aggressive Pattern

Parenting an aggressive-patterned son

> *"How do we help our nine-year-old son who does this aggressive pattern? We would like to change the course of his increasingly louder explosions, both for his future and for our family relationships."*

Short answer — all children need to feel that they are being energetically contained by something good and kind, but bigger and stronger than them. That means by their parents, their family, and their society. They need that because they need to feel their power and test their power, but they're not ready to face the whole world by themselves.

A nine-year-old definitely wants someone else to be bigger and stronger and guide him. So try to get him into situations, maybe in sports or something similar, where there is an older man who also has a big energy and is able to contain the boys on his team. Someone who is kind, but also firm. Someone who can say, *"No, there are rules. You can do this, but you can't do that. If you do that, you sit out the game."* Get him into situations that offer him a strong but kind container, so that he can feel his energy and let it flow, but also know he's not in danger of blowing things up.

There's much more you can do, but it's too long to include here. Look at the chapter on the aggressive pattern in my earlier book, *The 5 Personality Patterns*, and read the beginning section on what an aggressive-patterned child needs from his parents. That will help you see what you can do as parents to help your son learn how to manage his big energy. Also, at the end of that chapter, look at the section on healing the aggressive pattern. That will give you a sense of the wounds that need to be healed and the skills that he needs to learn.

> *"Thank you. Yes, one problem is his father does the aggressive pattern and doesn't have the empathetic gene. But he just recently started Boy Scouts, so Yaay!"*

Great. And any inner work his father can do to learn more about himself and heal some of his inner wounds is going to make him more able to not just contain his son but also love him at the same time. And that's what aggressive-patterned children need while growing up. They need parents who can both love and contain them, and that's a tough job when the kid has such big energy.

Orphans

> "I've worked as a nurse for thousands of foster youth that should have the aggressive pattern, yet do not fit these characteristics. Why is that?"

I wonder what criteria you're using to decide that they should do the aggressive pattern. The fact that they lost their birth parents and then spent time with foster parents or in an orphanage does not mean that they had to develop the aggressive pattern. They each found their own ways to try to feel safer, and shifting into the aggressive pattern is only one way. So don't think that the only solution to feeling scared or distressed is the aggressive pattern. All five of these patterns are ways to try to feel safer.

Compensated aggressive

> "Can you talk about how compensated aggressive works?"

There isn't any such thing as a compensated aggressive pattern. There is a compensated merging pattern that has an aggressive flavor to the compensation. The difference between the compensated merging pattern with an aggressive flavor and the real aggressive pattern comes down to core. *How real is the person's core?* An aggressive-patterned person has a strong felt-sense of their own core, while a compensated merging-patterned person has only a pretend core. So under pressure, a compensated merging-patterned person will collapse and give up, whereas an aggressive-patterned person will not collapse or give up. They will dig in and fight.

Core to core over the phone

> "How would you speak from your core to their core when having a phone conversation?"

You imagine and intend it in exactly the same way. Just imagine that they're standing in front of you, and send it directly to their core. One of the amazing things about energy is that it doesn't depend on physical distance. You can send your energy to someone who is a thousand miles away, and you can send it <u>at</u> someone who's a thousand miles away. In just the same way, you can drop your heart connection to someone who's a

Relating to the Aggressive Pattern

thousand miles away, and if they are sensitive to it, they will feel it. So don't let the fact that you're used to thinking in terms of physical space fool you. Imagine it and intend it.

Protecting yourself

"In both my personal and professional life, people who do this pattern have left me feeling used and mangled. I find them very predatory. They take the position of being the predator animal, not the prey animal. How do you have a relationship with someone who is always playing power games?"

Well, our purpose here is to help you have a better relationship with them, but only if you choose to do that. I'm not saying it's going to be perfect, or even something that you'll want to continue. To protect yourself from a person who is completely lost in this pattern, you may need to cut them out of your life. That may be the only way to protect yourself. But if you choose to stay in contact with someone who runs this pattern, my hope is that some of these approaches and techniques will help you keep yourself safe while you do that.

Asking them to see you

"How can an enduring or leaving-patterned person ask the aggressive-patterned person to see them and allow them to exist in their presence?"

You can certainly say that to them. But if they haven't studied this map of personality, they won't know what you're talking about. If they haven't done much inner work on themselves, they may not even realize that they often run more energy than you can tolerate and they're putting you into overwhelm. That's true for all of us. So keep their limitations in mind — along with your own limitations — as you ask them for what you want. If they cannot do what you're asking, you will need to find another way to protect yourself.

Behavior toward those without core

> "Do aggressive-patterned people get more aggressive in the face of the patterns that don't have a felt-sense of core? How can you be in their presence, if you don't have that?"

They don't necessarily get more aggressive toward people who don't have a felt-sense of core, but they may disregard you or just brush aside what you're saying as unimportant. In fact, they may not even see or hear you. So you will be doing yourself a service by developing a strong felt-sense of your core. And that's true in all parts of your life. Developing a stronger felt-sense of your own core will bring you many benefits. That's why I recommend that you practice the Centering Breath every day.

Enduring-patterned anger vs aggressive-patterned anger

> "What is the difference between the aggressive pattern and the enduring pattern who uses anger to have people leave them alone?"

I would guess you're looking at a person who does both the aggressive and the enduring patterns. And I would guess that the enduring pattern is the pattern they go into first as they try to get away and get you to leave them alone. And then, if you're bothering them so much that their distress rises past their inner threshold, they switch into the aggressive pattern and get angry at you.

Tracking vs other referencing

> "What's the difference between tracking and other-referencing?"

In other-referencing, you are actually sensing into their core to see what they are feeling. In tracking, you are just monitoring their location in space and time. It's like tracking your dog by using a GPS collar and an app on your phone that shows you where your dog is located. It doesn't tell you if your dog is happy or scared or hungry, or even whether it's alive or dead. It just tells you about their current location.

Preferred drugs

> *"What kind of drugs do people who are caught in the aggressive pattern tend to use? And how about preferred drugs for the enduring and rigid patterns?"*

Aggressive-patterned people typically don't turn to drugs, because they very much value being in control, and being on most drugs will feel to them like being out of control. So they're more prone to seeking power — being rich, famous, powerful, admired, feared — that kind of thing. Maybe owning a big truck, an AR-15, or some other badge of power. If they do use a drug, it's more likely to be cocaine, since cocaine makes you feel more self-confident.

On the other hand, people who do both the aggressive and leaving patterns may be more into psychedelics because they want to have adventures in other realms. But without the leaving pattern, I doubt they would be into psychedelics.

Getting out of the aggressive pattern

> *"How does a person get out of the aggressive pattern?"*

The main thing needed to get yourself out of the aggressive pattern is to acquire a felt-sense of safety. You may have no body memory of actually feeling safe, so this possibility may sound foreign to you. First, you will need to have a felt-sense experience of feeling defended and protected by someone else. Secondly, you will need to feel energetically contained by someone or something that's bigger and stronger than you are, but also kind and caring. As you feel safer, your body will gradually come out of the fight-or-flight state and you'll once again be able to feel your heart and your many disowned feelings and needs. The process will most likely take a long time, with much back and forth as each new feeling of safety allows your body to relax a little more, which then reveals a bit more of the old terror, prompting alarm and the need to re-check your protection before retreating inside to digest the fear.

This book is on how to relate to others and their patterns, so we can't go deeply into how to get yourself out of pattern. But my earlier book, *The 5 Personality Patterns,* has much more information on this.

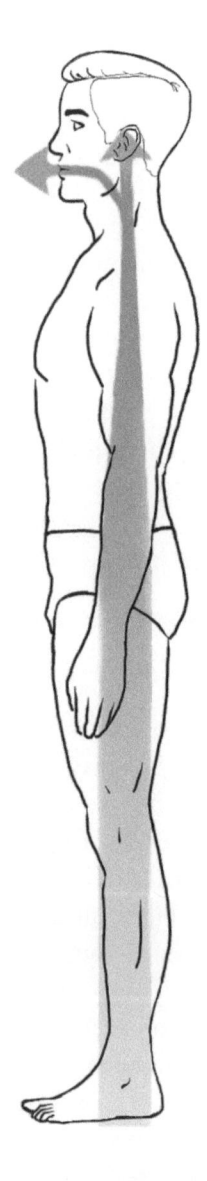

The Rigid Pattern – body and energy flow

- 10 -

Relating to the Rigid Pattern

Like all the survival patterns, the rigid pattern is a way to buffer the self from feelings of overwhelm. It is a habit of attention, fueled by trauma held in the body. The habit here is to shift attention away from internal experience and onto an external set of rules and standards. The emphasis is on correctness: both on being correct and on finding what is incorrect and fixing it. This creates a negative bias of attention: it shifts the person's attention away from what's right and toward what is wrong, away from satisfaction and pleasure and toward improving whatever is not yet perfect.

Unlike the first four patterns, this survival pattern is usually not precipitated by an identifiable traumatic event. In many cases, these children are simply indoctrinated into the Church of the One Right Way. If this is the only reflection they get from their parents and community, they grow up thinking, *This is who I am.*

We're focusing on one pattern at a time because that's the clearest way to study them, but keep in mind that, in life, people do more than one pattern.

> **Centering Yourself**
>
> Before we get into the chapter, let's practice the Centering Breath and Core again. Each time you do this practice, you're developing the

core skills you need to get out of whatever patterns you do and become an emotionally healthy adult.

Imagine a column inside your body, from the crown of your head down to the bottom of your torso. And imagine that you can breathe in through the bottom of that column and fill it up. Now, breathe in through your nose and fill the whole column with breath, from the bottom up to the top. Then, breathing out through pursed lips, send all that breath down and out the bottom of the column. Do it again several more times: in and all the way up, then out and all the way down. Again, in and up, and out and down. And up once more, all the way up to the top, and then back down and all the way out.

And now put your awareness on your Core, that column in the center of your body. Maybe gently breathe into it and feel into it, or imagine that you can see it. Notice what you find there. This is the part of your body where you are the most you. This is the place to look to get the answers to your questions about *What do I feel? What do I want? Do I like this one better or that one?*

And notice, how do you feel inside now? Did something shift for you? Do you find yourself coming more into your body and into alignment with yourself? I encourage you to do these practices repeatedly, throughout the day, to bring you back to yourself.

Your aim is to get used to putting your attention there every day, and eventually every minute of every day, until you have embodied a felt-sense of your core and it is part of your awareness all the time. This is where we want to get to with all of the basic energy skills: feeling your core, grounding into the earth, holding an energetic edge, and differentiating me from not me.

Wiggle Your Butt

Before we get into the serious stuff, I want to teach you one other very simple practice, which is surprisingly helpful for getting out of the rigid pattern. It's called Wiggle Your Butt, and it's just that simple. All you do is wiggle your pelvis left and right. You can be sitting down or standing up. It doesn't matter. Just let your butt wiggle back and forth. Try doing it right now. Just let your butt wiggle side to side. And then notice whether anything has changed in your inner state. Sometimes doing it makes people laugh. What does it do for you?

Many people find this very helpful for getting out of pattern and not being so serious about everything.

What would your life be like now if . . . ?

What would your life be like now, if back when you were a child, no one was interested in your heart or feelings? What if your parents never talked about their own emotions or asked you about your inner experience? And what if the only thing they did notice was your performance? For instance, what if they always asked, *"Did you win the spelling bee? Did you get an A on the test? How did you do in the swimming meet?"* But they never asked how you *felt* about winning or not winning. And they never noticed how you felt about having to report your every success and failure the moment you got home.

What if they noticed only your appearance, so all their attention was on *Is your hair combed? Are your teeth brushed? Are your clothes clean? Are you standing up straight?* As children, we learn to care about what our parents care about. Our attention follows their attention, so we see ourselves and the world through their eyes, as well as through our own. If their attention was mainly focused on being correct and performing well, you may have come to believe *I am my performance.*

If your parents had ignored your heart, what would you have learned about trusting yourself? Would you have discovered and developed a sense of inner wisdom or guidance? Would you have learned to trust that? Or would you have learned to trust only the guidance you received from outside yourself?

And what would you have learned about love? If your love for them had caused you to abandon your self in order to be the child they wanted and win their love, how would you feel now about falling in love? Would you fear that falling deeply in love would mean once again losing your self?

The Origins of the Rigid Pattern

The other patterns are a way of dealing with a childhood wound, but the rigid pattern is a little different, because it is often intentionally taught by a parent to their child.[1] The rigid-patterned parent believes that the most helpful thing they can teach their child is how to perform well. For them, teaching their child to perform well is an act of love, and many children who adopt the rigid pattern receive it that way. So the rigid-patterned child doesn't think they have been wounded, even though they have lost touch with their own heart and feelings. Their belief is more likely to be, *They loved me and taught me well.*

The Problem: only performance was valued

The problem for this child was that only their performance was valued and reflected back by their parents. Their heart and their feelings were ignored. And since, as kids, we see ourselves primarily through the eyes of our caregivers, if they don't see, value, and reflect back our heart and our feelings, unconsciously we conclude that our heart and our feelings aren't important. If only our performance is noticed and valued, we come to believe that only our performance matters. If our parents care mostly about doing everything the right way, we care about that, too. We then become identified with our inner critic, and it runs our life. This typically happens between about three and five years old, as the inner critic develops.

As kids, we see ourselves through the eyes of our caregivers.

The Solution: be correct and perform well

If you're taught that you shouldn't have the feelings that you naturally have, how can you suppress them? You can constrict the muscles around your core in order to mute your feelings. You can learn to distrust and ignore your own inner experience and instead trust an external set of Rules, a Right Way to behave that you're taught by your parents and your culture. This becomes your safety strategy.

Relating to the Rigid Pattern

In order to perform well, you learn to mute your inner experience and control your self-expression, so that you feel and do and say only what is correct. Gradually, you come to believe, *I am my performance. I'm not my feelings or my heart. I'm not my essence or my beingness. I am my performance.*

Attention and energy are: narrowed and constricted

With this pattern, the flow of life energy through the body has been narrowed to help them stay focused on the Rules they have been taught to follow, not on their core or feelings. Remember that with the leaving pattern, attention and energy goes away from people. With the merging pattern, it goes toward people to connect with them and get help from them. With the enduring pattern, attention and energy is pulled in and sent down in order to hunker down and hide. With the aggressive pattern, the person brings up as much life energy as they can to appear big and intimidating. Here, the person contracts inside to mute the sensations in their core, which allows them to ignore what they feel and focus on performing correctly according to the Rules. That habit becomes the person's safety strategy and the root of the rigid pattern.

The effect of this Safety Strategy: performing instead of feeling

The Rules become your guide, and you learn to control your inner experience by constantly correcting yourself. Now, it's actually your inner critic who's doing the correcting, but since you are identified with your inner critic, you think that you are correcting yourself.

You learn to act appropriately, rather than authentically. In order to act authentically, you would have to know what you feel, but you have lost touch with what you feel. Instead, your inner critic tells you what you *should* feel and how you *should* behave.

So you're unable to feel yourself, and you're unable to trust your own inner wisdom to guide you. Instead, you trust the Rules, and obeying the Rules becomes your safety strategy. Earlier we discussed how a person caught in the merging pattern only references others and how a person caught in the aggressive pattern only references themselves. Here, a person caught in the rigid pattern only references the Rules, not themselves or others. And their inner critic becomes so fierce and enforces the Rules so strongly that they come to believe their inner critic is their self. Instead of feeling hurt or oppressed by it, they become identified with it.

What is the Inner Critic?

All of us have an inner critic, but we don't all develop the rigid pattern. So what is it? It's the recorded voices of your mom, your dad, and whoever else taught you how to behave. Your inner critic is all their voices, still inside you and still telling you how they want you to behave.

Here's a way to understand it. When we're very young, how do we know what to do and not do? Well, whoever is raising us tells us what to do and not do. They say, *"Do this. Don't do that. Good boy, good girl. Bad boy, bad girl."* And our little brains record their voices, verbatim. Over time, we blend all those recordings together and they become the voice of our inner critic. So your inner critic is just all those recordings being played back, without wisdom or kindness. It doesn't mature as you grow up. It's just your parent's voices played back, telling you to be the Ideal Child they wanted you to be.

Now, the creation of your inner critic is actually a good thing. It's a big step forward in your psychological development. Before it emerges, there is no boundary inside you between having an impulse and acting on it. But with the development of your inner critic, you have your first mechanism of self-control. It's your first inner structure standing between having an impulse and taking action on it, and that's very important.

Most people are still identified with their inner critic and think it's voice is their own voice.

Ideally, as you develop psychologically, your inner critic (and your super ego) will gradually separate from your central ego, and you will begin to hear your own voice as separate from the voice of your inner critic. You'll learn to distinguish between your own voice, telling you what you actually feel and want, and the voice of your inner critic, telling you what you *should* feel and want. This gradual separation and disidentification from your inner critic is the last major step in the process of developing a healthy, mature ego structure.

Relating to the Rigid Pattern

Unfortunately, this separation does not happen for most people. I would guess that over 95% of the general population has not finished this separation process. So most people are still identified with their inner critic. Because of that, they don't hear their own voice, or at least, they don't hear it clearly. Instead, they hear the voice of their inner critic, and they think of it as their own voice.

If you listen closely to the words people use, you can tell who is talking. A person's own voice will say, *"I feel"* and *"I want."* But the inner critic will say, *"I should"* and *"you should."* Or they will say something like, *"I'm hard on myself."* Ask yourself, who is the "I" in that statement? It is their inner critic. If they had separated from their inner critic, they would say, *"My inner critic is hard on me."* But most people don't say that, because they remain identified with their inner critic and think that its voice is their own voice.

However, the processes that cause a person to develop their personality patterns generally happen at a much younger age than the separation from their inner critic, so failing to separate from the inner critic does not determine which patterns a person adopts. Fortunately, you can still complete the process of separating and disidentifying from your inner critic. See "Disidentify from Your Inner Critic" in Chapter 2 of this book, and also see Chapter 11 of my earlier book, *The 5 Personality Patterns*.

Their Inner Critic is running their life

Because rigid-patterned people believe that their inner critic's voice is their own, authentic voice, it runs their life. It censors their feelings and controls their behavior, so they do only what's 'right.' That's good for developing manners, but it's not so good for being an authentic human being.

Also, the inner critic doesn't have a 'good enough' meter. In discussing the aggressive pattern, we talked about how their fear meter was broken. Here, the rigid-patterned person's good-enough meter is broken. Without a good-enough meter, they can't tell if the job they're doing is good enough. They have only two states to choose from: either it's perfect or it's nothing. Their thinking is very black and white. Because a rigid-patterned

The inner critic doesn't have a 'good enough' meter.

person can't perceive 'good enough', they're stuck with either doing it perfectly, or totally failing.

It's also important to remember that, because the inner critic is a critic, it's not doing a fair assessment. It cannot praise or even be neutral. It's looking only for what's incorrect or imperfect. For instance, when looking at this page, it will automatically focus on any typos or errors. When you're looking at yourself in a mirror, it will see every detail that is less than perfect. And if you remain identified with your inner critic, that's what you will see, too.

Because of all this, the attention of a person caught in the rigid pattern is biased toward the negative. They tend to be critical of everything they see, and they want everything to be improved and made perfect.

For those of you who have not experienced this from the inside, I want to let you know that it's a little bit like living in a police state. But the police are not outside, watching you. The police are in your head. And you believe that whatever they say is true, and you should do what they tell you to do. So it's a little hellish inside there.

The Gifts of the Rigid Pattern

As we've said before, the process of developing any of these personality patterns involves successfully using the safety strategy that underlies that pattern many, many times. But in order to make that safety strategy work for you, you have to have the talents and skills needed to pull it off. If you can't make it work, you'll abandon it and try a different safety strategy. But if you can make it work, you'll continue using it, and each time you use it, you'll be practicing and improving those skills. After years of practice, you become an expert, and those skills become the gifts of the pattern.

The gifts of the rigid pattern are order, form, and structure. People who do the rigid pattern become Masters of Form. They can perceive and work with forms and patterns. Those could be forms and patterns of space, time, sound, color, or language, to name a few. For example, architects work with forms in space. Drummers and dancers work with forms in time. Poets and writers work with forms in language. I don't mean to say that everyone who does those things necessarily does the rigid pattern, but the best among them often do.

Because they value form, they also respect boundaries and make clear divisions between things, including things like ideas, space, and time. For them, everything has a place, and they want to put everything in its place. They also make a clear distinction between self and other and usually hold a strong energetic boundary around themselves, which you may be able to feel.

People who do the rigid pattern are also Masters of Order, that is, of categories, lists, maps, systems, and analysis. They know how everything fits together. They know how to give clear instructions and how to follow clear instructions. However, they need any instructions they receive to be clear. If the instructions aren't clear, they'll get confused and frustrated because they won't know what to do.

They tend to be head-centered and left-brained, which makes them good at linear, logical, methodical thinking. Because they have a very strong point-focused attention, they're able to focus on one thing at a time. That means they're good at seeing details, analyzing the situation, and making plans. They can break a big job down into its parts and lay it out, step by step. They have a strong will and want to complete any task they start. This is part of keeping the world in order. The trade off is that they are not so good at opening up their attention to see the larger picture.

Rules are very important to them. They are always aware of The Rules and want to follow The Rules. (I'm capitalizing it to give a sense of how they regard The Rules as almost sacred.) If you need someone on your team to keep track of The Rules, give that job to a rigid-patterned person.

Similarly, agreements are very important to them. They organize their life around agreements, so they will keep their agreements with you, and they want you to keep your agreements with them. That includes being on time.

Rigid-patterned people want to be high performers and achievers. They believe they are their performance, so they have been working at performing well their whole life. Now, that doesn't mean that everybody who does the rigid pattern performs every task perfectly. But it does mean that many of the top performers in their field do this pattern, especially when form and order are valued. Think of the Olympic figure skaters and gymnasts who practice for years in order to perform their routine perfectly once at the Olympic games.

How to Have Better Relationships

Mitt Romney is the poster child for the rigid pattern. He's a little stiff and formal at emotional communication, but he made millions of dollars, which is one way of performing well. And he has a perfect house, a perfect wife, and a perfect family.

Fears

Rigid-patterned people fear making a mistake. They believe that all mistakes must be punished, because you can't restore order until you find the mistake and punish the person who made it. Notice that detail. They're afraid of mistakes, because they believe that all mistakes — both theirs and yours — must be punished.

They're also afraid of imperfection in general, because only perfection is good enough. That makes them afraid of uncontrolled experiences, that is, experiences that don't go through the inner censorship process, because if you're not censoring yourself to be appropriate, you might do something wrong. Like when you're being spontaneous, or when you're playing and having fun. That tends to make them a little afraid of playing and a little stiff in playful situations. In fact, rigid-patterned people are afraid of change and uncertainty in general.

Emotions

All emotions tend to be muted because the inner censoring process tones everything down in order to make sure it's appropriate. All the inappropriate feelings and desires are blocked and forced back into the unconscious, where they morph into an angry resentment that others are allowed to have and do what is forbidden to them. The inner contraction required to contain all those buried feelings creates a chronic inner tension and a background anxiety that often leaks out as judgment and criticism.[2]

The default emotion for rigid-patterned people is anger, just as it is for aggressive-patterned people, but usually with less force and more of the flavor of criticism and righteousness. And the emotions under the anger are suppressed, not because they fear appearing weak, but because expressing them is against the rules. Whenever their system gets overwhelmed, they will likely start to act critical and judgmental.

Relating to the Rigid Pattern

Beliefs

Rigid-patterned people believe there's One Right Way for everything. It may be unconscious, but if you dig down, there is a conviction that there is a Right Way, we have to find the Right Way, we have to do it the Right Way, and there's only One Right Way.

For them, the idea that *You have your way, and I have my way* is just not true. There is almost a religious fervor about it. There's only One Right Way, and we all have to find it and do it. Otherwise, we'll be wrong, and we'll get punished.

They also believe that *A person is their performance*. Because of that, personal feelings don't matter. All this boils down to one idea: the purpose of life is not to have fun, love, or grow. The purpose of life is to improve. Now, that might include healing and growing, but really, it's about improving. It's about you becoming a better you, and it's about helping others become a better them. So, for rigid-patterned people, relationships tend to become a project, and the goal of the project is to improve you, them, and the relationship.

They believe that the purpose of life is to improve.

Examples

- Inspector Javert in *Les Miserables*
- Jessica in *Kissing Jessica Stein*
- Annette Bening's character in *American Beauty*
- Richard Gere's character in *Shall We Dance*
- The black and white town depicted in the movie *Pleasantville*
- Mitt Romney
- Hillary Clinton
- The archetypal librarian, trying to keep everything in order and everyone quiet

Communicating with Someone Caught in the Rigid Pattern

To communicate successfully with a rigid-patterned person, you need to know that you're mostly interacting with their inner critic, not their heart. They're not focused on feelings, play, beauty, self-expression, or just enjoying your company. They're focused on facts. They tend to reference only the Rules, not themselves or others. And their attention gravitates toward improving everything. The upside is that they often focus on solving problems, and they're good at it.

Understand their Rules

To understand them, you first need to understand their Rules. All rigid-patterned people are obeying a set of Rules, but they're not all obeying the *same* set of Rules. There are many different sets of Rules.

In politics, on the left end of the political spectrum, there are communitarian parties, with an emphasis on cooperation. And on the far right, there are authoritarians, who focus on competition and believe that whoever holds power gets to make the Rules. Those two sets of rules are completely different. In between, you've got center-left and center-right parties and many other distinctions.

In terms of religions, there are the mainstream religions, like Christianity, Islam, Judaism, Hinduism, and Buddhism, which all have their own sets of rules about how to behave. Each religion has fundamentalist versions, which have much stricter rules about who you're supposed to be and how to behave.

Then there are various philosophies, including ones that champion personal freedom. Maybe this particular rigid-patterned person grew up in a free love commune, and they were raised to follow that set of rules.

So when you want to have a better relationship with someone who does the rigid pattern, you first need to identify and understand their Rules, because their Rules are very important to them, no matter how strange they may seem to you.

If you find yourself getting judgmental about their set of Rules, try thinking of it the way you would think of a different language. If they spoke a different language, you could probably accept that you will need to speak to them in their language, rather than insisting that they learn yours. Try bringing that same attitude to understanding their Rules.

For much a more detailed discussion of this pattern, please see the book, The 5 Personality Patterns.

How to Relate to Them Successfully

Respect their rules

You don't have to adopt their rules for yourself, but when interacting with them, you do have to respect their rules. And here's why: if you violate one of their rules, their attention will go to your rule violation, and they won't be able to process what you're saying. They may be so distracted that they aren't even able to hear what you're saying anymore. Their inner reaction might sound something like: *"Oh, my God, how could you wear that shirt with those pants?"* Or *"How could you phrase it that way?"* Or if they're reading and there's a comma in the wrong place, it might be, *"Oh no! This isn't right. We have to fix this."* If you violate their rules too much, they won't be able to take in what you are saying, and your attempt at communication will fail.

Don't violate their rules.

So don't violate their rules. Say it the Right Way, according to their rules and forms. I'm not saying it's morally correct; I'm only saying it's practical. In order to communicate effectively with rigid-patterned people, you have to do it according to their rules and their forms. Again, think of it as speaking to them in their language, rather than insisting that they learn yours. This includes when and where you talk to them. It includes how you dress for the occasion. Many people in corporate culture have taken workshops on how to "Dress for Success," which have taught them that, in order to succeed in a corporate environment, you have to follow the corporation's rules about what to wear. Some rigid-patterned people have rules about what everyone should wear. Not all rigid-patterned people have rules about that, but some of them do. That's why you need to know the rules of this particular person.

You also have to respect their rules about how to begin the conversation. In many cultures, there's a ritual you have to go through before you can get down to the substance of whatever you came to say. Often, you have to go through a greeting ritual. In many Western cultures, you shake hands. In Asia, you bow. Whatever it is, you have to do it. If you skip it, you'll throw them off track, and they won't be able to listen to you.

You also have to address them in the right way. Are you allowed to call them by their first name, or is that too personal? Are you supposed to call them by their last name, their family name? Should you use a title, like Doctor, Professor, Mr. or Ms.? So you've got to learn their rules, and you've got to respect their rules. You don't have to adopt their rules for your life. But you have to recognize that, for them to fully receive your communication, you have to package it in a way that they can receive, a way that doesn't cause them to have a critic attack which distracts them from your message.

Put your communication into words

Rigid-patterned people communicate in words. They usually aren't listening on the psychic or energetic channels, so if you want them to receive your message, you have to put it into words.

If you think of a song as having both words and melody, they will mostly hear the words and may not really notice the melody. In contrast, a person who does the merging pattern (but not the rigid pattern) will probably mostly hear the melody. They will be moved by the melody, but they may not notice the words. Here, with the rigid pattern, the words are what's important. If you want them to receive your message, you have to put it into the words — not the feelings, the melody, the pictures, or a psychic message you're sending — the words. This may not be your native way of communicating, so you may need to adjust how you communicate in order to translate it into their native language. Their language is words, so to be heard clearly by them, you need to adopt their language.

Similarly, when they communicate with you, they will put their message in the words. The melody and the feeling behind what they're saying may be quite different — and therefore confusing to you — but they may not even notice that discrepancy. What they are consciously intending to say is in the words.

Relating to the Rigid Pattern

Keep your agreements with them

Rigid-patterned people use agreements to organize their world, so if you break an agreement with them, they will get upset and will probably have a critic attack.

That critic attack may be internal, attacking them, or it may be external, attacking you. If their inner critic starts attacking them, their inner voice may say something like, *"Oh my God, I can't believe I'm so stupid that I depended on this person. What's wrong with me?"* Or, their critic may start attacking you and telling you everything that's wrong with you. When you're going to interact with them, be on time, be prepared, and follow their rules so that you don't cause them to have a critic attack, either against themselves or against you. Again, think of this as speaking to them in their language, rather than insisting that they speak to you in yours.

Help them manage their inner critic

Remember, their inner critic is running their life. They're afraid of being attacked by it, so they're afraid of being wrong or making a mistake.

You can help calm their fear by frequently agreeing with them. While you're listening to them talk, keep part of your attention on what part you can agree with, no matter how small it is. Then start your reply with that agreement. It can be a small, simple agreement like, *"Yeah, I can see your point."* Or *"Okay, I get that."* Or maybe just say the word, *"Okay"* and then go on with the rest of your reply. I'm not suggesting that you lie or manipulate them. I'm just suggesting that you focus on agreeing whenever you can, especially at the start of your reply.

If you can, start your reply with a small, simple agreement.

Simply put, your agreement helps them relax. It gives them some space inside so they can listen to what you have to say. I'm suggesting this as a practical matter, not as some kind of moral standard. Your agreement will help them take in what you're saying so that the two of you can have a productive conversation. They have an unconscious habit of attention that highlights the negative. For them, the negative usually looks big and bright, while the positive fades into the background. So you're just balancing that out a little bit.

Also, be aware that the words *"You're right"* can have an almost magical effect. They're wonderful. Don't say them every time, but notice that the words *"You're right"* tell them that, right now, they're safe from being attacked by their inner critic.

Conversely, the words *"You're wrong"* suggest that they're in danger and scare them. That's often how their own inner critic attacks them, and they'll fear that you're about to attack them, too. Remember, they believe that all mistakes must be punished, so hearing *"you're wrong"* will scare them and activate every defense they have.

Re-frame a conflict into a problem that we can solve together

When there's an emotional conflict between the two of you, another thing you can do is to shift the conflict from being a problem 'between us' to being a problem 'out there' that we can face and solve together. If the problem is between us, then someone is wrong and they must be punished. In that case, the need to protect ourselves by blaming the other will likely turn it into a fight. On the other hand, if the problem is not between us, but out there somewhere, we can face it together and solve it together.

So, as we've done before, go through the movements of physically grabbing the problem and moving it out of the space *between* the two of you and off to one side, somewhere *out there*. As you do, turn to face the problem out there. Invite them to turn, also, so that, instead of the two of you facing each other, you are now standing shoulder to shoulder.

Now, there's still a problem, but you can face it together. You may want to say something like, *"You know, we're pretty smart. And I know you're good at solving problems. Let's solve this one together."*

You have re-framed the problem from being a conflict between the two of you, to being a problem out there that you can solve together. You have reassured them that the problem is not in them, and they don't have to be afraid they're going to be blamed and punished. And you have reassured them that the problem is not in you, so they don't have to blame or punish you. Instead, the problem is out there, and the two of you can fix it together.

Rigid-patterned people like solving problems, and they're good at it, so move the problem from 'between us' to 'out there' and invite them to collaborate with you in solving it.

Asking for their help in solving a problem

Suppose that you have a problem, and you want their help to solve it. First of all, tell them that you have a request. Say something like, *"I have a problem, and I'd like to ask for your help. Is that okay?"*

Don't just launch into it. Orient them first. They don't like to be surprised, but they do like to help. Helping other people is considered a good thing by almost every set of rules around the world. So they love helping, they probably want to help you, and they are actually good at solving problems.

However, you need to be careful to keep it as *your* problem. Because if you let it morph into becoming *their* problem, it may start to seem like there is something wrong with them. And if that precipitates a critic attack in them, the critic attack will grab their attention and the whole process will get derailed. So when you talk about your problem, be very careful to make it *your* problem. Tell them what's going on with you that you wish were different. Use 'I statements,' not 'you statements.' If you can avoid it, do not even say the word 'you.' Say something like, *"When somebody says or does XYZ, I have this feeling inside and I don't like it. But I don't know how to change that in myself. What do you think I can do?"* Don't make it something wrong with them, or their inner critic will jump in and start to attack someone, either them or you. Just lay it out as *your* problem, and then let them wrestle with it.

Now, they may have a solution instantly. Or they may need to go away and think it over for a while. But when they come back with a solution, remember to look for what is good in their solution and agree with that first. Praise whatever you can in the solution that they offer. At least praise the effort they put into trying to find a solution. Then, tell them about the part that doesn't work for you, and again, make it an 'I statement.' Don't say, *"Well, you forgot about this part."* As soon as you make them wrong, you are triggering their inner critic and providing the fuel for a critic attack. So use 'I statements' as you tell them what part does not work for you. Then let them wrestle with it some more.

The two of you may go through quite a few rounds of this, but they will likely stay focused on solving the problem. They like solving problems, and they're good at it. An unsolved problem is kind of irritating to a rigid-patterned person, so they will keep coming back to it, looking for a solution. For them, an unsolved problem is a defect in the order of the universe. They want the whole universe to be in order, so they've got to fix it.

Be aware that, as they help you solve your problem, they will gradually start to regard it as *their* problem. As they get emotionally attached to solving it, they will start to take responsibility for finding a solution. And they may start to implement their solution without even asking you. So, if you want to retain control over how your problem gets solved, you will have to say that clearly. You'll have to say something like, *"I want to have control over what solution I use and over when and how I implement it. So I'm asking you for help and advice, but I'll do the implementation part myself."* It's okay that you want to do that. But you have to explicitly tell them that because otherwise, without even thinking about it, they will start to take on the responsibility for implementing a solution.

> *If you want to retain control over how your problem gets solved, you will have to say that clearly.*

For example, suppose that you live with them and you say, *"I'm late to work a lot. What do you think I can do to get to work on time?"* Even though you didn't ask them to prompt you, for days afterward, they will be sticking their head around the corner and reminding you to get to get going so you get to work on time. They are implementing a solution, even though you didn't ask them to.

Just remember, they're good at problem solving, and they like to solve problems, but they have a tendency to claim a problem as their own, even when no one asked them to. So to retain control over your solution, you'll have to explicitly say that you want to implement the solution yourself.

Their way of asking for help or complaining about something

When rigid-patterned people want something, their want (just like all their feelings) is vetted for correctness by their inner critic before it reaches consciousness. If it is deemed appropriate, it is allowed to become conscious. If it is deemed inappropriate, it is shoved back down into the unconscious. It may still get expressed somehow, but its expression is likely to be distorted. As a result, the whole process of wanting and asking can get pretty convoluted for rigid-patterned people.

Relating to the Rigid Pattern

If what is desired is deemed correct and appropriate, it can be expressed directly. For example, *"Can you please pass the salt?"* or *"May I ask a question?"*

If what is desired is deemed to be incorrect, bad, wrong, immoral, or simply inappropriate, it is more likely to be expressed as an attack on others who have what they desire. For instance, a religious fundamentalist who unconsciously wants to have sex but cannot consciously know that fact may rail constantly against *"those Godless fornicators"* and later get caught with a prostitute.

Or what a rigid-patterned person wants may get expressed as an attack on what they don't want. This usually takes the form of criticizing and devaluing what is not wanted, often without even mentioning what they do want. So instead of saying, *"I want this,"* they will say *"Well, that other thing is wrong."* For instance, a rigid-patterned person who wants to get their driver's license but fears they won't pass the test may criticize the test, saying, *"That test is so stupid. It doesn't prove anything. I don't know why they even make you take a test."* Notice that they never said *"I want to get my license"* and may be totally unaware of their fear of failing the test. You may be able to figure out what they do want by noticing what they judge and criticize.

Because they think that personal feelings are not important, they're not used to asking for something they want. In their world, only the Rules matter, so they're more likely to present their desire as *"You should,"* than as *"I want."* They will then build a case for why you *should* do what they want, instead of just asking for what they want. They will also talk about what people in general *should* do, but not exactly say what they personally want. So they may say, *"People should be honest,"* rather than say, *"I want you to be honest with me."* It will be more about *"you should"* or *"I should,"* than *"I want."* Listen for the personal feeling or need hidden beneath their complaint, and reply to that, if you can.

Asking them to do something

In this situation, you already know what you want them to do. Once again, remember that they don't like to be surprised, so start by informing them that you have a request. Ask if this is a good time. If they say it is not, ask when would be a good time and come back then. When it is a good time, tell them exactly what you want. Lay it out in clear, logical instructions.

How to Have Better Relationships

They like to follow instructions, because then they know they're doing it the right way. So give them clear, step-by-step instructions. Tell them, in words, exactly what you want them to do and say. Do not ask them to read your mind. They're not good at mind-reading. You may have that skill, but they don't. So, don't assume that they can read your mind and figure out what you want them to do and say. You have to figure out what you want them to do and say, and then tell them that.

You have to give them clear, step-by-step instructions.

To clarify for yourself exactly what you're asking of them, you may need to write out your instructions beforehand:

> *I want you to do X.*
> *And then I want you to do Y.*
> *And then I want you to do Z.*

Give them a clear, step-by-step path to follow.

Lastly, make sure to tell them how they can know that they have succeeded. They always check their work, and they will be looking for this confirmation, so tell them what to look for. Each time they see it, they will get a good feeling, and it will motivate them to continue doing what you've requested. You can say something like, *"Whenever I see you doing that, a big smile comes to my face. So when you see that smile, you'll know you did it."* If you help them check their work, they will do an excellent job.

Their response to your request

So you've told them exactly what you want to do. How might they respond? They will respond according to whatever rules they follow. It will be a correct response. Not necessarily a heartfelt, emotional response, but a polite response according to their rules.

Now there's something unconscious going on here that you need to be aware of. When you asked them to do something for you, they automatically and unconsciously checked their rules for how to respond. Because most rules say they're supposed to help people, they probably said *"yes."* But they did not check themselves. They skipped referencing their own core to find out, *How do I feel about doing this? Do I like doing this? Do I want to do this?* Typically, rigid-patterned people have never practiced

Relating to the Rigid Pattern

referencing themselves, because that gets in the way of performing well, so they are not good at self-referencing.

If they skipped that step, they may later come to resent doing what you asked, because they didn't really want to do it in the first place. To prevent this, be sure to ask them to take a moment to check inside. Maybe you can say something like, *"Can you check inside to see if this is really something that you feel good about?"*

You're giving them permission to reference their core and discover whether they want to do this, whereas their set of rules probably does not give them permission to look inward and discover that, much less say it. Doing this extra check at the beginning can spare you both a lot of tension and difficulty later on.

Giving them a compliment

As we've said before, put the compliment in their language and compliment them on what they value. They value order, correctness, and achievement, that is, good performance, in all its forms.

They will be able to take in your praise more easily if you compliment something specific that they did, rather than how it made you feel. If you say, *"When you hit that home run, I felt so happy for you,"* that's not really about their achievement. Hitting the home run is their achievement, but your happiness is about you. So, if you want to compliment them, say, *"It was great how you hit that home run. That was a tough pitch, and you really caught it."* Make it specific. And be aware that they will check inside to see if they really did the thing that you admire. In their world, praise has to be earned, so they probably have a rule that prohibits accepting praise for something they didn't actually do. So they will check inside and ask themselves, *"Do I deserve this praise? Can I accept this praise?"*

That means you have to be specific about exactly what you're praising. They may ask, *"What moment are you talking about?"* They want to find the exact thing you're praising, so they can cross-check it inside and make sure they really did it. That's typically one of their rules. They aren't allowed to just accept praise for something without making sure that they really did it. This is another example of the constant self-correction process going on inside them.

During a conflict

At the first hint of conflict, a rigid-patterned person will start to contract inside in order to mute their feelings and control their response. Their awareness will tend to shift up into their head to their left brain. They will become more logical, and their attention will narrow to a point focus on the facts. Then they will use reason and logic to try to solve the problem, even though it's an emotional problem. They won't think of letting the emotion show them how to solve it.

At the first hint of conflict, their attention will narrow to a point focus on the facts.

If there was a heart connection between the two of you, they will likely drop the heart connection, because they're not able to hold a heart connection while they shift up into their head in order to solve the problem logically. So you may notice that very soon after they feel a little unhappy or frustrated, you can no longer find the love connection between the two of you. Don't take this personally. They're not doing it to punish you. It's automatic.

In their attempt to use logic to solve the emotional problem, they may minimize your feelings and try to talk you out of them. They may say, *"Oh, it's really not that bad. You shouldn't feel that way. I mean, come on. It wasn't that big a deal."* You may find this wounding, especially if you're more heart-centered than head-centered.

They're not doing it to personally hurt you. They do this to themselves all the time, or rather, their inner critic does it to them all the time. This is how their inner critic keeps them behaving appropriately. It minimizes and talks them out of their feelings. It tells them they can't have those feelings unless they can justify them. This goes on inside them all the time, and you're just getting a taste of their personal inner hell.

It's also possible that they may feel angry during this upset, but not even know it. I've known rigid-patterned people who were angry about something for months, but could not express it because they didn't even know that they were angry.

When their anger does come out, it tends to be righteous, because they have a belief that you have to be able to justify a feeling before you have the right to have that feeling. You don't just get to have feelings because you have feelings. They have to be the right feelings, and that means they have to be justified. So a rigid-patterned person can't really know they have a feeling until they can justify it. Because of that, when a feeling does rise into their conscious awareness, it arrives with a righteous justification. And that is often doubly true of anger. Try to look underneath that justification for the buried feeling. Remember, in all people, anger is almost always a sign of a hidden personal need. Look for that need, and name it if you can.

The anger of a rigid-patterned person is usually pointed and sharp, and their aim can be quite precise. An aggressive-patterned person's anger is like a bomb; it's just a big explosion that flattens everything in the vicinity. But a rigid-patterned person's anger is different. Their anger is more precise, and may even be intimate, like a dagger to your heart. They have good aim, and if they know you well, they know exactly where to slide the knife in.

You may also feel the drip, drip, drip of their daily corrections, their little suggestions to help you become a more perfect spouse, a more perfect friend, or a more perfect person in general. You're seeing the action that comes from their desire to improve everything. They're attempting to help you become a more perfect version of yourself. In their world, the purpose of life is to improve things, and they're just trying to help you do that. Since for them, "Criticism is caring" they think of this as a form of caring, It's just one more way to help you improve yourself.

Of course, it may not feel to you like caring, and you may not like it. You may want them to love you just the way you are. But loving you the way you are is probably out of reach for a person who is caught in the rigid pattern. Maybe they would like to do that, but it would require that they get out of pattern enough to love someone who is not perfect. That's a big order for them, but if you can frame it as a good thing for them, as an improvement, they may want to achieve it. They may decide to improve themselves enough to be able to do that. But it's not part of the rigid pattern.

So if you feel this drip, drip, drip of little corrections to help you improve, don't take it personally. Again, you're getting a taste of the inner experience that they have all day, every day, as their inner critic tells them what they should do to be a better person. If it's upsetting to you, you may want to limit it in some way. One friend of mine negotiated an agreement with his rigid- and aggressive-patterned girlfriend that she was allowed only three corrections a day. This is an example of how you can use one part of a pattern to control another part. In this case, the rigid pattern's loyalty to agreements was used to modulate the need to improve a boyfriend. As we've said before, when you're expressing your anger, don't send it straight into their space or at their core. (Only a person who does the aggressive pattern can tolerate that.) That becomes an energetic attack, and it's likely to put them into overwhelm and provoke a patterned reaction, in this case, a critic attack. Instead, turn you body at least 90 degrees away from them and send your anger somewhere away from them. If you're inside, send it at the wall. If you're outside and there's a big space, send it out there. They will still see and hear your anger and your complaint, but they won't have to deal with being hit by a blast of your energy. That will make it much easier for them to take in your complaint and respond to it constructively.

In Romance

Just like all kids, kids who are developing the rigid pattern want to please their parents, so they try to be whoever their parents want them to be. If their parents teach them to value performing well above all else, they may learn to abandon their own feelings and needs in order to perform as expected. This habit of abandoning themselves to win their parent's love will leave them with a fear, consciously or unconsciously, that surrendering into love as an adult means losing themselves once again.[3] That scares them and makes them cautious, so their expressions of love are likely to be controlled and appropriate, rather than impulsive and passionate.

They will sincerely feel love, and they will express it, but they will use the approved and accepted forms, such as Hallmark cards or gifts of flowers, instead of some wild and impulsive gesture. Similarly, in sex, their attention will be on doing it well, rather than on surrendering to passionate impulses. If they haven't learned how to do it well, they may be somewhat stiff and mechanical. Or if they have studied sex, they may have become quite a skillful lover. But again, it will be studied and intentional, rather than impulsive or surrendered.

They believe that love has to be earned. Earlier, we talked about their belief that praise has to be earned. They have the same belief about love. In their childhood, love was not freely given. It was awarded for good behavior, and it had to be earned. The idea that someone could love them freely, just as they are, seems strange to them, and they may find it hard to accept. If you're more heart-centered and love people easily, you may feel confused and hurt by their inability to simply let your love in. Again, don't take it personally. You are getting a glimpse of the censoring process that dominates their inner world.

Lastly, you need to be aware that they're in a lifelong romance with perfection. They believe that, if they can just finally make everything perfect, it'll somehow solve everything. So they may be seeking an ideal spouse and an ideal relationship. They may want you to be their ideal spouse, and they may be working hard to make themselves into a person who would merit such an ideal spouse, along with their efforts to improve you. In a romantic relationship, their automatic need to improve everything tends to turn the relationship into a project and makes it something you both have to work on, instead of something to enjoy. To get out of their lifelong romance with perfection, they would need to get out of the pattern.

Summary

The situation that usually leads a person to adopt the rigid pattern is simply that their heart and feelings were ignored, while their performance was constantly monitored, assessed, graded, and corrected. By watching what their parents notice and comment on, a child learns what their parents value. Rigid-patterned people learned that their parents valued their performance, but hardly noticed their feelings.

Often one or both parents did the rigid pattern themselves, sincerely believed it was the Right Way to Live, and diligently taught it to their children. In fact, they saw this teaching as an act of love, and the child received it as an act of love. As a result, the child developed a fierce inner critic and became a faithful believer in The Church of the One Right Way.

When relating to them, the main thing to keep in mind is that they believe that there is only One Right Way for everything and that we must all follow the Rules, lest we disrupt some grand universal order. And since they received all those parental corrections as acts of love, they now expect that you will receive their corrections as acts of love. They may sincerely believe that "Criticism is caring" and therefore be confused when you feel hurt by their corrections. They may also believe that mistakes must be punished, and so devote a great deal of time to finding and correcting even the smallest mistakes.

Remember, this is the internal experience that they have all day, every day, and they have no other experience to compare it to, so they think it is normal. Now, we all make the classic mistake of thinking that everyone else is experiencing life the same way we are, but the faith of rigid-patterned people in The Church of the One Right Way takes this mistake a step further. It not only makes them unaware that other people have different ways of living, it also makes them believe that all those other people are wrong and must be corrected. This is the source of their constant attempts to correct others and convert them to their One Right Way.

> **Tips for Relating to the Rigid Pattern**
>
> - do the Centering Breath and Core practices daily
> - respect their rules and forms
> - put your communication into words
> - keep your agreements with them
> - help them manage their inner critic by agreeing where you can
> - re-frame a conflict into a problem that you can solve together
> - ask them to help you solve *your* problem
> - make your instructions clear and explicit

Relating to the Rigid Pattern

Questions

The need for a plan

"This is textbook my boyfriend. He doesn't want to improve the relationship because there's no clear end goal."

Yes. People who do the rigid pattern need to see the destination and all the steps needed to get there before they can take the first step. They need to see where we are and where we are going so there won't be any surprises. They don't want to just jump in and see what happens. Too scary.

Fear of making mistakes

"Could you please talk a little about fear of making mistakes and the rigid pattern?"

Yes, it's a really big deal. Because, you know, mistakes have to be punished. So if you make a mistake, punishment is coming your way. If you were raised in a rigid-patterned family, then when there was a mistake, somebody had to be blamed, so immediately, the hunt was on. Who did it? Who's to blame? We've got to find them and punish them. So, as soon as anyone discovered a mistake, even if it was a small one, everyone scattered, saying *"I wasn't there." "It wasn't me." "I didn't do it."*

Improving others

"Any tips on how to stop trying to improve friends, romantic partners, etc.? I do this pattern, and I see it's hurting my relationships."

Yes, you have to give up your lifelong romance with perfection. And you have to learn how to know when you're in the rigid pattern and how to get out of it.

Trying to improve everyone hurts relationships because people who do not do the rigid pattern do not believe that the purpose of life is to improve. They don't want other people trying to improve them. If they want to improve themselves, that's one thing. But they don't want others deciding that for them. Just like all of us, they value their own autonomy, and they don't welcome intrusions on it. My guess is that none of us want someone else to come up to us and say, *"Oh, by the way, you're not up to par on this, so I'm going to help you improve it."* So, the way to stop trying to improve others is to get out of the rigid pattern. It's that simple. There's a whole section on this in my earlier book, *The 5 Personality Patterns*.

A vicious inner critic vs rigid pattern

> *"I used to have a vicious inner critic, and I was certainly identified with that, but I don't have rigid as either one of my two patterns."*

Yes, so the question here is this: How does the inner critic show up in the rigid pattern versus other patterns? It's a great question and an important question.

First, notice that everyone has an inner critic. It's a normal and necessary part of ego development. Some inner critics are mild, some are fierce, and some are downright vicious, but everyone has one, no matter what patterns they do.

The difference is this: People who don't do the rigid pattern usually don't regard a critic attack as a good thing. They feel hurt or shamed by it, and they don't like it, especially if it's vicious. They wish it would go away. In contrast, a person who is deeply caught in the rigid pattern regards an attack by their inner critic as a good thing, because it is restoring correctness and order to their life. They regard the voice of their inner critic as the voice of Truth, so they see it as helpful and they try to obey it. That's a big difference.

Relating to emotion

> *"The enduring pattern and the rigid pattern seem to have many similarities in relating to emotion."*

It's true that both patterns restrict emotional expression, but they do it in different ways and for different reasons. Enduring-patterned people feel their feelings, but usually don't express them because doing so would draw attention, which might draw an attack. Their energetic habit is one of holding in. In contrast, rigid-patterned people hold back their expression, check it against their internal rules, and then express the part that is correct. Their energetic habit is one of holding back.

Anxiety and the rigid pattern

"What is the relationship between anxiety and the rigid pattern? Would you say that rigid-patterned people are more prone to be anxious?"

Yes, I would. I think the diagnosis of Generalized Anxiety Disorder was invented for rigid-patterned people. The anxiety is caused by the voice of the inner critic, constantly judging and punishing you for doing anything against its rules. It's like having the correctness police in your head. So yes, I would say that rigid-patterned people tend to be more prone to anxiety than others. But anyone who has a fierce inner critic is likely to also feel a lot of anxiety, no matter which patterns they do.

The need for structure

"Could a heart-centered child, growing up in an unstructured environment, develop the rigid pattern as a way of controlling their world?"

Yes, kids need enough structure to feel safe. They want to be able to predict what's going to happen and know that it'll be okay. And developing the rigid pattern is one way for a kid to give themselves more structure. So a child who needs structure, but is growing up in a very unstructured environment, may try to make more structure by developing the rigid pattern inside themselves. However, I think this is more likely for a head-centered child than a heart-centered child.

Pattern vs skills

"I thought I did the enduring and leaving patterns, but the rigid pattern sounds so familiar — it's my mother and ex-husband of 40 years that I chose to leave. Could I have adopted the rigid pattern as a self-protective measure, living in the world they controlled?"

To figure this out, it's important to notice that a person can learn the skills of a pattern, but not actually adopt the pattern as a safety strategy. For instance, if you were being raised by two rigid-patterned parents, you'd have to learn to follow their rules just to get by. You'd have to learn to keep things in order, be on time, be responsible, keep your agreements, etc. So you would most likely adopt the rigid pattern. But if you're strongly heart-centered, you may not adopt the pattern, but just learn the skills.

Rebelling against the rules

> *"Does rebellion against the rules fall within the rigid pattern? For example, bringing up an emotional topic among people who belong to a culture that deems that to be inappropriate? Or is that the enduring pattern self-sabotaging, or something else?"*

Well, it depends. It could be that this person who is rebelling believes in a different set of rules, so they're rebelling against *this* set of rules. Or, if they do the aggressive pattern, it could be that they don't like rules in general, so they're making a show of breaking the rules. I doubt this would be the self-sabotage of the enduring pattern, because this rebellion is too obvious an act. It's active-aggressive, not passive-aggressive, and people who are caught in the enduring pattern will usually avoid that.

Rigid vs enduring in relating to authority

> *"What's the difference in ways of relating to authority, rigid versus enduring?"*

The rigid pattern respects authority and wants to obey authority. The enduring pattern will say they're going to obey, but then will subtly undermine it by passively resisting. In contrast, a rigid-patterned person will want to do what the authority deems proper.

Fundamentalist religions and cults

> *"Are religious upbringings and cults more responsible for producing rigid-patterned people?"*

I haven't seen any hard data on that. But I do know that the rigid pattern is passed down from parent to child more than any other pattern, apparently because it is intentionally taught to the child, rather than being a reaction to early wounding. And it does seem that fundamental religions and cults would have that attitude when teaching their children. On the other hand, it also seems that many of the people who join fundamental religions and cults already do the rigid pattern, and they join because the strict rules fit them and give them a set of rules that they can believe in. So it may be that rigid-patterned people are simply more likely to join groups with strict rules, rather than that the groups produce them. Or perhaps both are true.

Disregarding boundaries

> *"It seems rigid-patterned people disregard other people's boundaries. They point out a problem they want me to change, and even if it's not a problem for me, they force their perspective and take license to run things the way they want to. In that way, they are aggressive at times. How can we set boundaries?"*

Yes, they believe they have the One Right Way, and you should get on board with their way. However, I haven't seen that the rigid pattern necessarily disregards other people's boundaries. In my experience, the rigid pattern tends to make people more respectful of the boundaries that they're aware of. Often that means that they're aware of and respectful of psychological boundaries, but because they're not energetically sensitive, they don't notice energetic boundaries and tend to violate them. I wonder whether the person that you're talking about runs both the rigid and aggressive patterns. That could be the source of what you're seeing.

Asking for instructions

> *"My husband often states that he has a problem, and I try to provide a solution. That is frustrating to him. Really, he just wants empathy."*

It sounds like maybe you are caught in the rigid pattern, so you think all problems must be solved, but he is not caught in rigid pattern; he just wants to say he has a problem, tell you about his feelings, and then figure it out by himself. So, when he says he has a problem, I would suggest that you ask him for instructions. Ask him, *"Now, are you asking me to simply listen to you as you tell me about your feelings and hold space for you? Or are you asking me to help you solve this problem?"* Then he gets to say which one he wants. If he says he doesn't want your help solving the problem, he just wants you to listen while he talks about how he feels, then that's what you do. Don't assume that he's asking for your help just because he says he has a problem.

Taking ownership of the other person's problem

> *"It seems like merging-patterned people will also take ownership of another person's problem. How do the rigid and merging patterns differ on that?"*

A merging-patterned person will want to help the other person feel good, whereas a rigid-patterned person will want to take ownership of their problem, but it could easily lead to the same behaviors. And many people do both of these patterns.

Getting out of the rigid pattern

> *"How can we get out of the I Am My Performance way of thinking? I'm so attached to the idea of success. I feel like it's really holding me back. I'm gripping so hard that I'm getting in my own way."*

Yes, you need to get out of the rigid pattern. In my book, *The 5 Personality Patterns,* there's a big chapter on each of the patterns, and the last two sections of each chapter are about how to get out of that pattern and how to heal the pattern, so I invite you to consult that. Overall, you need to dis-identify from your inner critic, learn how to tell when you're caught in the pattern and how to get out of it, and develop a stronger felt-sense of presence to avoid going into the pattern so easily. Simply put, you need to practice noticing your feelings and let them guide you, rather than your inner critic. In the first lines of her poem *Wild Geese,*[4] Mary Oliver says it beautifully:

> You do not have to be good.
> You do not have to walk on your knees
> > for a hundred miles through the desert, repenting.
> You only have to let the soft animal of your body
> > love what it loves.

Relating to the Rigid Pattern

- 11 -

The Personality Patterns in Romantic Relationships

Centering Yourself

Before we get into the chapter, let's practice the Centering Breath and Core again. Each time you do this practice, you're developing the core skills you need to get out of whatever patterns you do and become an emotionally healthy adult.

Imagine a column inside your body, from the crown of your head down to the bottom of your torso. And imagine that you can breathe in through the bottom of that column and fill it up. Now, breathe in through your nose and fill the whole column with breath, from the bottom up to the top. Then, breathing out through pursed lips, send all that breath down and out the bottom of the column. Do it again several more times: in and all the way up, then out and all the way down. Again, in and up, and out and down. And up once more, all the way up to the top, and then back down and all the way out.

And now put your awareness on your Core, that column in the center of your body. Maybe gently breathe into it and feel into it, or imagine that you can see it. And just notice what you find there.

Now let your attention remain on that column in your body, from the crown of your head all the way down to the bottom of your torso, and gently let that column begin to extend down deep into the earth and form an energetic connection between you and the earth. This is the Grounding process. I recommend that you do these practices frequently, throughout the day, to bring you back to your center and stabilize yourself.

Your aim is to get used to putting your attention there every day, and eventually every minute of every day, until you have embodied a felt-sense of each skill and it is part of your awareness all the time. This is where we want to get to with all of the basic energy skills: feeling your core, grounding into the earth, holding an energetic edge, and differentiating me from not me.

How the Patterns Interact in Romantic Relationships

So far, we've talked about primary and secondary (or backup) patterns. A person's primary pattern is the first one they go into, and their secondary or backup pattern is the one they switch to if their distress gets high enough. But many people are so caught in one of those patterns that, when you first get to know them, you may think it's their only pattern.

We're going to talk about the different relationship combinations as if person A has only one pattern and person B has only one pattern. We're going to do it that way for several reasons, even though, in reality, both people do two patterns and maybe even three.

First, since most people have not done much inner work, they're probably in only one of their patterns at a time. They're either in their primary pattern or their backup pattern, but not in both. Also, if you look at only one pattern for each person, there are only 15 combinations, but if you look at two patterns in each person, there are 55 combinations, which is so many that it becomes confusing rather than clarifying.

When you get down to that level of detail, there are many other factors that are important, factors like: Which patterns were their parents caught in? How about their siblings? Were they the oldest child, the youngest child, or a middle child? Did they have older brothers or sisters who were beating them up, running away from them, or parenting them? What cultural and religious environment did they grow up in? And what did their culture and religion tell them about how they should behave? All of those details can be important, as well. If you're exploring this for just yourself and your lover, I think you can get into that level of detail quite productively. But I doubt it would be useful to try to lay out 55 different combinations of patterns in the abstract, without considering all those other factors.

So, as we go through the 15 possible combinations, we'll be focusing on each person's 'main pattern'. By 'main pattern', I mean the pattern that the person identifies with the most and stays in most of the time, whether it's their primary or backup pattern. Many people have a main pattern. Often they do it so much that, when you first get to know them, you may think it's their only pattern.

The Ideal Relationship is *Presence + Presence*

The first question everyone asks is, *"What's the best combination for me? Who shall I look for to have a good relationship?"*

And my answer is always the same: the best relating happens when neither of you are in pattern, but when both you and your partner are present. Your presence interacting with their presence creates the best relationship. That happens only when both of you are present in the here and now, creating responses attuned to what's really going on, here and now. You're not automatically replaying conditioned responses from the past, which is what our personality patterns do. They are patterns of thinking, feeling, and behaving that were created in the past to respond to difficult situations in the past.

Presence relating to presence creates the best relationship.

So when you're caught in a pattern, you are literally caught in the past. Your perception of the present is replaced by thoughts, feelings, and impulses from the past. That's not optimal. It's much better to be present here in this moment and able to compose a response designed for this moment.

The best relating also happens when both people have the skills needed to inquire into their own current feelings, needs, and desires, and also to hold space for their partner's inquiry. And they'll find the best solutions to their problems through intentional collaboration, that is, when they can design their response together and implement it together.

The Personality Patterns in Romantic Relationships

So what creates the best relationship? It is presence relating to presence, not some particular combination of the five patterns. I will say that over and over again. Notice also that in saying it, I've used a verb — *relating* — rather than our usual noun — *relationship*. I say it that way to emphasize the fact that relating is something that we *do*, not a static thing that exists on its own.

Same-Pattern Relationships

So let's look at the 15 different combinations. The first five are same-pattern relationships, such as leaving and leaving, merging and merging, etc. They are relationships in which both people do the same main pattern.

No matter what sort of relationship it is, if you both do the same pattern, you have an innate understanding of each other. Whether the other person is your partner, your friend, your child, your parent, or your co-worker, if you both do the same pattern, you have certain commonalities. You both use the same safety strategy, value the same things, and communicate in the same way on the same channels. Those are big advantages, and they make your interactions much simpler.

If you both do the same pattern, you have an innate understanding of each other, but you are also missing the same skills.

You also have the same set of skills and understand each other's skills. Unfortunately, that also means that you lack the same skills. Each pattern requires that you practice and develop certain skills, and those skills become the gifts of the pattern. But there are other skills that it does not require and that you do not develop. So those skills are missing, and, sooner or later, you will need to develop them. That's the situation in same-pattern relationships.

Let's go through them.

Leaving + Leaving

Here we have two people who like to play, create, and wander through lots of different dimensions. Not just this physical dimension of time and space, but lots of dimensions. So it's quite possible that they will get into playing and creating together in various dimensions and have a lot of fun together. And they may especially love delving into the worlds of magic and fantasy, like the Harry Potter books.

They're both head-centered, so they're both really into ideas, especially generalized, abstract ideas. But not ideas about personal feelings. Not *This is how I feel about you.* That's a little too close to home. Both of them are ignoring their bodies and their feelings, so they won't ask each other about that much, but instead will silently agree, *"No, we're not going there."*

Since they both communicate mainly on the psychic channel, they're probably pretty good at sending ideas and pictures back and forth, and that's their way of communicating with each other. And it's actually a more efficient way to communicate than using words. So they probably have a great time communicating psychically and not saying much in words. When they do use words, their words may get jumbled up, but they don't care, because the words aren't important to them. They already got the message on the psychic channel, so it doesn't matter. They know exactly what they're talking about. But a third person listening to them — a person who hears only the words and isn't on the psychic channel — has no idea what they're talking about. So that person may feel lost and frustrated.

Neither of the leaving-patterned people will be good at navigating time and space, unless their other pattern does that well — for instance, the rigid pattern. But failing that, you have two people who often get lost and arrive late, but probably don't care. They're on an adventure and having a good time finding out what will happen next.

Merging + Merging

Now let's look at two merging-patterned people together in a love relationship. For them, the most important factor is that they are heart-centered people in a heart-centered relationship. So they agree that feeling connected is the most important thing and they provide that for each other.

Both of them feel a lot and want to talk about it. There's a lot of talk, and it's about feelings — good feelings, bad feelings, feelings about me, feelings about you, feelings about my friend, my co-worker, my parent, my child, everybody. Lots of talk about feelings and lots of taking care of each

The Personality Patterns in Romantic Relationships

other's feelings: small gifts and favors, presents and praise. Connection and feelings will be their main focus.

While there will be lots of talk, they will probably not take much action. Neither of them has a felt-sense of self, and the skills of will and strength are not developed, so taking action toward a desired goal is not easy for them. Feeling the desire is easy, but taking effective action is not.

Both of them are missing a lot of developmental skills, including the basic energetic skills, like Core, Ground, Edge, and Me/Not Me. So navigating through the physical world and through life may be very difficult for them. Perhaps even more difficult than it is for leaving-patterned people, because merging-patterned people often have trouble with the basic life skills, like earning a living and taking responsibility for their actions. It may be that neither person in this couple is good at navigating life. They may be experts at feeling and relating skills, but not good at life skills.

There are two forms of this pattern, simple and compensated. A person who is more in the simple merging pattern usually takes a child role in interactions, while a person who is more in the compensated merging pattern usually takes a parent role. So the interactions of this couple may appear to be child-child, child-parent, or parent-parent, depending on the couple and the moment.

Enduring + Enduring

Here we have two people who are both belly-centered. Not head-centered and not heart-centered — belly-centered. And since the enduring pattern respects other people's space and privacy more than any other pattern, these two people are really good at respecting each other's space. They don't invade each other's space, and they don't want anyone invading their own space. They don't mess with each other, and they don't want anyone messing with them.

In contrast to the merging + merging couple, neither of these people wants to talk about feelings. They don't want to express their feelings. They don't want to take a position on anything. They don't want to argue. And they really don't want to talk about it. In fact, they will be happy to not talk at all for hours. They may both be very happy standing 50 yards away from each other, fly fishing in a river all day, while nobody says a word. No one is bothering them, and they love it.

Both people are deeply grounded. As a couple, they are terrific at grounding. However, it's also possible for them to go down so deep that they get stuck and can't move. So there may be a kind of heavy, ponderous quality in their relationship, a sense of slogging and plodding. Conversations may move slowly. In general, things just don't go very fast. People who do the enduring pattern have the slowest internal pace of any of the patterns. People who do the leaving and rigid patterns have a faster internal pace, but the enduring pattern is the slowest.

There may be a fair amount of complaining in their conversations. It's important to know that, for them, complaining can have two different meanings. There is the one that most people think of, which is, if you're complaining about it, you're saying, *"I don't like it, and I want you to change it. I want you to do it differently."* And that may be what these two are saying. But for them, complaining is also a way to talk about a feeling without actually saying that they're having the feeling. It's an indirect, protected, passive-aggressive way to talk about your feelings. They can imply that they're having the feeling, without ever taking responsibility for having it. So that may also be what they're doing.

Doing it that way may be just fine for them. They may feel good about it. Whereas a third person, someone who doesn't do the enduring pattern, may think they're saying that someone should change something, and then may feel confused and frustrated when nothing changes.

Are you seeing how different these couples can be from each other?

Aggressive + Aggressive

Here we have two people who naturally have a big flow of life energy through their bodies. They enjoy the big flow, but it often becomes a problem when they're around others who are not also aggressively-patterned. They have to continually dial down their energy flow so that it does not put the other people into distress. If they don't, the other people keep saying, *"Can you tone it down, please? It's too much!"*

But when they're with another person who also does the aggressive pattern, or even better, with a whole group of people who all do the aggressive pattern, they get to turn up the dial as far as they want. If they're in an aggressive + aggressive love relationship, they get to let it fly. They get to just let their big energy run, whether the two of them are playing, having sex, or fighting. Whether they're competing against each other, or they're on the same team competing against someone else. Whether they're working together or separately, they get to just let it go. For aggressive-patterned people, this is a huge relief, and they love it.

Both these people are good manifesters: they have will, strength, and focused attention. And their attention is focused on power and dominance, so they are good at wielding power and manifesting what they want in the world. They may be known as a power couple. As in the previous couple, both people are belly-centered, but here they are not well grounded. Their lack of grounding makes them unstable, like a tall building with no foundation, so their big manifestations may collapse.

They're both probably addicted to adrenaline and action, so their bodies stay adrenalized all the time, with lots of force and action, but no resting or down time.

Unless they're psychologically sophisticated, they tend to use force to solve every problem. You can imagine them as a couple who have only one tool in their toolbox, and it's a hammer. So to them, every problem looks like a nail, and they just hit it as hard as possible.

Rigid + Rigid

Both people in this couple have joined the Church of the One Right Way, and their rules tell them what that right way is. However, they may have different sets of rules, each with their own One Right Way.

For example, if one was raised in a very rigid, rule bound, fundamentalist religious community, and the other was raised in a free love commune, they will likely have totally different sets of rules, especially about sex. Or if one is a democratic socialist, and the other is an authoritarian, again they will have completely different sets of rules, especially about good government. When these two people get together, their first fights will be about the rules, and their first task will be to sort out which rules are the right ones, the rules that they will obey together.

But after they get the rules hashed out, things will get easier. Once that is done, they will probably be quite productive together, because both of them are committed to improvement and achievement. They want everything they do to be excellent, so they will work tirelessly together to make things excellent.

How to Have Better Relationships

They are going to work hard and achieve a lot. But they will play very little, unless one of their rules says that they should play — and play in this way, at this time and place. Maybe they believe that they should go dancing at least once a week, or play dominoes or cards together. If they have a rule about how and when to play, they'll do it. If not, play will be a little dicey for them, because being playful is being spontaneous. And if they're being spontaneous, they're not being careful about what they say and do, which means they might do something wrong or inappropriate. So, play may be rare for this couple.

As they attempt to always be correct and appropriate, both members of this couple will tend to hold back their feelings, so their emotional connection will probably be a little bit formal and muted. They are more likely to express their affection for each other in conventional, approved ways, like giving flowers, a card, or a present on a birthday or holiday. It's unlikely that either will be seen standing out on the street, below the other's window, loudly singing them a love song.

They will communicate mostly in words. Words are the main channel for rigid-patterned people, so their meaning will be mostly in the words, and very little will be happening on the psychic channel. For them, even the melody may not be important. They will be listening to the words.

And they will use their words to make agreements with each other about what they're going to do and not do, about what's important and not important. Since they organize their lives according to agreements, to them, those understandings will have the importance of contracts. They will strive to keep those agreements, and breaking one will be regarded as a major transgression. Agreements will be a very big deal for this couple.

The Personality Patterns in Romantic Relationships

Questions

Introducing the patterns to clients

"How do we present the patterns to clients? Saying 'you're an aggressive pattern' does not go well."

Yes, I learned this myself when I was first studying these patterns. So first, don't tell someone that they *are* a pattern. When you do that, you've turned them into an unchanging thing, instead of an evolving process. You've told them they're a type, which means they're stuck there. This is not a typology, but a map of personality.

People are not their patterns, but their presence. Their presence is who they really are. and their patterns block their presence from shining out into the world. Each pattern starts out as a safety strategy, but it becomes a mask covering our presence. So our goal is not to be in pattern more efficiently. Our goal is to get out of our patterns and be present.

In terms of introducing it to clients, don't start talking to them about the map, but about themselves. If you suspect they do a certain pattern, ask if they do the safety strategy of that pattern to feel safer. Ask if some of the feelings and beliefs of that pattern apply to them. After a while, they'll probably be impressed with how much you seem to know about them. I have had clients ask, *"How do you know this about me? Are you psychic?"* And I say, *"No, but there's a map of personality that makes it easy to understand what's going on inside a person, and I know that map."*

That conversation will make your client curious and they'll want to know what else it says about them. Then you can give them something about the personality patterns to read, or suggest that they look at the 5 personality patterns website, where there's a short summary of each pattern. So don't tell people what patterns they do; ask them questions about their life, based on which patterns you suspect they do.

Asking questions works better than asserting something because, if you declare that something is true, some people will automatically want to argue that it's not true. Even when they know it is true, they may need to argue the point just to defend their autonomy. So instead of asserting something, ask people questions like, *"Is this true for you? Do you do this?"*

Shared patterns

> *"With merging and merging, I find the second pattern becomes more important, and we take the merging pattern for granted."*

Yes, when the two people do the same pattern, they will meet in that pattern and often take that for granted. For them, it will be like, *"Well, that's just the way we are. That's natural. Doesn't everybody do that?"* And then any misunderstandings between them will most likely arise from the differences between their other patterns.

Three patterns

> *"I think I have three patterns: merging, enduring, and rigid. Is this common?"*

No, it's relatively rare that a person does three patterns, but it does happen sometimes. What's more common is that people who do the compensated merging pattern appear to do three patterns because the compensation layer has the flavor of a third pattern. They're not actually doing the third pattern, but they have the flavor of it, because the compensation is an imitation of it. And the way you can tell whether it's the compensation layer is that under pressure, the compensation will dissolve.

Aggressive-patterned couples communication

> *"How do aggressive-patterned couples communicate with each other?"*

Short declarative sentences and big energy. Sometimes there's yelling, so things can get loud. I remember a client whose 5-year-old son did the aggressive pattern, and she had discovered that, if she matched his energy, that would actually reassure and calm him. So when he would yell *"Mom!"* as loud as he could from the other room, she would just yell his name back at the same volume, as if to say, *"Yeah, I'm here."* She didn't say, *"What do you want?"* or ask him not to shout. She would just yell his name back. It's sort of like returning the serve in tennis.

Each pattern communicates in the way that feels comfortable to them, and for aggressive-patterned people, that often involves big energy.

The Personality Patterns in Romantic Relationships

Effects of Grounding

"What does it mean for an aggressive couple that they have no grounding? And what follows for the enduring couple that they are grounded?"

Being grounded is good for everybody. It gives you a strong foundation, and it makes you stable. When aggressive-patterned people are running big energy, but they're not grounded, they can easily get top heavy and unstable. Think of it the same way you would think of a tall building — you want the building to have a strong foundation so that it doesn't fall over. The same is true for a person — being grounded gives you a strong foundation and makes you stable.

Since an enduring-patterned couple are both deeply grounded, they are both very stable. But they're using their connection down into the earth as more than just a foundation. They're using it as a refuge, a place to hide, and because of that, they can get stuck down there, unable to move or take action.

Everybody needs to learn to energetically ground themselves into the earth. If you already do that, great. But if you don't, you need to learn it.

A grounded aggressive couple

"What would the behavior of an aggressive couple look like if they were well grounded?"

They would be stable as well as powerful, and so more effective in everything they did. They would be more present and less unconsciously scared, so they would be more aware of the needs of others and would likely turn down the volume on the amount of energy they're sending out.

Different-Pattern Relationships

Now let's explore relationships in which the two individual's main patterns are different. If the other pattern that these two people do is the same one, they will probably do a lot of their communication through their shared pattern. It gives them a common language and world view, as well as a way to understand and communicate with each other. So they may shift to their shared pattern when they really need to communicate with each other.

Couples who do not share any patterns lack a common language and world view. However, each has skills the other lacks.

On the other hand, couples who do not share any patterns lack a common language and world view, so they find it more difficult to understand and communicate with each other. For them, learning about the personality patterns can make a huge difference in their relationship. Understanding their own patterns will help break the control their patterns have over them, and learning about their partner's patterns will help them understand, perhaps for the first time, how their partner experiences the world. Many couples have emailed me to exclaim that learning about the personality patterns *"saved our marriage."*

So let's go through all 10 combinations, starting with the developmentally youngest patterns and moving through the various possibilities.

Leaving + Merging

Both these people like to play games, be happy, and have fun. So, this couple is probably going to play a lot of games and have a lot of fun together. Because joy is a heart-centered state, merging-patterned people are able to experience it more easily than most, and they tend to draw their partners into also feeling joy. So this couple may have happy times together more often than couples with other combinations of patterns.

Because both patterns want to avoid conflict, both people will avoid expressing unhappy feelings and may not even be aware of them. So it is unlikely that this couple will be good at exploring their disputes and resolving them. Instead, their problems may just get swept under the rug and ignored for years.

The Personality Patterns in Romantic Relationships

Both people are perceptive on the energetic channel, so they will likely do most of their communicating there, while regarding the verbal channel as less important. But they have somewhat different agendas in their communication. The leaving pattern wants creativity, while the merging pattern wants connection. So one person will be more focused on creativity and the other on connection. When they have a conflict, it's likely to be over that difference.

The merging-patterned person's agenda will often be, *How much time are we spending together? Are we connecting about personal feelings? Is there enough cuddling and lovey-dovey stuff?* However, that much focus on personal feelings can be scary for a leaving-patterned person. They're more comfortable talking about something impersonal, like big, abstract ideas. So they may want to move away from personal feelings and toward ideas and creativity.

This dynamic will probably play out physically as well. The leaving-patterned partner will move away to feel safer, and the merging-patterned partner will move closer to feel safer. They will disagree about what psychologists call 'optimal distance' — how close they want to be, both physically and emotionally. So they may find themselves in a dynamic that goes like this: one moves away → other moves closer → one moves away → other moves closer. If the merging-patterned partner initiates it by moving in closer, the leaving-patterned partner will respond by moving away. If the leaving-patterned partner initiates it by moving away, the merging-patterned partner will respond by moving in closer.

Neither of these people have much in the way of developmental skills, so they will both struggle and often feel overwhelmed by life. And that will be more true if the merging-patterned person prefers the simple merging form. If they prefer the compensated merging form, they at least have a pretend core. It's not a real, felt-sense core, and it will dissolve under pressure, but it's a start. They've got the beginnings of will and strength — not yet real will and strength — but it's something. So they will have more developmental skills and be more able to deal with life.

The compensation will also cause the merging-patterned partner to take the good parent role toward their partner. So, this couple may develop a parent-child dynamic, with the compensated merging-patterned person in the parent role and the leaving-patterned person in the child role.

Leaving + Enduring

Suppose you have a leaving-patterned person and an enduring-patterned person in a love relationship together. Both of these people have a strong awareness of energy in general, and they're watching for other people's intentions, because they don't want to get hurt. They both want to avoid conflict and trouble, but they have developed different ways to get away from it.

Neither of them is paying much attention to their heart center, so they may have difficulty even knowing what they feel and want. And both are somewhat inhibited in talking about their feelings, especially their unhappy feelings. So neither person is good at talking about what they don't like about the relationship and what they wish would change.

Many relationships are based on a trade, and the trade is what holds the relationship together. Here, the enduring-patterned person provides grounding for the leaving-patterned person. The leaving-patterned person is a bit like an untethered balloon, a balloon that's in danger of being blown away by the wind. By providing grounding, the enduring-patterned person holds the string to that balloon and keeps it from blowing away.

In return, the leaving-patterned person gives the enduring-patterned person a lot of space. Since they don't want a lot of contact, they don't bug the enduring-patterned person with questions about their inner experience. They're not over there all the time, asking, *"What do you feel about this? What do you feel about that?"*

Remember, as an adult, there are two ways you can get the benefits of a skill you failed to develop as a child. One way is to develop the skill as an adult so you can do it for yourself. But the other way is get someone else to do it for you, often as part of a romantic relationship. In this couple, the leaving-patterned person is getting grounding in exchange for giving the enduring-patterned person space, and that trade is the basis for their relationship.

Leaving + Aggressive

Here we have a situation in which the two people both have awareness of energy, but they're watching for very different things. The leaving-patterned person uses their awareness of energy to see conflict coming and get away from it, while the aggressive-patterned person uses their awareness of energy to measure who has power and how to win the fight. They're used to winning and don't avoid conflict. So this couple will disagree about what to do regarding danger, because one person wants to flee and the other wants to stay and fight.

There's another problem in this pairing that often makes being together difficult. The aggressive-patterned person's energy flow is so big that it's often more than the leaving-patterned person can tolerate. Let's say they're playing a game together and having a good time. If the aggressive-patterned person gets excited, their flow of energy will probably get so big that it scares the leaving-patterned person. Even when it's all positive feelings, it's still so much that they feel overwhelmed and need to leave. Then the aggressive-patterned person feels abandoned and says, *"Hey, I thought we were having a good time together. Why did you leave?"* This is a real problem for this couple. And it's even more of a problem when the aggressive-patterned person is angry about something, even if their anger is totally separate from the relationship. Maybe the bill for repairing the car was bigger than expected, and they're mad at the mechanic and the garage. Even though they're mad at someone else, the mere presence of angry energy scares the leaving-patterned person, and they flee.

So, this particular combination can make for a relationship that's very rocky and difficult to sustain, because they habitually run very different amounts of energy through their bodies. And the fact that neither of them is grounded only makes it worse.

As we've said before, in order to be an emotionally mature adult, every person needs all of the basic energy skills: Core, Ground, Edge, and Me/Not Me — all of them.

Leaving + Rigid

In terms of the stages of psychological development, the leaving and rigid patterns are as far apart as you can get in terms of age and skills. That means that the two people in this couple have very different sets of skills and abilities, and that makes it hard for them to understand each other. One is communicating mostly on the psychic channel, and the other is communicating mostly on the verbal channel. And neither is good at listening to the other person's channel, which can lead to a lot of misunderstandings.

But the fact that they have such different sets of skills also means that they can help each other out by doing what the other person can't. For instance, perhaps only the rigid-patterned person is able to reconcile a checkbook, so they do that task for both of them. Or the leaving-patterned person is more comfortable with play, so they coax the rigid-patterned person into playing with them, which the rigid-patterned person wants to do, but feels wary of. Typically the leaving-patterned person will take the lead on fun and games, and the rigid-patterned person will take the lead on work and structure. Here again, a trade is part of the foundation of the relationship.

Neither member of this couple really wants to tune into their feelings, and they both hesitate to express them. They both think, *"My feelings aren't important. No one cares about my feelings."* So they may also unconsciously help each other ignore their feelings as much as possible.

Lastly, both of these patterns tend to be head-centered and visual, which causes them to have a very rapid inner pace. So when these two are together, their pace will pick up, and they may do a lot together fast.

Merging + Enduring

Again, we have conflicting agendas. The safety strategy of the merging-patterned person depends on connection, so they're frequently sending their little feelers into the enduring-patterned person's body to discover, *How are you feeling? How do you feel about me? Do you want to get closer right now?* But the safety strategy of the enduring-patterned person depends on disconnection, on solitude and space, so they regard those little feelers penetrating them as a threat and an invasion. That scares them, and they don't like it.

So this couple will tend to fall into conflict over the optimal distance between them. Each time the merging-patterned person moves closer, the enduring-patterned person takes more space by moving away. Each time the enduring-patterned person takes more space, the merging-patterned person tries to move closer. And, since neither one understands the other's real motives, they tend to take it personally and feel hurt.

But there are benefits in this pairing, as well as problems. If they can learn to respect their partner's space, the merging-patterned person's tugging can get the enduring-patterned person to come out of their hiding place and engage more in life, which is good for them. And the enduring-patterned person is providing grounding for the merging-patterned person, who definitely needs it.

This process of grounding through another person's body is ideally the way a child learns how to ground themselves. As a young child is held and carried, they naturally ground to their parent's body. If their parent is grounded, by the time the child goes to grade school, their body has learned this skill from their parent's body, and they can do it on their own. But, since most of our parents didn't know how to ground themselves, most of us never learned this and still cannot do it. But we still need it to feel supported and stable, so finding a partner who can ground us is the next best thing.

Lastly, both of these people try to avoid conflicts, and they both do it by accommodating and agreeing with the other person, at least superficially. To avoid a fight, they'll say they agree, even when they really don't. So while each person may be sincerely trying to keep the other happy, they also may be ignoring a real problem between them. It can be difficult for them to finally get down to the real problem, explore it, and resolve it.

Merging + Aggressive

Here, the most energetically feminine pattern is in a relationship with the most energetically masculine pattern. That creates a lot of sexual spark and a lot of heat in this relationship. But remember that we're talking about their *energy* being feminine and masculine; we're not talking about their bodies, so this remains true, no matter what bodies they're wearing. They can both have male bodies; they can both have female bodies. It can be female and male; it can be male and female. So don't think this is only about their bodies. It's mostly energetic.

Now, it is also true that, if you're wearing a female body, your body runs feminine energy more easily. And if you're wearing a male body, your body runs masculine energy more easily. But we all run both feminine and masculine energy, so there are couples in which the woman is running more masculine energy and the man is running more feminine energy. We've all seen examples of that.

In this couple, where the energetic polarity between their patterns is creating so much sexual spark, it's often the sex that's holding the relationship together, even though they have a hard time understanding each other. And they will often acknowledge that by saying something like, "*We don't really get along, but man, the sex is great.*" It's the energetic polarity that's keeping them together.

Again, they each contribute something to this. The merging-patterned person, no matter their gender, is opening the door to the heart center. They're contributing heart qualities, like beauty and love, to the relationship. They've probably decorated the house beautifully. And the aggressive-patterned person, no matter their gender, is contributing will, strength, and action. They're getting things done. The aggressive pattern is belly-centered, and these are belly-centered attributes. Neither person in this couple is grounded, but there's a lot of energy and heat and action.

Couples with this combination of patterns often get together quickly for the hot sex, but may blow apart just as quickly because they just can't figure each other out. Along with the heat, there may be a lot of explosions and drama. Because they're experiencing the world so differently, they find it very hard to understand each other and communicate productively. For this relationship to last, each person has to make peace with how different they are and learn to look for similarity elsewhere. They will each need friends with whom they can do the things that their patterns like to do, because they cannot get that from their partner.

They can reduce the drama by learning to ground themselves. As each of them becomes more grounded, they will feel more calm and stable as individuals, and their relationship will become more calm and stable as well.

Merging + Rigid

Here we have a situation where both patterns, and therefore both people, lack a felt-sense of core. So neither person is able to self-reference, at least not through these two patterns. Instead of self-referencing to get information about what they feel and want, they both reference something else. The merging-patterned person references others, and the rigid-patterned person references a set of rules.

But while they're not good at referencing their own core and being true to themselves, they are good at doing and being what's expected. So these two people are being who others expect them to be, both as individuals and as a couple. That means they're likely to be a pretty conventional couple, not a unique or quirky one. They've been practicing this for a long time, and they're probably pretty good at it. They perform as expected by their culture and religion, and are likely successful in many different arenas of life. One or both of them may be professionally and financially successful, and they are likely well-liked by their colleagues and peers. They may even be famous for giving the best parties.

However, emotional depth and authenticity are minimal or missing for this couple. Neither person is good at that skill, but they also aren't wishing that they had a more emotionally intimate and vulnerable connection. It's probably not something that either of them has experienced, so they're not complaining or wanting more of it. They may not even be aware that it's possible.

They will likely communicate their love for each other in relatively formal, conventional ways, such as Hallmark cards, flowers, and gifts on birthdays and holidays. Both will strive to do what's expected, make the other happy, and just be normal.

Enduring + Aggressive

This is a very different couple, because here we have two people who do have core. This is the only combination where both patterns have a felt-sense of core and are therefore able to self-reference. Notice how different this is from other couples, where neither has a felt-sense of core.

On the other hand, these two people try to feel safer in opposite ways. One person tries to feel safer by acting and the other tries to feel safer by not acting. The aggressive-patterned person tries to be an irresistible force, a force that makes everyone else bend to their will and do what they want. But the enduring-patterned person tries to be an immovable object, an object that cannot be moved by any force. They refuse to bend to anyone's will and automatically resist everything, just for the sake of resisting.

So in this couple, we have a situation where the irresistible force meets the immovable object. What happens? Over time, this opposition proves helpful to them both. That's because the aggressive-patterned person, as they keep pushing to get what they want, is providing a lot of initiative and energy, which helps the enduring-patterned person get going and do something in life. And the enduring-patterned person refuses to be intimidated by the aggressive-patterned person's threats, so they don't respond or comply — they just ground more deeply. (In fact, they are providing grounding for the whole situation.)

Eventually, the aggressive-patterned person realizes that their method isn't working, and they think, *"I need to find some other way to get what I want. I want to be with this person, but trying to dominate them isn't working."* That is typically what causes the aggressive-patterned person to start looking for an approach besides just using force. And that opens up a whole new way of relating, both for them and for their partner.

So this combination is often beneficial for both partners in this couple. Not easy, but good for both of them.

Enduring + Rigid

Both of these patterns tend to be cautious, and both tend to be emotionally inhibited. So it's quite likely that both people in this couple will avoid expressing personal feelings and needs. Expressing personal feelings would be a risk, and they avoid risks, so there isn't much emotional expression going on.

Neither of these patterns opens the heart center, either for themselves or for the other, so their love connection may often be unspoken. It may seem tenuous on the surface, even if underneath it is strong. They may love each other deeply, but they probably don't talk about it much. They don't get effusive about it, and big, romantic gestures are unlikely for either of them.

On the other hand, when they set out to do something together, they'll probably be great at it. The rigid-patterned person will jump right in and start organizing and planning it. They may say, *"Okay, first, we need to do A, and then B, and then C, and then D, and then E. And by the way, I've already ordered all the stuff we'll need. It'll be here tomorrow."*

The enduring-patterned person will ground the whole project and provide the deep strength to keep going, no matter what — to be undeterred by obstacles or setbacks, and not get reactive if somebody else objects. Together, the two of them will just keep pushing through, so they may be very, very successful in accomplishing things together.

When they're out in public together, the rigid-patterned person is likely to do the talking for both of them, and the enduring patterned person will likely be happy to let them.

The thing they're most likely to disagree about will be their pace and speed. The inner pace of the rigid-patterned person is fast, while the inner pace of the enduring patterned person is slow, so they may have trouble agreeing on how fast they want to move through life.

Aggressive + Rigid

Here we have one person who has a big flow of energy and another person who has good aim. So together, they have both big energy and the ability to aim that energy in exactly the right way to make things happen. With this combination, they can accomplish their agenda, whatever it is.

On the other hand, the heart center is not well developed in either of them. They're both kind of blind to feelings — they don't notice their own feelings, their partner's feelings, or anyone's feelings. So as they're out there in the world, accomplishing big things, they may often be running over other people without even noticing it. In general, their relationship is much more focused on action and accomplishment than on tenderness and connection. And it may be that both of them are totally okay with that.

Neither of them is good at grounding. So with all this big energy, their projects can get top heavy and unstable, and that can lead to problems. The energetic principle is this: in order to remain stable as you build a bigger and bigger flow of energy, you must be able to ground the charge you are building, and your energy field must be strong enough to contain and hold all the charge. If you try to hold and use more charge than you can contain and ground, you will become top heavy and unstable, and your project may collapse or explode, either literally or metaphorically. This principle is true for an individual, a group, or an organization, no matter its size. So in order to accomplish big things together, both members of this couple need to learn all of the basic energy skills, and especially Grounding.

Summary

Let me say it again: the best relationship is presence meeting presence. No one is in pattern. Both people are present, able to feel their feelings, state their feelings, hold space for the other person's feelings, and cooperate in making decisions and solving problems. That's what I recommend you look for. But to attract it, you will have to cultivate those skills in yourself.

So your first task is to learn about the five personality patterns, discern which patterns you get caught in, and develop the energy skills you need to help you shift out of pattern and back to presence, again and again throughout the day. And since the traumas still stuck in your body fuel your patterns, you will also need to clear out of your body as much of that old trauma as you can.

Fortunately, energy psychology now has many tools to do that. These tools have been missing in traditional psychology and talk therapy for a hundred years, but energy psychology has finally developed them. Clearing the old traumas out of your body is still work and will take some time, but it is finally possible.

Questions

Healing the patterns

"Does one focus on the primary pattern to heal? Or do you need to address both?"

You'll need to address both, but start with whatever is up and causing you trouble at the moment. And remember that embodying the basic energy skills and developing a felt-sense of presence is a necessary part of healing any of the patterns.

Parenting

"How can parents use their understanding of this work to make adjustments in how they parent their children so that no patterns are created?"

I think it's very possible to use your knowledge of the patterns to understand your child better and be a better parent to them: to understand their habits of attention, how to interact with them, and what they need to thrive.

But I don't think it's possible to create a childhood in which no patterns are created. And I don't know that it's even desirable, because as you develop your patterns, you're also practicing the skills needed for those patterns. Frequently those turn out to be the skills that you will need in order to accomplish something big in your life. So instead of trying to create children without patterns, aim to help them be more present and wear their patterns lightly.

How other patterns might effect you

"How would we feel being next to a person who does a different pattern?"

You might have very different feelings, depending on which patterns you do and which patterns they do. People who do the same pattern often feel a kind of familiarity and connection, while people who do very different patterns may feel scared or overwhelmed. For example, a

The Personality Patterns in Romantic Relationships

leaving-patterned person who sits down next to an aggressive-patterned person may feel scared and want to get away from their big flow of energy. On the other hand, an aggressive-patterned person who sits down next to another aggressive-patterned person may feel excited by their big flow of energy, and they may think, *Oh, boy, this is fun! Let's go! Let's boogie!* So what you feel when sitting next to someone depends on which patterns you do and which patterns they do — along with other factors, of course.

Switching patterns during a conflict

"Can people change patterns during a conflict? How does the backup pattern replace the primary pattern?"

Yes, as their distress rises during a conflict, people do change patterns. As they reach their internal threshold, they will switch from their primary pattern to their backup pattern. If they haven't done much inner work, their entire attitude and approach will shift. In some people, the change is dramatic, and you can see it clearly as their first safety strategy is replaced by their second safety strategy.

I know a married couple who demonstrate this clearly. Her primary pattern is the rigid pattern, but under pressure, she will switch into her backup, which is the aggressive pattern. His primary pattern is the leaving pattern, but under pressure, he will switch into his backup, which is also the aggressive pattern.

Most of the time when they're interacting, they're in their primary patterns, so it's her rigid pattern interacting with his leaving pattern. He's getting more vague as he tries to get away, and she's getting more focused as she tries to pin him down. But if their distress rises to the point where their disagreement turns into a fight, both of them will switch into their backup, which is the aggressive pattern, and then it becomes a completely different dynamic. Then it's war.

If this kind of switch happens within you, take note of it and use it as a signal that you're very upset, and you need to do something to soothe yourself and return to being present. Or at least pause for a moment and then try to handle the situation more skillfully. If somebody close to you switches dramatically, you will need to recognize their change of patterns and change your behavior so that it works with their new pattern. So you'll need to be nimble.

Presence and skills

> "Ideally, what would each pattern look like when the person is not in pattern, but in presence?"

As we become more present, we keep all the gifts that we have developed by doing our patterns. So a person who does the rigid pattern would still have terrific gifts for organizing and ordering. A person who does the aggressive pattern would still be good at manifesting. A person who does the enduring pattern would still be deeply grounded. A person who does the merging pattern would still be skillful at knowing what other people are feeling. And a person who does the leaving pattern would still be very creative and aware of the big picture.

You bring all your skills with you as you become more present. And then, while being present, you can apply those skills to making things better — to solving the problems, healing the wounds, or doing whatever is needed. Learning how to get out of pattern opens the door to being present, so I urge you to learn how to get out of your patterns and practice that as much as possible.

Practice, practice, practice — even when you're not in pattern. You have to practice each skill until you embody it and it becomes second nature for you. Your goal is to be as present as possible, which means that you don't go into pattern easily and, when you do, you can get out rapidly.

Merging and rigid in relationship

> "Can merging-patterned and rigid-patterned people have a successful relationship? The rigid pattern doesn't believe in feelings and feelings are everything to the merging pattern. This is the loop I'm in with my rigid-patterned boyfriend and I'm at a loss. How do I make a very personal problem, like communication breakdowns in the relationship, an out-there problem?"

Sure, people with any combination of patterns can have a successful relationship, especially the more they're able to get out of pattern and relate to each other from presence. Relating from presence allows you to understand what's actually going on, here and now, in this situation, whereas a person caught in a pattern is actually responding to a situation from the past and automatically doing, again, whatever they learned to do back then.

The Personality Patterns in Romantic Relationships

Now what can you do to solve this problem with your boyfriend? First, you have to recognize that your boyfriend has not spent years practicing how to notice feelings and please others, like you have. You have unconsciously mastered those skills, but he hasn't. He has unconsciously mastered a completely different set of skills, the skills needed to know the rules and follow them. In order to faithfully follow the rules, he has learned to devalue and ignore feelings, both his own and those of others. So the core problem is that your two patterns have taught the two of you to have completely different priorities: feelings for you, and rules for him. And from within your patterns, each of you believes in your own view and tries to get the other to join you. You want him to value your feelings, and I would guess that he wants you to value his rules.

Fortunately, there is a way out of this impasse. His rules probably include something about making his girlfriend happy. But, since he doesn't know how to sense your feelings, he doesn't know how to make you happy. He learned how to follow his parents' rules and make them happy, but that doesn't make you happy, so he probably feels lost and scared that you'll leave him.

The specific problem is that he learned how to please a rigid-patterned person, but not a merging-patterned person. But he is good at following instructions, as long as they're clear to him. You can give him those instructions, step-by-step, as long as they're simple and clear. However, since you notice feelings and please others automatically, you may not know *how* you do it. If so, you will have to figure out how you do it, step-by-step, so you can teach him how to do it.

The two of you will also have to deal with the fact that he does not have some of your perceptual skills, like feeling into the other person's core to know what they want. Instead, you will have to tell him — in words — what you feel and want. In order to do that, you will have to develop a strong enough felt-sense of your own core to reference it inside yourself.

Doing all this will be a big project for both of you, but it will draw you closer together and make you both more skillful at relating in general. It can be the big, "out-there problem" that you asked about. And, of course, the larger solution for both of you is learning how to get out of your patterns and developing the energy skills needed to stay present.

- 12 -

How to Create Healthy Relationships

THESE GUIDELINES APPLY TO ALL the different kinds of relationships, including friends, co-workers, lovers, etc.

Begin learning the skills in chapters 2 and 3

Begin learning and practicing each skill daily. Some you may already know or be able to learn quickly. Mastering the others may take years of practice, but begin now.

Learn about and develop healthy psychological boundaries

Traditional psychology has produced many good books on psychological boundaries. Read several of them and do the exercises. The classic is *Boundaries* by Cloud and Townsend. A more recent good one is *Set Boundaries, Find Peace* by Nedra Glover Tawwab.

Develop your own ability to set and enforce healthy boundaries:

- decide what boundaries are right for you in each kind of relationship
- figure out how to enforce those boundaries
- practice doing so

Learn what real safety feels like in your body

You may never have experienced real safety. Many of us grew up in unsafe, even dangerous, environments and our bodies became accustomed to such environments. You may not even notice feeling unsafe, especially if you've never actually felt safe, so your body has no felt-sense of safety for comparison. You may think that feeling unsafe is just a normal part of life.

Being unsafe may feel normal to you.

To cope with feeling unsafe, you may have adopted one or more defense strategies — you may fight, flee, accommodate, manipulate, endure, or try to be perfect. In situations of real safety, none of these strategies are needed, because you're safe and protected to begin with. When you're actually safe, there is no need for defense.

Some signs that your body has no felt-sense of safety are:

- constant fear or anxiety
- hypervigilance, that is, constantly scanning for danger
- continually needing to be active or in motion, restlessness
- discomfort with or avoidance of stillness, silence, or peace
- inability to relax into rest or deep sleep

If your body doesn't yet know what real safety feels like, then you also don't know what a safe relationship feels like. Without the ability to reference that feeling, assessing your relationships accurately will be difficult.

If you have no bodily experience of real safety, you need to develop that, either through psychotherapy or through some other safe, holding experience. Unfortunately, traditional talk therapy is unlikely to clear the old trauma out of your body and give you a bodily felt-sense of safety, because it does not focus primarily on the body. Some form of somatic or energy psychology is more likely to give you what you need.

Then, when getting to know someone and considering some sort of relationship with them:

1. Assess their capacity to:

- self-soothe and regulate their own internal state
- recognize when they are in a defense pattern and come out of it
- control their words and actions toward you and others
- control the energy they send to others (the blast of anger, the tug of need . . .)
- set and maintain their own healthy boundaries

It's your job to assess them and keep yourself safe. Do not put this task on them and then blame them for not doing it. They may be able to describe their own capacities accurately, but then again, they may not. None of us are able to see our own blind spots. They don't have to be perfect. None of us are. They only have to be able to do what is needed for the particular kind of relationship that you want to have with them. Think of it this way: if you're about to drive your car across a small bridge, and the sign says "Weight limit 1 ton," it's your job to read the sign and compare the weight of your car to the bridge's capacity. If you overload the bridge, it will let you down, every time. In the same way, if you expect others to do for you things that are beyond their abilities, they will let you down. Every time.

Unless they're engaged in serious inner work, don't expect their capacities to be different in the future than they are today. The same goes for you. Without serious inner work, personalities and defense strategies are more likely to stay the same than to change. Trust in that fact, not in your fantasy of an ideal future.

2. Negotiate the norms of the relationship with them.

Whether you're becoming friends, co-workers, lovers, or something else, the ways you are allowed to behave toward each other now will become the ways you routinely behave toward each other in the future. The negotiations between you about what is acceptable may be conscious or unconscious, verbal or non-verbal, but they will happen, and they will set the norms for how you treat each other in the future.

How to Create Healthy Relationships

Notice in particular how power, respect, time, and space are handled between you. Notice what each of you contributes and what each of you receives.

- When, where, and how are each of you available to the other? Who decides?

- How do each of you express your needs and wants? How does the other respond?

- How do the two of you handle misunderstandings, differences, and conflicts?

- How are decisions made? Who makes them?

Again, unless the two of you are engaged in serious inner work, the ways you interact today will predict how you will interact tomorrow. The way the two of you resolve (or don't resolve) your first disagreement is a good indicator of what will happen with future disagreements. Unless you each take action to change and grow, the limitations you each have today will be the limitations you have tomorrow.

If you want the other person to change in some way, *ask* them (don't command, manipulate, or threaten). They may be willing, they may not. They may be able, they may not. Be prepared for a response of *"no"* or *"I can't"* or *"I don't know how."* This is their decision. Also, figure out how you're contributing to the problem and offer to change your part.

3. As you get to know the other person, and only to the degree that you have established healthy ways of interacting, gradually begin to be more vulnerable.

Do not lead with vulnerability, hoping that this will make them want you, love you, or take care of you. Open this door only to the degree that you have determined that this person is capable of the sort of relationship you desire and after the two of you have negotiated a set of norms for the relationship that are healthy for you.

You may feel a strong desire to lead with your vulnerability, before you've even had a chance to assess their abilities. If so, be aware that you're taking the posture of a child interacting with a parent. You're putting yourself in the role of the child — smaller, weaker, helpless, needy, not responsible for your own actions and your own care — and inviting the other person into the role

How to Have Better Relationships

of the parent — bigger, stronger, wiser, more capable, and responsible for you. This is not a healthy basis for an adult-to-adult relationship.

If you lead with your vulnerability, to maintain an adult-adult dynamic with you, the other person will have to be aware enough to recognize your behavior as an invitation to a child-parent dynamic and remind you that you're actually an adult now and able to take responsibility for yourself. Most people aren't be able to do this. Most people will unconsciously shift into the parent role and the child-parent dynamic will become the norm in the relationship. They may tend to be the good parent or the bad parent, and you may tend to be the needy child or the rebellious child. And over time, your roles may become fairly steady or the two of you may oscillate between good and bad, needy and rebellious. Such a relationship may include lots of drama or relatively little.

If you tend to do this, notice that by leading with your vulnerability, you have created a child-parent relationship when you intended to create an adult-adult relationship. Ask yourself why you're doing this. If there is a child part of you that needs attention from a parent (and there is in most of us), it will be much better for you to consciously parent your own inner child and then negotiate to get those needs met within an adult-adult relationship, rather than unconsciously trying to get what you need by creating a child-parent relationship. By taking responsibility for meeting the needs of your own inner child, you will be strengthening your sense of yourself as an adult and inviting the world to see you as an adult. You are much more likely to get what you need this way, and you will feel better about yourself while doing it.

- 13 -

Moving from Me to Us
from Negotiating to Collaborating

After you develop a strong individual sense of self — with a strong sense of grounding, core, boundaries, and the other skills — there is one more step you can take. You can begin to expand your sense of self to include others. You can expand it from 'me' to 'us'. But you'll need to be solid in the individual skills named above to be able to maintain a solid sense of yourself as an individual while you expand your sense of 'me' to include others.

Enlarging your sense of self this way may sound strange to you, but you probably do it already in some situations. You do this whenever you identify with a group so much that you consider your well-being to be dependent on its well-being. You may think of your family this way, and maybe also your community or nation. You may identify this way with your favorite sports team, especially if you're one of the fans shouting *"We're number 1!"* One of the benefits of playing team sports in school is that it trains you to take on this attitude, at least in that situation. You learn to think about what is good for the team, instead of only what is good for you. It shifts you from seeing yourself as separate from others to seeing yourself as part of something larger.

The same shift happens within you when you first recognize another person as being equally important. When making decisions, you begin to consider what's good for both of you, not just for yourself. Instead of thinking only of 'me', you think of 'us.'

When people treat each other this way, their way of making decisions evolves from negotiating to collaborating. Instead of bargaining to only get

301

their own needs met, they consider everyone's needs and then cooperate to create the greatest good for all. They enter into a process of deciding together, instead of deciding separately.

You can cultivate this shift within yourself. You can learn to see each person you meet as just as important and valuable as yourself. To do this, practice identifying with the larger body of humanity and thinking of each other person as a cell within that larger body. Would you think of your own body as healthy if some parts of it were attacking other parts? If your stomach was keeping all the food for itself? If your nerves were misleading your brain? No, because you would be identifying with your entire body, not with just one cell or organ.

Seeing yourself as part of something larger does not mean merging with others and losing your sense of yourself as a distinct individual. In fact, maintaining your individual sense of self is essential to the health of the group. When moving from 'me' to 'us,' you must be able to maintain your individual self within the larger group, just as every cell within a larger organism retains its own individual structure. By always maintaining your core, ground, and edge, you can expand your sense of self to include others without losing your sense of yourself as an individual.

When you think of every person as a cell within the larger body of humanity that we all share, harming others no longer makes sense. Lying, cheating, and stealing are just hurting yourself. War is an attack on yourself. Huge differences in wealth are a sign of illness in the larger body, not of individual success.

This is how your sense of self can shift if you choose to identify with the larger body of humanity, along with your individual self, family, and nation. If you practice thinking of others this way, it will transform not only your relationships, but also every interaction you have with others.

- 14 -

Conclusion

We have seen that, while we perceive the world in different ways and communicate in different ways, we are all trying to feel safer.

We have discovered that there are many levels of relationship and communication, and to become a healthy adult, each of us needs to develop a whole range of psychological and energy skills, including how to manage our own inner state.

We have seen that, in order to interact successfully, we need to be able to listen, speak, and negotiate with others skillfully. And we need to know how to approach them in ways that respect their autonomy, norms, space, and timing.

We have reviewed the five personality patterns, focusing on what each pattern needs to feel safe, how to communicate and relate to people caught in that pattern, and how our own patterns may interact with those of others.

And lastly, we have looked at how to create healthy relationships and how to go beyond negotiating to collaborating.

Now it is time to ask yourself: How are you going to apply all that you've learned? How are you going to embody this knowledge and use it to relate more skillfully to those around you, especially those you love?

Don't fool yourself into thinking that you're not important. Your every action ripples out across the world, and how you treat others matters.

So act like you make a difference.

Or as Mary Oliver[1] puts it:

> *What is it you plan to do*
> *with your one wild and precious life?*

Endnotes

Chapter 6 – Relating to the Leaving Pattern

1. Linda Kohanov, *The Tao of Equus* (Novato, CA, New World Library, 2001), pp. 160–161.

Chapter 8 – Relating to the Enduring Pattern

1. Stephen M. Johnson, *Character Styles (New York, Norton, 1994)*, p. 219.
2. Johnson, *Character Styles*, p. 228.

Chapter 10 – Relating to the Rigid Pattern

1. Johnson, *Character Styles*, p. 271.
2. Alexander Lowen, *The Language of the Body* (New York, Collier Books, 1971), p. 255.
3. Johnson, *Character Styles*, pp. 283–284.
4. Mary Oliver, "Wild Geese" in *New and Selected Poems* (Boston, Beacon Press, 1992) p. 110.

Chapter 14 - Conclusion

1. Mary Oliver, "The Summer Day" in *New and Selected Poems*, p. 94.

Bibliography

Almaas, A. H., *Essence: The Diamond Approach to Inner Realization* (York Beach, ME, Samuel Weiser, 1986)

Almaas, A. H., *The Pearl Beyond Price: Integration of Personality into Being: An Object Relations Approach* (Berkeley, CA, Diamond Books, 1988)

Brennan, Barbara Ann, *Hands of Light: A Guide to Healing Through the Human Energy Field* (New York, Bantam Books, 1987)

Brennan, Barbara Ann, *Light Emerging: The Journey of Personal Healing* (New York, Bantam Books, 1993)

Brown, Byron, *Soul Without Shame: A Guide to Liberating Yourself from the Judge Within* (Boston, Shambala, 1999)

Cloud, Henry, *Changes That Heal: How to Understand Your Past to Ensure a Healthier Future* (Grand Rapids, MI, Zondervan Publishing House, 1992)

Cloud, Henry, and Townsend, John, *Boundaries: When to Say Yes, When to Say No to Take Control of Your Life* (Grand Rapids, MI, Zondervan Publishing House, 1992)

Heller, Laurence and LaPierre, Aline, *Healing Developmental Trauma: How Early Trauma Affects Self-Regulation, Self-Image, and the Capacity for Relationship* (Berkeley, CA, North Atlantic Books, 2012)

Johnson, Stephen M., *Characterological Transformation: The Hard Work Miracle* (New York, Norton, 1984)

Johnson, Stephen M., *Humanizing the Narcissistic Style* (New York, Norton, 1987)

Johnson, Stephen M., *Character Styles* (New York, Norton, 1994)

Judith, Anodea, *Eastern Body, Western Mind: Psychology and the Chakra System as a Path to the Self* (Berkeley, CA, Celestial Arts, 1996)

Kohanov, Linda, *The Tao of Equus: A Woman's Journey of Healing and Transformation through the Way of the Horse* (Novato, CA, New World Library, 2001)

Levine, Peter, *Waking the Tiger: Healing Trauma* (Berkeley, CA, North Atlantic Books, 1997)

Lowen, Alexander, *The Language of the Body* (New York, Collier Books, 1971)

Lowen, Alexander, *Bioenergetics* (New York, Penguin Books, 1976)

Newton, Michael, *Journey of Souls: Case Studies of Life Between Lives* (St. Paul, MN, Llewellyn Publications, 1994)

Newton, Michael, *Destiny of Souls: New Case Studies of Life Between Lives* (Woodbury, MN, Llewellyn Publications, 2000)

Oliver, Mary, *New and Selected Poems* (Boston, Beacon Press, 1992)

Palmer, Wendy and Crawford, Janet, *Leadership Embodiment: How the Way We Sit and Stand Can Change the Way We Think and Speak* (San Rafael, CA, The Embodiment Foundation, 2013)

Pierrakos, John C., *Core Energetics: Developing the Capacity to Love and Heal* (Mendocino, CA, LifeRhythm Publication, 1987)

Reich, Wilhelm, *Character Analysis* (New York, Farrar, Straus and Giroux, Third, enlarged edition, 1949)

Tawwab, Nedra Glover, *Set Boundaries, Find Peace: a guide to reclaiming yourself* (New York, TarcherPerigee, 2021)

Index

A
aggressive pattern, 84-85, 203-235
AK 4-point Rubbing Technique, 37
Arrien, Angeles, 50
attaching to the body, 105-107

B
basic energy skills, *see* energy skills
beliefs:
    aggressive pattern, 211-212
    enduring pattern, 175
    leaving pattern, 111
    merging pattern, 146
    rigid pattern, 247
boundaries,
    energetic, 32, 145, 159, 223
    psychological, 32, 223, 296

C
Caesara, Lynda, 86
Centering Breath, 18-20
centers of intelligence, 59-63
channels of perception, 63-66
character structure, 228
Communication 101, 58-59
communication skills, 50-59
communicating with:
    aggressive pattern, 212-215
    enduring pattern, 176-177
    leaving pattern, 112-115
    merging pattern, 147
    rigid pattern, 248-249
compensated merging pattern, 83, 140-142, 206, 275
complimenting:
    aggressive pattern, 221
    enduring pattern, 188
    leaving pattern, 122-123
    merging pattern, 156-157
    rigid pattern, 257-258
conflict with:
    aggressive pattern, 221-223
    enduring pattern, 188-189
    leaving pattern, 123-124
    merging pattern, 157-158
    rigid pattern, 252, 258-260
control:
    of others, 85, 92, 100, 206-208
    of self, 101, 241, 242, 258
core, 18-24
    pretend core, 140-142, 206, 283

D
discerning patterns, 90-94

E
embedded statements, 55-56
embodiment, 81, 105, 106, 125
emotions:
    aggressive pattern, 210-211
    enduring pattern, 174-175
    leaving pattern, 110-111
    merging pattern, 145-146
    rigid pattern, 246
enduring pattern, 83-84, 167-201
energy skills,
    Centering Breath, 18
    Core, 20
    Edge, 32
    Grounding, 25
    Me/Not Me, 34
    see also boundaries
examples of each pattern:
    aggressive pattern, 212
    enduring pattern, 175
    leaving pattern, 111
    merging pattern, 146
    rigid pattern, 247

F

fear meter, 210-211, 228
fears of:
    abandonment, 210
    being bad inside, 210
    feeling empty, 144
    fragmenting, 81, 106-107, 109
    imperfection, 101, 246
    invasion, 174
    losing heart connection, 99, 145, 147, 148, 150
    loss of control, 100
    mistakes, 246, 252, 262
    self-expression, 100, 171, 188, 191, 241
    shattering, 81, 106-107, 109, 123, 126
    success, 174, 192
    vulnerability, 112
field focus, 117-119
fight-or-flight state, 207, 211, 213, 222, 225, 235
fragmenting, 81, 106-107, 109, 123
Freud, Sigmund, 1, 13

G

getting out of pattern:
    aggressive pattern, 235
    enduring pattern, 200
    leaving pattern, 132
    merging pattern, 165
    rigid pattern, 268
gifts of each pattern:
    aggressive pattern, 208-
    enduring pattern, 172-174
    leaving pattern, 108-109
    merging pattern, 143-144
    rigid pattern, 244-246
good-enough meter, 243
grounding, 25-31

H

Harley SwiftDeer, 86
holding space for someone, 69-73, 151-153

I

I statements, 52-55
ideal spouse, 261
inner critic: 13-18, 242, 251, 264
    attack, 14-18, 20, 250, 251, 253, 260, 264
    creation of, 242
    defending against, 17
    disidentification from, 15-17, 242-243
    identification with, 15, 242-243
inner witness, 9
invasion, 174, 186, 286

J

Johnson, Stephen M., 228

L

leaving pattern, 81-83, 103-133
levels of communication, 47-50
levels of relationship, 43-46

M

me/not me, 34-35, 137
merging pattern, 83, 135-165

N

narcissism, 228-229
negotiating, 56-58

O

One Right Way, 89, 237, 247, 261-262, 277
origin of:
    aggressive pattern, 205-208
    enduring pattern, 169-172
    leaving pattern, 105-107
    merging pattern, 137-142
    rigid pattern, 240-244

P

patterns:
    creation of, 79-80
    distortion of perception, 87
    discerning, 90-94
    in romantic relationships, 270-295
    overview of, 80-86
    primary vs secondary, 86-87
    vs presence, 74-76
    vs true self or essence, 77
presence, 74-77, 272-273, 279, 291, 294
primary and secondary patterns, 86-87

Index

R

rapprochement phase, 140
referencing, 142-143, 151-153, 160, 256-257
Reich, Wilhelm, 1
relating to:
    aggressive pattern, 215-227
    enduring pattern, 177-191
    leaving pattern, 115-126
    merging pattern, 148-161
    rigid pattern, 249-262
rigid pattern, 85-86, 237-268
romance:
    aggressive pattern, 225
    enduring pattern, 190
    leaving pattern, 124-125
    merging pattern, 158-160
    rigid pattern, 260-261

S

safety strategies, 77-78
self: coalescing of, 81
self-sabotage, 192
self-soothing, 37-38
space:
    awareness of, 172-173
    defending, 32-35, 85,
    holding, 69-73
    need for, 100, 170-171
    respecting, 68, 100, 176-181, 183-184, 186-188
superego, 13-18

T

True Self, 77

W

wiggle your butt, 238-239

About the Author

Steven Kessler has been a psychotherapist for over 40 years and has studied many different maps of personality and many healing modalities, including Character Structure, the Enneagram, NLP, energy work, Thought Field Therapy, and EFT (emotional freedom techniques). He is a certified EFT Expert and Trainer and maintains a private practice in California.

Since 1984, Steven has taught hundreds of groups and workshops in the U.S. and internationally, helping men and women heal their wounds and grow into their full adult selves. More recently, he has taught over a hundred classes and workshops training other therapists in the use of EFT. From 2006 to 2010, Steven left his private practice for 2-3 months a year to work on U.S. military bases in both North America and overseas, helping soldiers and their families recover from the wounds of war.

Steven holds a Masters Degree in Transpersonal Psychology from John F. Kennedy University and has spent many years studying mythology, anthropology, and the evolution of human consciousness. For over 50 years he has pursued various spiritual and meditation practices, including many years in the Diamond Heart meditation school. For over 20 years he has been a student of Lynda Caesara, studying character structure, the direct perception of energy, and shamanism in the lineage of Grandfather Two Bears and the Southern Seers tradition.

For information on speaking, workshops, and trainings, please visit *www.ThePersonalityPatterns.com*
or contact Steven Kessler at
info@ThePersonalityPatterns.com.